MOONSHOTS
IN EDUCATION

Moonshots in Education: Launching Blended Learning in the Classroom
By Esther Wojcicki and Lance T. Izumi with Alicia Chang, Alex Silverman, and Elliott Parisi

ISBN-13: 978-1-934276-20-4

Pacific Research Institute
One Embarcadero Center, Suite 350
San Francisco, CA 94111
Tel: 415-989-0833
Fax: 415-989-2411
www.pacificresearch.org

Download copies of this study at www.pacificresearch.org.

MOONSHOTS
IN EDUCATION

Launching Blended Learning in the Classroom

By
Esther Wojcicki and Lance T. Izumi
with Alicia Chang, Alex Silverman, and Elliott Parisi

*To teachers everywhere who work tirelessly and whose
influence affects eternity for the benefit of all of us.*
—Esther Wojcicki

*For April, who nursed me during the writing of this book, and without
whose care and love this book would not have been possible.*
—Lance Izumi

*For my parents, Tony Jaung and Mui Thi Chang,
whose moonshots became my reality. Thank you.*
—Alicia Chang

CONTENTS

Foreword by James Franco..1

Part I

1. The Online Learning Revolution..................................7

2. What Is a Moonshot?... 13

3. Trick in the Blended Classroom 17

4. Beyond the "3 Rs": 21st-Century Skills in the Classroom 27

5. Online Search Skills Matter:
   Tips on How to Teach Them to Your Students 43

6. Get Inspired: Real-Life Examples of Moonshots in Education............... 57

7. Moonshots in Music Theory 83

8. STEM Success: Programming "Outside the Box" in
   AP Computer Science 91

9. Journalism and Media Studies: Teaching through
   Freedom, Relevance, and Respect 95

10. The Magic of Motivation.................................. 119

11. Apps and Tools for Teachers................................ 123

12. Google Apps for Education 153

13. Uses of Google Apps.................................. 183

14. Networks that Support Teachers............................ 187

PART II

15. An Overview of Digital Education In America...................... 201

16. An Overview of Teacher Training in Digital Education in the U.S....... 209

17. How Other Countries Are Training Teachers in Digital Education 235

Conclusion.. 253

Endnotes.. 255

Acknowledgements.. 272

About the Authors.. 274

About Pacific Research Institute 279

Foreword

By James Franco

When I was at Paly I was part of the school newspaper, *The Campanile*, which was overseen by Esther Wojcicki, known to the students as, "Woj." This was before Woj was mother-in-law to Sergey of Google, but we had Lisa Brennan-Jobs (daughter of Steve Jobs) and Ben Hewlett (grandson of Hewlett of Hewlett-Packard) in our class. I was just James Franco of the South Palo Alto Francos, son of two Stanford grads, one a Silicon Valley something or other, and the other a children's book author.

Let me give you a picture of her, Woj, because she is my childhood figurehead for a particular kind of participatory learning. She is a tall, former swimsuit model with a deep, goofy laugh that pours out easy. I have known her for twenty years and she hasn't aged since that first beginning journalism class when she taught us how to structure a news story. She is at ease amongst her students, and treats them like peers, which isn't hard because she gets the smartest students in the school. Her actual children went to all the Ivy League schools and now run half of Silicon Valley while being mothers. She is as easy going as they come and would give up her soul to further education. She probably already has.

Today there is a media empire at Paly: the newspaper, about five magazines, a television station, and a media center that rivals the J School at Columbia. Basically they have a mini-Google office right on campus. This building stands for, and *is*, everything Woj has dedicated her life to: teaching through project-based classes.

Back in 1995 and 1996, when I was on *The Campanile*, we didn't have the media building, we met in an old auditorium oddly flanked with posters of Luke Perry's bull riding film, *8 Seconds,* and the obscure Matt Dillon/Danny Glover film, *The Saint of Fort Washington*—neither of which have I seen. But despite the facility, the core of Woj's teaching approach was firmly in place: the paper was overseen by four senior editors (Lisa Brennan-Jobs was one of these, I wasn't even close), under whom were fifteen odd page editors (I was not one of these either), who managed forty or so student writers (I was one of these). Every three weeks this student organization would put a paper together and the school would read it.

My year was special because the paper actually got a scoop before all the commercial papers. Good ol' Ben Hewlett, of the Hewlett-Packard lineage, somehow discovered that the school district was misappropriating funds. You should have seen the joyful/mischievous flash in Woj's eyes as she pushed Ben and the student staff to get the story out. Two decades later she still talks about that story because it was her teaching philosophy in action: the students were no longer doing exercises in class. Ben Hewlett's story was not something that would be read by a teacher and then locked in a drawer, it was a story that engaged with the outside world. It was a story that was important outside of the classroom.

At *The Campanile* I was not Ben Hewlett and I was not Lisa Brennan-Jobs, I was a weird, quiet kid who wanted to be deep, but I didn't know how. My list of stories makes me sound like a Jack Kerouac wannabe, which is what I was: I wrote stories about Buddhism; circus freaks; and hiking trails at the The Baylands, the local nature conservatory. But the important pedagogical aspect of working on the paper, that I understood subconsciously then, and that I understand explicitly as a teacher now, is that my work was being seen by a public, and that that changed the work. I wasn't writing for a school grade as much as I was writing for independent readers. At Paly the readers didn't pay for *The Campanile*, but if they didn't like the stories, they wouldn't read it; one step away from writing for the *New York Times*: if the readers don't like it, they won't buy it.

Now, after two decades as a professional actor, and multiple MFA programs where I was trained to make work that would ostensibly be consumed by a public (fiction, poetry, directing, art) I realized that I had already been trained in such practice by Woj back in high school. Her classes had one foot in the classroom and one foot in the real world.

Now I teach at UCLA, USC, and CalArts—directing, writing, acting. My classes are always project based and collaborative. The entire class will work on a feature film together, or mount a live performance together, which brings them as a unit of disparate parts. Like Woj's student-run paper, my classes push the students to make a product that individually is out of their reach, but as a group is well within it.

I hate wasted time and energy. And as a teacher I hate reading material that will go nowhere beyond me. I don't want students to create work that will please me; I don't want them to feel the safety of knowing their work will be read simply because I am their teacher, and *have* to read it; I want them to make work that can stand up in the real world. And the pressure of creating work that is public makes all the difference: the students are accountable for what they've made, and they will get a more thorough, and representative idea of how their work is engaging with others. They will learn that their work, no matter how complex, is about communication. None of us lives in a vacuum, and neither should our work.

Thanks, Woj.

PART I

THE ONLINE LEARNING REVOLUTION

BY ESTHER WOJCICKI

Alan November, a leader in education technology, tells a story in his well-known book *Who Owns the Learning?: Preparing Students for Success in the Digital Age* about a young boy named Gary who breaks into a computer lab at the beginning of summer vacation. The boy only wanted to use the computer lab to learn programming. He did not steal the computer since it was a heavy desktop; he just wanted to use the computer to work on his project. He wound up completing the entire course in a single week with no interaction or help from his teacher. It was an epiphany for November. He couldn't believe that this student could complete an entire semester course in a week, but when Gary showed up with the assignments completed and they were all perfect, November changed his mind. He realized that "computer technology may have truly broad implications in the education process." The key to Gary's success was that the computer supplied immediate feedback. In addition, he felt he was completely responsible for his work and therefore had the enthusiasm kids do when they play computer games.

These three characteristics of online learning are what makes it so powerful: 1) there is immediate feedback; 2) the student owns the learning; and 3) the teacher does not play the central role. Being in control of one's learning is key to the effectiveness for students.

This book is about blended learning and project based learning in which online learning is used in conjunction with classroom learning. Blended learning is defined by Michael Horn of the Innosight Institute as "a formal education program in which a student learns at least in part through online delivery of content and instruction with some element of student control over time, place, path or pace, and at least in part at a supervised brick-and-mortar location away from home."

● MOONSHOT TOOLS

Visit www.edutopia.org to hear an explanation from Professor Linda Darling-Hammond of Stanford University on why social and emotional learning is a crucial part of teaching a child.

The opportunity for blended learning is now. It is a moonshot moment. President Barack Obama is seeking $68.8 billion for a federal program that will support educators in creating and using digital-learning resources, including mobile devices. It will also expand collaboration and engagement among parents, teachers, and professional networks. This would be the largest amount allocated to education ever and would truly open the door to remarkable achievements. Another support for the moonshot moment is the Future Ready Schools movement announced by the White House in October 2014 to help districts transition to personalized learning.

This book is called *Moonshots in Education* for several reasons, but the main reason is that it will take courage for teachers and administrators to change the entire culture of the classroom away from the way education has been delivered for centuries—the lecture method—and toward something truly interactive.

Changing the culture involves first of all *trusting* students. Historically, students were never trusted; the premise was that they could not be trusted. The school system is *built around* not trusting and not respecting students. But, as Gary's story illustrates, adding *trust* to schools will make learning more effective. Educational studies have confirmed this insight, showing that when students own the learning, they are more engaged and learn more.

While teachers need to trust students to own their learning, teachers need to be trusted too. The lack of trust in our schools starts at the top and ripples downward. In all too many districts today, teachers are scripted every day of the school year—told exactly what to teach and how—because the school boards don't trust them. Then, to make sure teachers are doing their job, we test students repeatedly.

> 66 Education today needs moonshots to allow a major culture change. Changing the culture is the hardest thing to do in any situation—but it desperately needs to be done in our schools. 99

No wonder the students are bored; no wonder we have 50 percent of teachers leaving after five years.

The problem is made worse by the fact that we live in a nation of fear. The kidnapping of eleven-year-old Jaycee Lee Dugard in 1991 and the kidnapping-murder of twelve-year-old Polly Klaas in 1993 traumatized a generation of parents. People are afraid to let their kids walk to the neighborhood store. We never see kids walking alone to school. Even in towns like Palo Alto, California, where crime is low, parents walk their kids into the classroom every morning. We are afraid to let them leave our side in the grocery store because there might be a predator lurking around every corner. When is the last time you heard an announcement over the loudspeaker that there was a lost child?

The fear has extended to other areas of American life—notably education. We are afraid our kids will not get the right education, so those who have the resources send them to private schools. In the public schools we are afraid the teachers are slacking on the job, and so we test and test. Parents don't trust administrators or teachers, and in turn administrators and teachers don't trust students or parents.

We need to break this cycle and work together to raise children, as Hillary Clinton said in her 1996 book *It Takes a Village*. "Children are not rugged individualists," Clinton wrote. "They depend on the adults they know and on thousands more who make decisions every day that affect their well-being. All of us, whether we acknowledge it or not, are responsible for deciding whether our children are raised in a nation that doesn't just espouse family values but values families and children."

Education today needs moonshots to allow a major *culture change*. Changing the culture is the hardest thing to do in any situation—but it desperately needs to be done in our schools. More than 70 percent of teachers today are using the traditional lecture model, the way people have been teaching for centuries. But today, they teach directly to the tests because test scores are tied to their evaluations. They may have computers, tablets, or even cell phones in the classroom, but having the devices alone does not change the culture. The worksheets may now be on a computer instead of on paper, but the culture remains the same: the teacher is in charge, the teacher is the director, and the teacher controls the learning.

Many teachers now have electronic whiteboards, but that just reinforces the image of the teacher as the "sage on the stage" and the person in charge of learning. Although many studies have shown that students learn best when they are in charge of their learning, we continue to reinforce the teacher as oracle.

> **"To transition to the 21st century, schools need to take a risk—they need a moonshot. "**

To transition to the 21st century, schools need to take a risk—they need a moonshot. They need to find a way to change the culture of the classroom from a teacher-directed model to a student-directed model. That is the basis of blended learning. The students, with the support of technology, can own and direct at least some of their own education. Students today have a whole library in their pocket on their cell phone. Whatever they want to know, they can look up in a minute. And yet, in many school districts, including some of the largest in the nation, cell phones are banned, the web is censored, and computers and tablets are minimally used. Los Angeles Unified, one of the largest districts in the nation, censors Google and blocks Facebook and YouTube. It distributed iPads to students in a $1 billion plan in 2013, only to take them back weeks later because the students hacked the Facebook site.[1]

Google+ is not used in schools because of the fear of violating federal laws such as the Children's Online Privacy Protection Act (COPPA) and the Children's Internet Protection Act (CIPA). Google+ would be an excellent tool, permitting circles of students to meet online for homework in a Google Hangout. But it is not encouraged because of these laws. While we are all concerned about protecting our children from predators, we should also be concerned about overprotecting them in ways that inhibit real learning.

Students should be taught to search intelligently and understand the results of their searches. They should be taught how to differentiate between fact and opinion, how to tell who is the creator of a site, how to determine if the information is credible. Students need to know how to navigate the web, how to deal with bullying, how to be intelligent, responsible digital citizens. These are among the skills needed for lifelong learning.

There are several chapters in part I dealing with these topics, and many books and articles have been published on the importance of digital technology in the education process and in preparation for life. We cannot afford to be held back in a world that is changing rapidly.

What will it take for our nation's schools to teach for the 21st century—to teach students how to navigate the real web, not a censored version? It will take the kind of energy and courage that it took for a moonshot.

WHAT IS A MOONSHOT?

BY ESTHER WOJCICKI

(2)

*We choose to go to the moon in this decade and
do the other things, not because they are easy,
but because they are hard.*

—John F. Kennedy

The Original Moonshot

On May 25, 1961, President John F. Kennedy addressed Congress on
"Urgent National Needs." These needs included the goal of landing
a man on the moon and bringing him safely back to earth by decade's
end. Skeptics declared Kennedy's timeline overly ambitious. Just one
month before the president addressed Congress, Russian cosmonaut
Yuri Gagarin had become the first human being to ever journey into
space. Gagarin had orbited the earth, and now Kennedy was shooting
for the moon.

Within a year, two American astronauts traveled into space.
The following year, four additional Americans had orbited the earth.
Space exploration continued through the 1960s, each mission bring-
ing us one step closer to the goal: landing on the moon.

On July 20, 1969, history was made, as Neil Armstrong became
the first person to walk on the moon. The term "moonshot" has come
to represent bold, audacious thinking that can lead to new discoveries
that propel society forward.

Modern Moonshot Thinking

Moonshots involve goals that are difficult to achieve, perhaps seemingly impossible. When you think of present-day innovation, the work of Google may come to mind. Having built a search engine used by over one billion people monthly, researchers at Google are now working on bold new ideas like designing self-driving cars and providing Internet service through balloons in the stratosphere to the two-thirds of the earth's population that does not already have it.

You might be wondering what space exploration and self-driving cars have to do with your life as a teacher. Perhaps your school is implementing a 1:1 tablet initiative, or has turned its focus to aligning its curriculum with the Common Core State Standards. You might feel that you have much to learn in a short period, and that all this new knowledge is overwhelming. That is where this book can help you. Teaching is an inherently challenging career. You are not alone in finding it challenging. In this book, I not only discuss tools and methods that have worked successfully in other classrooms, but also provide you with resources and networks that you can use when you feel you need some advice or when you want to share ideas. My main goal is to help teachers "shoot for the moon," despite how difficult it may seem. To paraphrase President Kennedy, we choose to teach not because it is easy, but because it is hard. And as research has consistently shown, learning also is not easy—success in school and beyond is related to one's ability to face challenges and overcome obstacles.

How to Use Part I

The theme of perseverance through difficult times will appear throughout part I. First, we will discuss recent research findings on what are called "non-cognitive skills"—grit, tenacity, and perseverance—that have been shown to be critical for success. Media coverage of education often focuses on domain-specific achievement in areas such as math or reading, but we highlight factors outside of academic skills that can be cultivated and integrated into classroom experiences.

Next, we provide examples of successful blended learning in classrooms around the United States and the world. You will notice that while there are common threads in many of the programs we discuss, each scenario is unique to its teacher as well as its students. We invite you to consider which of these methods might fit best in your classroom, and how you might be able to craft a personalized experience that suits the needs of each student.

We then present a curated list of tools and technologies that we have found to be effective in teaching and learning. This list is not meant to be exhaustive, but rather just a starting point for you to begin experimenting to see what works best for you and your students. As innovative technologies are by definition always evolving and changing, we'd love to hear about the interesting ways you've integrated apps, software, and

● MOONSHOT TOOLS

The non-profit organization For Each and Every Child at www.foreachandeverychild.org is working to provide one overarching framework for educators, researchers, and policymakers to help support equity and excellence in all public schools in this country.

other supplemental resources in your classroom. We'll also continue to add to our list of tools on our website and online forums, so we can keep the discussion going.

We believe that interacting in an active community is a key component of successful teaching and learning, and in the next section we discuss networks that support teachers. We have found great inspiration in speaking with other educators in both online and offline settings. We understand that change can be intimidating, particularly when it comes to implementing brand-new technologies. Remember, *you are not alone.*

In chapter 14, we provide some guidance on where to stay updated on the latest education-technology news, and where to find advice and help from fellow teachers who have likely shared similar experiences. It is our hope that after reading this book, you will feel equipped to try some new techniques and tools in your classroom—not because it is easy, but because it is hard.

Why Do We Need a Moonshot Now?

As the saying goes, there is no time like the present. The state of education in the United States is in need of major change. Fewer than half of American children from low-income families are ready for school at the age of five. By age four, low-income children are already trailing their higher-income peers. With just 51 percent of three-year-olds enrolled in pre-school and 46 percent of schoolteachers leaving the profession within five years, public schooling is in a perilous state. These troubling statistics are not only the problem of those directly affected. When half of our students are not prepared for school and half of our teachers cannot meet the challenge, this affects each and every one of us. Systemic change is imperative, and we know that large-scale reforms are costly in both time and finances. But we strongly believe that change can start with the individual.

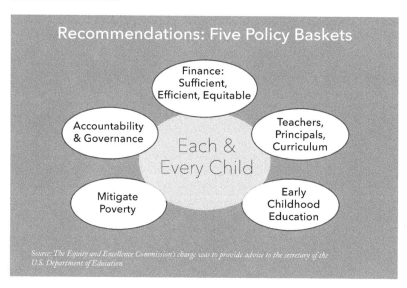

Source: The Equity and Excellence Commission's charge was to provide advice to the secretary of the U.S. Department of Education.

TRICK IN THE BLENDED CLASSROOM

BY ESTHER WOJCICKI

It all started in 1987, when I got a grant from the State of California. The state sent me eight Macintosh computers, never asking if I knew how to use them, and when they arrived I had no idea how to even turn them on. I realized then that I was going to fail if I didn't get some help quickly. I looked around for colleagues who could help, but none of them had any idea. Our school had no IT department. So I took a leap of faith and confessed to my students that I had no idea how to use the new computers and that I needed help. This turned out to be a stroke of good luck, even though I did not see it that way at the time. It was the beginning of my new teaching methodology.

The students were absolutely thrilled to help me (can you imagine being asked to help a teacher?!), and that was the beginning of my collaborative teaching model. Only, at that point, it did not have a name, and in fact I had to hide it from other teachers who might have frowned on what I was doing. The students and I ended up spending hours after school and on weekends figuring out the computers and how to network them. I had never even heard the word "network" in a computer context. I was one of the first teachers in California to use computers in the classroom, and possibly the first in the nation to use computers in a journalism classroom.

I was soon sold on the idea of collaboration, respect, and trust in the classroom. And it turns out that building a culture of collaboration, respect, and trust is key to a successful blended classroom. The first action a teacher needs to take in the fall when school starts is to *set up the culture*. On the surface, this may sound like a waste of time, but in fact its importance cannot be overemphasized. Part of such a culture is understanding that the teacher is not the only expert in the room; in fact, students can know more than the teacher about some aspects of what they will be doing together.

Computers, tablets, and other electronic devices alone are not going to change the classroom. It is the change in culture that will make the difference.

To help everyone remember what it takes to set up a culture that works, I have come up with an acronym, TRICK. Each letter stands for an important part of the culture.

T = trust
R = respect
I = independence
C = collaboration
K = kindness

Trust

The first thing to establish in the classroom is a culture of trust. That does not mean the students are given complete freedom to run wild and do what they want; it means the students trust each other to help in the learning process and the teacher trusts the students. The boundaries need to be established early in the semester. There are a variety of exercises to build trust that a teacher can use, ranging from the blind man's game to walking into walls.

Since the teacher is the one in control, it is he or she who must take the initiative. Teachers need to put themselves into situations that require students to be trustworthy. Opportunities arise every day. For example, having students work in teams and be responsible to the team teaches trust. Creating a group blog or website gives students a natural way to develop trust in the team, and, if the teacher trusts the team, it builds a community of trust in the classroom.

However, the key to building trust is *to actually trust the students*. While that may seem counterintuitive to many teachers, it is really the only way to effectively build trust. For example, in my advanced journalism class, the students each have an individual story assignment, so no two students are doing the same thing. Some of the stories are particularly sensitive about issues in the school, the district, or the city. It takes a leap of faith on my part to trust students to get the information right and to write it up in an objective way. We publish the results online—typically garnering thousands of views—and in hard copy for three thousand local residents. Students have told me that trusting them to write the stories is significant in building their self-esteem.

The students also put out a newspaper or magazine. The newspaper class has an enrollment of seventy students, who work in teams on the paper. Six editors-in-chief are in charge of the class, giving the students critical leadership experience and a sense of control over the publication. The magazine classes have an enrollment of thirty-five and an editorial board of three editors. Each student in each class has a title that correlates to his or her responsibilities. Examples are news editor, editorial-page editor, feature-page editor, or reporter.

Besides having the students produce actual publications, a second suggestion is to allow the students to teach the class on a regular basis. For example, the teacher can designate one day a week when the kids take over the class for an hour or so. Having kids teach each other in small groups on a regular basis also creates a sense of trust in the class.

I also encourage the students to help with the technological side of the program. I use Google Docs to create documents and Adobe software to publish. New products come out daily, and many of those might be useful for me, but I have little time to investigate them. Thus, I ask my students to watch out for new software that might be useful for the program, tell me about it, and, if it seems appropriate, learn how to use it. They then share it with the rest of the class.

A third suggestion to enhance trust is to give students your home phone number, cell number, and e-mail and tell them to contact you when they have problems, but not later than a specified time in the evening. Just giving out that information provides for a culture of trust and caring. All students also have the same contact information for all other students including home phones, cell phones and addresses as well as my contact information.

A fourth suggestion is for the teacher to laugh at his or her own mistakes on a regular basis. We all make mistakes, and teaching students that mistakes are part of life is an important lesson in helping them accept themselves. I do that every day in class, and the mistakes are not difficult to find: Every day there is something that does not go as planned. Teachers who are willing to show that they are not perfect, don't know everything, and can laugh at themselves can more easily develop trust.

Finally, and perhaps most important, is to put students in situations requiring them to think for themselves. They may stumble and have difficulties, but the key is to support them in their efforts while letting them solve the problem themselves. This builds trust in themselves, in the class as a whole, and between teacher and students.

MOONSHOT TOOLS

For a resource to help teachers develop respect in the classroom, visit www.ascd.org. ASCD is a leader in developing and delivering innovative programs that empower educators to support the success of each learner.

Respect

Teachers need to have sincere respect for their students, especially in today's world, where the members of a class may come from very different backgrounds and experiences. But each one has unique gifts even if he or she also has unique problems. As a teacher I know how difficult it can be to respect students who create problems in the classroom, but it is up to the teacher to show respect. It goes a long way in making the student feel better about themselves.

● MOONSHOT TOOLS

One of the obstacles to independence is the high stakes in correlating curriculum with the Common Core testing requirements; neither the teacher nor the students has much independence in what is studied. However, there is independence in how they reach the Common Core goals. To learn more, visit the blog post "Independence Day: Developing Self-Directed Learning Projects" by Dinah Mack and Holly Epstein Ojalvo on the *New York Times* Learning Network.

Respect is part of trust. I trust the kids and respect them, and in turn they trust and respect me. Someone has to start the process, and it cannot be the students, since the teacher is in charge.

Giving students respect does not mean letting go of expectations. In fact, it means the opposite.

Teachers need to respect them as individuals and expect them to achieve at a high level. My *expectations* are high and I encourage my students to reach those standards by giving them the opportunity to revise their work on a regular basis. I use the mastery system model (which means students work on a skill until they master it) and grade only when student have finally mastered the standard. An innovative internet company called MasteryConnect.com has software that supports this pedagogy. Grades can be very discouraging for kids but if teachers return an assignment with suggestions on how to improve or correct the errors and kids understand it is part of the process of learning, they will still be excited to learn.

● MOONSHOT TOOLS

To learn more about how you can improve collaboration in the classroom, visit www.academia.edu and read "Improving classroom learning through student collaboration: learning outcomes in a learnlab teaching environment" by Hans Peter Wachter.

Also check out "From Mirroring to Guiding: A Review of State of the Art Technology for Supporting Collaborative Learning," Proceedings of the First European Conference on Computer-Supported Collaborative Learning by Patrick Jermann, Amy Soller, and Martin Muelenbrock.

For more on kindness, visit the Pinterest page Random Acts of Kindness: Character Education.

Famed psychologists Albert Bandura talks about the power of self-efficacy and how a student's self image determines how they feel about themselves. He defines self-efficacy as a person's belief in their ability to succeed in specific situations and says that self efficacy plays a major role in how people (especially students) approaches goals, tasks, and challenges. According to Bandura's theory, people with high self-efficacy—that is, those who believe they can perform well—are more likely to view difficult tasks as something to be mastered rather than something to be avoided.

http://en.wikipedia.org/wiki/Albert_Bandura

David Kelley CEO of IDEO and head of Stanford University's D School has a similar philosophy which he calls Creative Confidence. He says the key to being creative and achieving is "believing in your ability to create change in the world around you. It is the conviction that you can achieve what you set out to do. We think this sel assurance, this believe in your creative capacity lies at the heart of innovation. Creative confidence is like a muscle---it can be strengthened and nurtured through effort and experience."

http://en.wikipedia.org/wiki/David_M._Kelley

Carol Dweck social psychologist from Stanford University talks about the power of "mindset" and how if people think their intelligence is flexible and can grow, they will achieve, but if they think it is fixed and their is nothing they can do about it, they tend to be afraid to try. People with a growth mindset, understand that their talents and abilities can be developed through effort, good teaching and persistence. They think that if they persevere, (mastery learning concept) they will succeed.

http://en.wikipedia.org/wiki/Carol_Dweck

This is nothing new but it is hard to do than to say. Students will rise to meet the expectations of their teachers and parents. By giving students the respect and having the expectation, teachers will be empowering kids. Students need be given the opportunity to practice skills (mastery learning) until they get them right, that is little bits of learning that finally add up to an important skill and self confidence. In my experience, students will achieve at levels far beyond what is expected if you give them the opportunity. Just believing in them helps them believe in themselves.

Independence

We all like independence; it is the foundation of our nation. For most children it starts when they are two years old and want to do everything themselves—to the chagrin of their parents. In elementary school, students want to be independent too, but as they progress through the system, they become more dependent on the teacher. By the time they are in high school—if they have been taught according to the old model—they are waiting to be told what to do. However, high school is a time when the students' drive for independence should be at its peak. One way teachers can encourage this drive is to give students an opportunity to come up with their own projects within defined guidelines. For example, students could have a writing assignment, but one in which they pick the topic. It could be a restaurant review, with each student reviewing a restaurant of his or her choice.

Collaboration

Collaboration is an important part of the culture of the blended classroom. Students love to work with their peers, especially if they are working on a project they selected themselves. In fact, the main attraction of school for most students is being with their peers. So if teachers can make the environment a friendly, collaborative work space in which students feel comfortable, more learning will take place.

This type of learning is important for several reasons: 1) most workplaces today require collaboration and students need to practice those skills at school 2) students learn more when they are responsible for another students work 3) collaboration increases student interest in learning especially if it is on a common project such as a newspaper, magazine, video, or website.

Kindness

Kindness is self-evident. If students feel that the teacher is kind, they want to learn. I can remember many instances of being kind to students who had made mistakes. It paid off a hundred times, because the students were so grateful, it made them feel relaxed and accepted.. Being kind not only in school, but in life in general, makes the difference. As the American religious leader William J. H. Boetcker (1873–1962) put it: "Your greatness is measured by your kindness; your education and intellect by your modesty; your ignorance is betrayed by your suspicions and prejudices, and your real caliber is measured by the consideration and tolerance you have for others."

James Franco published a famous poster with me in which he says just that. "She showed me I could take my dreams as seriously as I wanted."

Behind every famous person is a fabulous teacher.

Spider-Man's **James Franco** admires high school teacher **Esther Wojcicki** for treating her journalism students like true professionals. "She showed me that I could take my dreams as seriously as I wanted," he recalls.

Esther loves to inspire her students: "Some students are afraid they cannot succeed, but if the teacher believes in them, they will believe in themselves."

BEYOND THE "3 Rs": 21ST-CENTURY SKILLS IN THE CLASSROOM

BY ESTHER WOJCICKI

While the 3 Rs have been part of the curriculum for nearly two centuries, blended learning just emerged at the beginning of the twenty-first century with the advent of technology in the classroom. Blended learning incorporates the 3 Rs—reading, writing, and arithmetic—but with online support. The reading is stories and articles found on websites; the writing uses collaborative programs like Google Docs; and the arithmetic is supported by programs like Khan Academy.

Blended learning, as we saw in chapter 1, incorporates both online delivery of content, where the student works at his or her own pace, and classroom interaction with the teacher and other students. Students do much of their computer work at home, but they still attend a regular school in which they have the usual face-to-face activities mixed in with computer-mediated activities.

There are many proponents of blended learning, and it is being facilitated by Google Apps for Education, now a huge movement and growing fast, with over 20 million users worldwide. One of the main advantages of Google Apps is the collaborative feature, which enables a user to work together with others on documents, spreadsheets, and presentations from any computer anywhere, as long as it is connected to the web.[1]

The 3 Rs were first declared to be the foundations of modern, skills-based Western education in the early nineteenth century. In many ways, this skills-driven approach still permeates curriculum and assessment design well into the twenty-first century. Consider any of the "high-stakes" standardized tests: for example, the ACT, GRE, or SAT. What does each examine? Generally speaking, they all measure the 3 Rs. I do not want to understate the importance of these skills, as they remain critical to academic and career success to this day. However, attention is now turning toward "twenty-first-century skills," which has become a buzzword in education circles in recent years. What are these "twenty-first-century skills," and how do they differ from the 3 Rs approach that has ruled much of the past two hundred years of education?

In recent years, researchers and policymakers have turned their focus to skills beyond domain-specific knowledge (i.e., the 3 Rs) that have been found to be important for twenty-first-century success. These skills are considered "non-cognitive," and might be better described as individual characteristics, rather than specific skill sets; they are not easily measured or quantified by traditional tests. These characteristics involve personal attitudes and social skills, and are not necessarily tied to performance in a specific domain, such as reading. In a February 2013 report by the U.S. Department of Education, a core set of non-cognitive skills—*grit*, *tenacity*, and *perseverance*—was identified as a critical factor for success in the twenty-first century. In this chapter, we will review some of the seminal research findings that support these claims, and discuss the implications of these "twenty-first-century skills" for teaching and learning in the classroom.

What Are "Twenty-First-Century Skills"?

As the twenty-first century has been characterized by rapidly changing technologies, today's young students need to develop skills beyond basic reading, writing, and math in order to become tomorrow's innovators. The Partnership for 21st Century Skills[2] has developed a framework for teaching and learning that fuses fundamental skills (the 3 Rs) with skills that promote innovative thinking. These skills are referred to as the "4 Cs":

1. Critical Thinking
2. Communication
3. Collaboration
4. Creativity

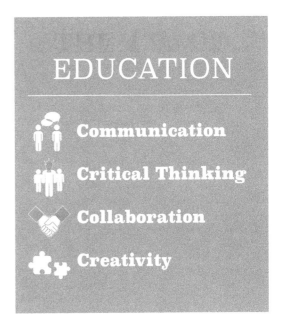

A key difference between the 3 Rs and the 4 Cs is that, while the Rs each refer to one specific type of skill or knowledge, the Cs cut across subject areas and are applicable to both academic and non-academic settings. As the 3 Rs are domain-specific, the 4 Cs are domain-general. Moreover, communication and collaboration require individuals to successfully interact with others. All four Cs require careful effort and analysis on the part of the student beyond rote memorization or procedures. As we examine a twenty-first-century learning framework, we will discuss the importance of social and emotional factors in learning, and how we as teachers can encourage and cultivate a fusion of the traditional 3 Rs with the 4 Cs of twenty-first-century learning in our classrooms.

Non-Cognitive Factors for Long-Term Success

'Tis a lesson you should heed:
Try, try, try again.
If at first you don't succeed,
Try, try, try again.
  —Thomas Palmer, *Teachers' Manual*, 1840

As it turns out, nineteenth-century educators had some solid foundations in their teaching methods that have withstood the test of time.

Between the 3 Rs and the sage advice to "try, try, try again," our predecessors have provided us with some strong ground to build upon as we devise our twenty-first-century "moonshot" in education. Although the adage to keep trying after initial failure(s) is ingrained in our minds from hearing it since childhood, what does it really mean in terms of learning? More specifically, how does "try, try, try again" apply to a classroom setting?

University of Pennsylvania professor of psychology and former middle-school math teacher Angela Duckworth has focused her research on two character traits that are positively correlated to success in life: grit and self-control. Grit is defined as sustained interest and effort toward long-term goals, and self-control involves the voluntary regulation of behavior, emotion, and attention in the presence of distractions or temptations.[3] Both of these characteristics involve perseverance through challenges (i.e., "try, try, try again"), which is applicable not only during the school years, but throughout the lifespan.

Angela Duckworth

Grit has been shown to be a trait that equips people to pursue challenging goals over years and even decades. As a teacher, Professor Duckworth noticed that effort was more closely tied to middle-school math achievement than sheer talent or IQ scores. Her later research has replicated her classroom observations across multiple measures of success. For example, grit has been found to predict, among many other things, graduation rates in Chicago public high schools, and rates of retention and performance of novice teachers as well as members of the U.S. Special Forces.

Policymakers have begun to take notice of the importance of grit in learning. The Common Core State Standards Initiative includes one measure for persistence on difficult problems.[4] The state of Illinois also measures social and emotional learning competency in its standards.[5] Although the integration of measures supporting grit and self-control into curricula is still in its earliest stages, we will discuss later in this chapter ways you can incorporate and support these measures in your classroom.

The study of self-control or willpower is not new. In 1972, Stanford psychologist Walt Mischel conducted a classic experiment[6] that has become known as the "marshmallow study." Thirty-two children, four to six years old, were told that they could have a treat (a marshmallow) immediately, or two treats if they were willing to wait until the experimenter returned after about fifteen minutes. The original participants in the study were followed throughout their lifetimes. Children who were able to delay gratification ("delayers") by waiting longer for rewards had better life outcomes, including higher SAT scores and educational attainment. Delayed gratification was also found to relate to physical measures of health such as lower body-mass index. There were also brain differences between the children who did not wait for their reward and those who did. Certain areas in the brain—the prefrontal cortex and the ventral striatum—were found to be more active in delayers than non-delayers. These brain regions have also been found important in studies of impulse control and addictive behaviors.

So far, we have pointed to research findings that suggest that overcoming challenges and being able to control one's impulses and delay gratification lead to better overall success in life, including measures of academic achievement like graduation rates and test scores. Great, you might be thinking, but this all seems a bit vague and abstract. How can support for "grit" and "self-control" be incorporated in my teaching practices?

"Desirable Difficulties" in Learning

Beyond the aforementioned studies that have shown positive associations between grit and willpower, on the one hand, and life accomplishments, on the other, researchers have also found direct evidence (as opposed to a correlation) that overcoming obstacles in the learning process can lead to improved retention of learned material over the

Robert A. Bjork
Professor of Psychology
UCLA

long term. Cognitive psychologist and memory expert Robert Bjork of the University of California, Los Angeles, has been conducting research on what he calls "desirable difficulties" in learning for over twenty years.

One of the most well-substantiated "desirable difficulties" in learning is the idea that spacing out learning sessions rather than massing them together leads to better long-term retention. Now, think back: In your student days, did you ever wait until the last minute to study for a test, leading to an all-night cram session? If you answered "no," I am very impressed! Study after study has shown that spacing out learning sessions makes you more likely to deeply process the information and remember it better and longer. If you crammed for an exam the night before, you might have been able to get a decent (or even excellent) grade on the test, but did you remember much about that course years later (or even a month or a week later)? According to scientific studies, the answer is probably not.

I know what you might be thinking. Science or no science, it would be a challenge to convince your students to quit cramming altogether, although we think it is definitely worth a try. After all, building good study habits in the earlier grades will help them in the long run. Fortunately, there are also several other desirable difficulties that you can introduce to your students that are supported by strong empirical evidence as being helpful for long-term learning and retention.

While tests are used principally for assessments or evaluations of learning, multiple studies have shown that the act of retrieving information from memory (e.g., during a test) enhances long-term retention of the learned material. Thus, a test is another beneficial opportunity to learn. According to many empirical investigations, something about the purposeful recall of information helps strengthen it in memory—a phenomenon known as *the testing effect* (e.g. Roediger & Karpicke, 2006).[7] The idea is that the retrieval of material from memory acts as an active type of practice where the learner re-familiarizes himself or herself with the information, which results in its reinforcement. One way you might be able to incorporate this type of active retrieval in your lessons is to schedule quizzes throughout a unit, rather than giving a summary assessment at the end. This way, students can revisit material throughout the course, and will hopefully not have to cram a marking period's worth of information into a last-minute study session right before the final exam.

> " Consistent review of material can also support students' understanding of how different concepts and lessons relate to one another, bolstering not only retention of material, but also the ability to apply it to other contexts. "

Consistent review of material can also support students' understanding of how different concepts and lessons relate to one another, bolstering not only retention of material, but also the ability to apply it to other contexts. We know that more testing might sound a bit unsavory—students get anxious before exams, and tests aren't exactly seen as "fun." This is where your expertise as a teacher and your experience with your students come into play. What are some interesting ways you can evaluate your students' knowledge throughout a unit without making it feel high-stakes? We are confident that your expertise and experience with your students will lead to great results. And as a bonus, you will be able to get quick snapshots of your students' understanding throughout the course or unit, rather than just at the end. These quick quizzes can serve as formative assessments, and can guide your lesson planning by highlighting topics that need review. You might also be able to pinpoint specific issues that a student is having, and be able to personalize his or her experience to make sure each learner is getting relevant feedback and reinforcements throughout the curriculum.

Another way to enhance the effect of regular tests involves the format. Multiple-choice tests are easy to grade and commonly used, but research has found that simply reading text does not activate one's memory processes as deeply as generating information independently (e.g. McDaniel et al., 1988).[8] These findings suggest that fill-in-the-blank, short-answer, or essay exams might engage students' memories

more than multiple-choice. Another way to support what McDaniel et al. call "the generation effect" is to have students come up with their own discussion questions after reading a text, and to collaborate with their peers to review the material. These types of assessments and activities are more challenging than your run-of-the-mill multiple-choice test, and your students will benefit from engaging more thoroughly with their course content, and might even find some personal inspiration from coming up with their own ideas and sharing them with others.

Simply changing routines might also enhance learning. Mix up the organization of materials; varying the order, presentation, or even location of learning has been found to present a desirable difficulty (e.g., Smith, Glenberg, & Bjork, 1978).[9] There have been countless studies on learning and memory, and one prominent takeaway message is this: It's not just the content, or *what* you're learning, but also the details of *when* and *how* things are presented. Varying these can be a subtle, but effective, agent for change in your classroom.

While "intellectual struggle" as a support for learning might be seen as counterintuitive in our culture here in the United States, researchers have found that Eastern cultures, such as Japan's and Taiwan's, consider struggle to be an integral part of the learning process. Jim Stigler, a psychologist and UCLA colleague of memory researcher Bob Bjork, once conducted a study with first-graders, where they were given an impossible math problem to solve. American students worked on the problem for less than thirty seconds on average before giving up, telling the researchers that they hadn't yet learned this type of problem. On the other hand, Japanese first-graders worked for the entire hour of the testing session, until they were told to stop. Stigler has found through his research of cross-cultural classroom differences that the act of struggling is framed differently by Eastern and Western cultures. In the West, he says, struggle is an indicator of low ability.[10] Americans tend to view intelligence as innate and fixed. However, in the East, struggle is seen as an opportunity to learn. Persisting through difficulty is used to measure "emotional strength" or, as Angela Duckworth calls it, "grit." In the following section, we review research on social and emotional factors in learning, and how they are critical for the development of twenty-first-century skills.

Social and Emotional Factors in Learning

At the beginning of this chapter, we touched upon the fact that policymakers are beginning to look at the influences of "non-cognitive" factors in academic success, and incorporating these ideas into their suggestions for education reform. In some schools, social and emotional learning, or SEL, has been implemented as a strategy to equip students with the emotional and psychological skills that will critically affect achievement both in and outside of the classroom. These schools, such as Garfield Elementary in Oakland, California, and Leataata Floyd Elementary in Sacramento, consider SEL as critical to academic

Sample Diagram measuring SEL

http://static.squarespace.com/static/513f79f9e4b05ce7b70e9673/t/522f344be4b06bf96fa45901/
1378825415158/social-and-emotional-learning-core-competencies

success, and strive to support emotion regulation in their young students, a key component of what they consider "psychological intelligence."[11]

At Garfield Elementary, kindergartners sit in a circle and discuss conflicts with parents at home and how to respond to them. "Mommy, I don't like when you scream at me," a five-year-old boy learns to express through role play, with help from his peers. Psychologists who study emotion have found that attention and memory can be greatly affected by emotions such as anxiety. A growing number of researchers and practitioners are now advocating that emotion regulation be taught in schools. Organizations like the George Lucas Educational Foundation[12] have spent the past decade lobbying for SEL to become commonplace in schools. A Chicago-based non-profit, the Collaborative for Academic, Social and Emotional Learning, evaluates emotional-literacy programs for their grounding in research-based evidence, and has approved several dozen as "evidence-based." It is now estimated that there are tens of thousands of emotional-literacy programs running nationwide. Early data do suggest positive academic, social, emotional, and behavioral outcomes from well-designed and well-implemented SEL programs,[13] (Society for Research in Child Development), though researchers caution against drawing broad conclusions, as these programs are not consistently implemented and there are few benchmarks on what constitutes effective integration of SEL into classroom practices.

However, researchers are optimistic that the addition and deep integration of SEL into daily interactions between teachers and students could greatly benefit children's lives. Strong non-cognitive skills developed during childhood have been found to predict positive employment outcomes, longevity of marriages, and better mental and physical health. Because children spend much of their time in school settings, these are a significant context for their social and emotional development. Rutgers University professor Maurice Elias, who serves as director of the Rutgers Social-Emotional Learning Lab, enthusiastically proclaims that emotional literacy could be the "missing piece" in the American education system. Other researchers are more cautiously optimistic about SEL integration into schools. Implementing and scaling programs in education broadly is quite difficult, and success is difficult to measure.

What we do know so far is that traits like self-control and empathy throughout life are closely tied to one's early-childhood environment. In addition to the robust research that links these characteristics to life success, kindergarten teachers have reported a direct relationship between emotion regulation and academic success in their students (Graziano et al., 2006).[14] Interestingly, it was emotion regulation along with quality of teacher-student relationship that uniquely predicted academic outcomes in one study, even after variations in IQ scores were taken into account. What this suggests is that being able to control one's emotions and relate well with others can have a strong influence on a child's academic performance, possibly even more so than scoring well on traditional measures of intelligence or skills like the 3 Rs.

These findings are particularly striking in the context of the focus on the 4 Cs of twenty-first-century learning. The abilities to keep calm under pressure and to relate well with others are crucial for productive communication and collaboration. Moreover, creativity involves taking chances, overcoming obstacles, and delaying gratification. And in order to think critically, one must undertake processes of analysis and problem solving, which can be challenging and unpredictable. Building empathy and strong communication skills at an early age will be important to students as they start to face the challenges of adulthood and the workforce.

Attention, Please!

We have spent quite a bit of time focusing on the non-cognitive skills that have been found to contribute to positive life outcomes—especially grit, self-control, and perseverance. We would be remiss if we did not discuss the cognitive skills that these qualities are most closely related to, which have also been researched at length for many years. Angela Duckworth's definition of self-control includes the ability to regulate one's attention in the face of many distractions. We are now going to discuss the cognitive process of attention itself, and how it can be taught as a skill.

In this rapidly paced world, where a never-ending stream of information flows across our computer screens, tablets, and smartphones, often in tiny bite-sized tidbits, maintaining one's attention on a singular focus might prove challenging, even for adult professionals who did not always think in 140-character fragments. In a recent article in *Slate.com*,[15] Swarthmore College psychology professor Barry Schwartz writes that his students seem to have shorter attention spans every year. But catering to these diminished attention spans is doing young students a disservice, Schwartz states, as maintaining attention is a skill that should be taught and reinforced, even in a culture where brevity is considered to be a highly attractive feature of online digital media—a presence that has become constant in our lives.

Schwartz believes that accepting short attention spans is a self-fulfilling prophecy, and simply offering materials based on the assumption that people cannot maintain attention is doing nothing to help them build this critical skill. He makes an analogy to bodybuilding: You can't expect someone to build up his biceps by lifting two-pound weights; by the same token, you can't flex your attention muscle by reading 140-character tweets. Here is where the cognitive aspects of attention tie in closely with the non-cognitive skills of grit and perseverance: If a student cannot maintain his attention in a single task, persevering through more difficult tasks until success is achieved will be virtually impossible. So how can we train students to sustain their attention in the classroom?

SLANT

Sit Up Straight
Listen
Ask Questions
Nod your Head
Track the Speaker

KIPP system

One technique has been implemented in the KIPP (Knowledge Is Power Program) charter schools, which have seen great success in graduation rates and college attendance. KIPP first-graders are taught to keep their focus by using a technique known by its acronym, SLANT:

*S*it up, *L*ook at and listen to the speaker, *A*sk questions, *N*od, and *T*rack the teacher. Having kids specify goals and plans to reach them have also been found by researchers to improve attention.

Attention and self-control have also been shown to relate to a set of cognitive processes called "executive function." Sometimes called "cognitive control," executive function is the regulation and control of processes including memory, reasoning, planning, and problem solving. It is related to an area of the brain called the prefrontal cortex, which is a region that does not fully mature until late adolescence or even adulthood. Executive function is measured by the ability to switch tasks fluidly, as well as the ability to focus on a single stream of information when there are multiple streams. Researchers have found a direct relationship between high executive function and academic achievement (Best, Miller, & Naglieri, 2011).[16] When executive function is measured through a standardized intelligence test,[17] evidence shows a strong correlation between executive function and both math and reading achievement, with similar patterns across age groups. This suggests that executive function is a domain-general skill that relates to overall academic achievement.

How to Encourage these Skills at Home and in the Classroom

This chapter has covered a variety of topics that are seldom discussed in teacher training, whether it be in a college lecture hall or in formal professional-development settings. For these reasons, we felt it was of utmost importance to discuss these concepts with you. Even if some—or all—of them are already familiar to you, we believe that there should be more conversation about how to encourage the development of skills such as grit, self-control, and executive function in classroom settings. This might be particularly important for school districts serving students from lower-income homes, a factor that has been well documented as closely correlated with lower academic achievement. One contributor to the income gap might be rooted in the early social and emotional environments of children. There is ample empirical evidence that children from lower-income families get less verbal interaction with their parents than children from higher-income families.[18] A recent study at Stanford has found this gap to be significant in children as young as eighteen months of age, with children from affluent families able to identify words much more readily than their peers from lower-income families. By age two, children from wealthier families had learned 30 percent more words (Fernald, 2013).[19] The implications are far-reaching, even at ages where kids might not be able to fully participate in conversations.

❝ Too many young children are entering school without the social and behavioral skills needed to succeed. ❞

While more language input from parents correlates strongly with cognitive-developmental milestones in language and concept acquisition, the emotional effects of the lack of social interaction with one's caregivers can also have great impact throughout a child's life. Researchers in social and emotional learning have cited numerous studies showing that too many young children are entering school without the social and behavioral skills needed to succeed (Gilliam & Shahar, 2006; Raver & Knitzer, 2002).[20]

Admittedly, there is still a lot of work to be done in trying to determine the best course of action in attempting to make meaningful changes in early-childhood learning environments, but there are some encouraging examples that show positive results. Dana Suskind, a pediatric surgeon at the University of Chicago specializing in cochlear implants, noticed that her patients from lower-income families lagged behind their wealthier peers in learning to speak post-surgery. Citing a landmark study (Hart & Risley, 1995)[21] indicating that children born into poverty had heard 30 million fewer words from their parents by age three than kids from higher-income families, with direct impacts on IQ measurements and academic outcomes, Dr. Suskind and her colleagues began The Thirty Million Words Project,[22] in which low-income mothers are trained in a "parent-talk" curriculum developed by Suskind and her staff. She is also conducting numerous studies on the impact of the quality and quantity of caregiver speech to young children. One recently published report indicates that even affluent children can benefit from more targeted interaction and speech. These findings indicate that social, emotional, and cognitive development are all intricately intertwined.

While some of this research is still in its infancy, we can conclude that the nineteenth-century focus on domain-specific skills like the 3 Rs needs an overhaul to take account of current evidence that clearly illustrates the importance of the 4 Cs and SEL. Research must continue into the best practices for integrating social and emotional learning into our curricula. In the meantime, we will discuss tools and methods that we and others have found to be effective in inspiring and engaging students. As always, this is an ongoing conversation, and we invite you to contribute what has worked best for you. In a later chapter, we will discuss some ways in which you can share your knowledge and learn from like-minded others as well.

The Role of Technology in SEL and the Classroom

In speaking with numerous teachers about the use of technology in their schools, we have found that one word seems to come up most frequently—"engagement." Perhaps you have seen a young child navigate a touchscreen with great fluency and gusto, or a middle-schooler come up with the answer to a question via the Internet before you even finish asking it. Technology seems to capture the attention and imagination of students, and can offer useful tools for enhancing their learning experiences. What types of tools can we use to engage students, as well as support the development of both cognitive and non-cognitive skills?

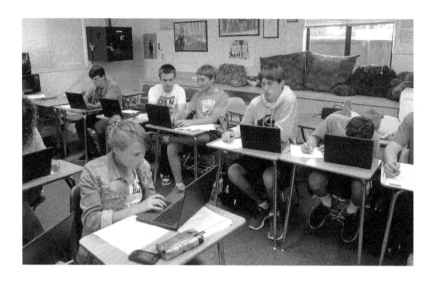

In the next chapter of this book, we will describe several examples of successful implementation of blended and project-based learning in schools across the country and the world. We will discuss both technological tools and methodologies teachers have used that provide scaffolding for students in learning both academic skills (like math) and social skills (like creativity and collaboration). As you read about what has led to positive outcomes in other scenarios, we invite you to consider both successes and challenges you have had in your own classroom, and what tools and tips might be most helpful to you. Again, we would like to emphasize that these anecdotes and suggestions are not meant to be read as "how-to" guides. We highly encourage experimentation—you will know what is working and what is not in your own classroom. Some results might take a bit of time to see. When it comes to moonshots in education, grit, tenacity, and perseverance are not only important characteristics for students to have—we teachers benefit from these critical skills as well. And as Thomas Palmer said so many years ago, if at first you don't succeed . . .

ONLINE SEARCH SKILLS MATTER: TIPS ON HOW TO TEACH THEM TO YOUR STUDENTS

BY DANIEL M. RUSSELL

5

It is the technology age, the age when everyone has a smart phone in their pocket or nearby, or a tablet or a computer. Phone is a 20th century concept since all you could do with it was make or receive a call. But today with the smart phone you can listen to music, find out how to get somewhere, find a restaurant for dinner and most important SEARCH for information. Thus, the most important skill that a teacher can give a student in the 21st century is how to search intelligently on the web, how to find the information you are looking for quickly. Many people don't even know the possibilities for information that can be found if you know how to search intelligently and that brings me to Dan Russell, the Guru king of search at Google. Dan is a Research Scientist at Google who is in charge of "User Happiness," an appropriate title since if you can find what you want, you will be happy. He is an outstanding speaker and also has an excellent website loaded with resources for teachers who want to teach about search in their classroom.

I was lucky enough to have Dan to write a chapter for this book on search to help all of you be better searchers yourself and better teachers of search. —E.W.

There's always been a gap between those who know how to use information resources and those who don't. Students who knew the ways to leverage a library for research could consistently do better research than those who couldn't.

But this gap is turning into a vast chasm of difference. Students who know how to use online resources efficiently and effectively will be able to massively outperform students who don't. This is a qualitative change from the days of paper-based libraries and information resources. Then, doing research was largely limited to what you could reach out and touch by hand. Now, it's possible for students to do research on information that's scattered across the entire planet; and they're not limited just to finding text in documents.

Here's my favorite example of this change. In the 1990s, I used to teach algorithms to my graduate students in Computer Science as a way to help them understand the details of artificial intelligence. If you can write a program to do some task better than a human can do it, then you're well on the way to understanding how this algorithm operates and in the process, you'd learn something about the nature of intelligence. I did this for years—handing out the assignment one week, and then expect the homework to be done four weeks later after we'd covered the material, discussed how things worked, and let them write the code. In the early 2000s, I noticed that my students were suddenly turning in their assignments weeks ahead of schedule. *Weeks ahead of the syllabus?* That didn't seem possible, until I asked around and found that they were just Googling for the code, finding that someone else had written it already, modifying it slightly, and then turning it in as their solution.

That was a few years ago, but it set the stage for what's happening now. It was never great educational philosophy to just shovel facts to a student and then ask them to pick the right one from the set of options, but now, with search engines and an immensity of online content available in milliseconds, it's a truly terrible idea. Students who are good researchers can find information on a topic faster than you can push it to them.

This is as true in the elementary grades as it is in graduate school. We all know sixth graders who can (with the aid of their phone and a quick search) name all of the signers of the Constitution in less than 10 seconds. Suddenly, what it means to know something has profoundly changed. There's a difference between knowing, and knowing how. There's a difference between knowing that something exists, being able to find it rapidly with a moment's worth of research, and then being able to pull together multiple sources of information into a coherent analysis.

> " Having research skills isn't just an optional part of your education— they're essential. "

In particular, the *research skills gap* is growing. Students (and teachers, and for that matter, employees) who are able to do rapid and accurate research on a topic have a substantial advantage in getting things done and deepening their understanding. What's more, there's an unexpected second-order effect: those that have developed and sharpened their research skills can grow those research skills over time, increasingly widening the gap from their peers who haven't mastered that self-teaching nuance. Having research skills isn't just an optional part of your education—they're essential. Especially once you know how to research to upgrade your research skills.

It's important to realize that there is a fundamental change going on in what it means to learn. We know that memorizing the US presidents in election order isn't really a useful skill for most students. It's rare that anytime after high school that you'll be asked if Chester Arthur was before, or after, James Garfield. It's even less likely that you'll be asked how many US presidents were in the Whig party. But it takes a student about 5 seconds to find the number. (I timed my students doing this. It does take around five seconds, limited mostly by typing speed. Their answer? There were four, the first was William Harrison, and the last was Millard Fillmore.)

But if you don't know the names of the presidents, if you have never studied them as a group, in a sequence, possibly with their party affiliations, then you won't recognize the name of Millard Fillmore as a Whig president, but perhaps only as the name of a trivia hunt game.

The very nature of what it means to know is shifting our understanding of teaching, and what's important for our students to command. Students still need to know about presidents, their policies, and the role they play in the history of the nation. For example, Fillmore wasn't elected president, but assumed the presidency when Zachary Taylor died in office. His attitudes about slavery influenced the course of the Civil War. Students still need to know these kinds of things, and is possible that learning the sequence of presidential elections is a good way to introduce those ideas. But just as important, they need to know how to find out more about a topic. They need to command the key ideas, and recognize the presidents, their policies, and their parties—but to answer most questions that will come up require the skills of research.

Motivating Questions

We have found that teaching research skills is best taught with genuinely interesting research questions. These don't have to be rocket science, but they do have to be compelling and interesting to the students. While every student population is somewhat different, there are a few guidelines for creating questions that move students to build their skills.

Great research questions for students:

1. ... *aren't just busy work, but lead to an unexpected insight about the world.* Excellent research questions for teaching are those that are actually of interest to the students and lead to a surprise. For instance, a question such as "Are any insects in your yard viviparous?" means that a student will probably have to look up the definition of the word "viviparous," and then spend some time listing local insects to see if any of them are. Since insects normally lay eggs, discovering that some actually are viviparous (that is, give birth to live young) is a surprise. By contrast, "busy work" questions are those that are clearly made to exercise a skill in a trivial way (such as "find the definitions of 20 words you don't know" or "what is the 100th digit in the decimal expansion of pi?").

2. ... *tap into something that's of interest to the students.* Almost every place has insects, some of which feed on humans. That's a topic of direct interest to nearly everyone. Other kinds of local interest are sports, local events, nearby historical locations, and so on.

3. ... *teach a specific research skill.* There are many research skills to learn. (A short list might include, how to find and access archival content, how to search out credible resources, when to stop searching, when to ask a friend for help, how to discover the specific terms that help identify a particular idea, or how to recognize and search for specific quotations.) We know how to write test questions that assess particular pieces of knowledge, but the art of writing research questions for students that exercise these skills, while also being insightful and inherently interesting, that's another skill for teachers to develop.

How to Write Questions for AGoogleADay

The website AGoogleADay.com gives students a chance to practice their research skills with several questions each day. Each question is a mini-research project that takes some time to work through. Writing them for students illustrates the craft of creating research questions to teach research skills.

The question I'll use as an example is *"What is the demonym for the inhabitants of the capital of Argentina?"* This question started life as just "What do people in Buenos Aires call themselves?" Once I looked that up, I realized that the answer is somewhat surprising. (Answer: *Porteños*.) That's one criterion ("unexpected insight"). But just asking that question was too simple. I made the question slightly more interesting by adding the uncommon term "demonym" (which means "name of the resident of a locality," such as "San Franciscan") and adding another subquestion, ".. inhabitants of the capital of Argentina?" Those make the question interesting and also teach a specific research skill.

To answer this research question, the student had to go through a multistep process. First, look up "demonym," then figure out what is the "capital of Argentina," then discover what citizens of Buenos Aires call themselves. The surprise twist comes from the observation that they do not call themselves "Buenos Airians" or anything similar.

More sophisticated research questions can have multiple parts, or require pulling together information from different resources into a single, unified answer. Just as shown above, more advanced researchers can find information from multiple sources, and then create a small analysis showing why one answer is better (or more credible) than another.

Again, details vary from classroom to classroom. Students are very different from year-to-year, from place-to-place. Teachers know from experience what triggers the imagination. Great research questions tap into this knowledge and motivate students to dig deeply.

Pragmatics

A key step to writing research questions is to first solve them yourself before handing them out as an assignment. You'll be surprised how often a much simpler approach (or at least one different than the one you're trying to teach) will lead to a quick solution. Most important, this verifies that the lesson you're hoping to teach will be the lesson that is actually taught.

While creating a good research question is important, writing background supporting materials for a research question is often key to generating interest and creating motivation for the students. Often students have no real expectations about the subject matter, so finding something that's *surprising* is difficult. They often don't have strong expectations, so the background material provides some context and understanding of what's important about the research question. The trick here is to write a compelling mini-story without necessarily giving everything away. As with writing the research question to begin with, an important part of the supporting materials is to communicate something that's surprising and engaging, given where the students are coming from.

For instance, a research question about Native American languages used as "code talking" languages would fit easily into many curricula as a way to talk about modern history (the use of code talkers in World War II), language (the way verbs are conjugated in Navajo), and so on. Supporting materials for the research question should give suggestions about directions that further research could go as well as providing context. In this example, the supplemental materials might give questions about what other Native American languages were used for code talking (it wasn't all only Navajo), or how the Axis powers tried to handle and decode the languages they heard on the radio, or why Native American languages are so different than Indo-European languages (and why that made decoding them so very difficult).

Sometimes questions that seem obvious can actually lead to some surprising results. More than one student has turned in a learned research paper about a topic that was very different than the one that was assigned. When students have access to the entire resources of search engines, disambiguation (that is, telling one "John Smith" apart from another person also named "John Smith") is an important skill. This is another reason to verify the research question by testing it yourself. This is a major change from the days when information resources were relatively static and unchanging. Now, a new person named "John Smith" might become dominant (say, due to a prevalent news story) and overwhelm the search results for "John Smith of Jamestown," which is the intended "John Smith."

As a consequence, research questions need to be written that tell students which of the possible interpretations is meant. Instead of "John Smith was given a knighthood by which royal person?" a better, less ambiguous research question might be "John Smith (1580-1631) was given a knighthood by which royal person?"

Evaluation Changes

For AGoogleADay.com, the ideal answer is one that can be checked quickly and by a short program. Unlike a multiple-choice question, these are open-ended, short answers; no essays are required. Since the responses are open-ended, this means that students typically can't recognize the correct answer hidden in a set of options, or just scan the text and spot the answer in the middle of the text. Instead, they have to actually *research* the question, read and understand some of the content they find, and then respond with a short, unambiguous answer. In the demonym example given above, unless you already know what the answer is, you can't just scan through a book about Buenos Aires looking for an answer that "looks right." You actually have to know what a demonym is, then read about how local people talk about themselves. You have to locate the appropriate text and then read carefully. If a set of options are given as a multiple-choice question, chances are good that a student could figure out the right answer from the spelling alone. ("Porteño" looks like a word from Argentina.)

But for more sophisticated research tasks such as those given in the classroom, the answer ideally has to be drawn from multiple sources. Interesting research questions thus demand a bit more from the teachers evaluating the answers. For a question such as "What Native American languages were used for code talking during World War II?" instructors need to not just carefully read the responses, but be prepared to learn something new themselves. It's quite possible that despite upfront testing during question preparation, there is something new, something more to be discovered. Like as not, the students will find it. Again, as information resources grow and evolve, teachers need to understand that new discoveries will be made—some of which will change the answers to research questions.

For a teacher evaluating the written report that draws on new information, this presents a new and interesting challenge. It's not impossible for a middle school student to discover, in the process of her research, some new item that has been recently added to the available resources on the web. As major institutions keep adding new and searchable materials, this high quality content from reputable sources might well change the way students write their reports. Recent examples include the University of Cambridge putting up all of Isaac Newton's handwritten notebooks, or the US Census release new data reports that give new information about immigration patterns, and the Smithsonian National Museum of the American Indian adding thousands of new images to their searchable online collection.

Several of the Common Core standards make these skills a requirement. The "English and Writing Arts" standards (CCSS. ELA-LITERACY.RH.6-8.1 and CCSS.ELA-LITERACY.RH.6-8.2) highlight the research skills of finding and using primary sources. An advantage goes to the student who can quickly find primary resources on topics of Native American languages used for code talking or locate original newspaper coverage of Millard Fillmore's attitudes about abolition. Good research skills are exactly what a student needs in order to be able to "determine the central ideas or information of a primary or secondary source; provide an accurate summary of the source distinct from prior knowledge or opinions." With efficient research skills comes additional time spent on doing the reading, analysis, and understanding.

What this Means for Teaching

It's clear that the skills of research are broad and varied, encompassing aspects of credibility assessment, query formulation, effective question-asking, and synthesis of information found from multiple sources. It's also clear that research skills are not being taught in any organized, centralized fashion. While some schools have media literacy courses, relatively few teach Research 101.

Just as reading, writing, and math are fundamental skills, so too are the broader Research skills. They too need to be a part of our lesson plans, for art history as much as world history, and for mathematics as much as for current events.

Writing your own research questions and reading through student answers to those questions is quickly becoming a fascinating part of teaching. The canon no longer stays still as it used to do in a traditional textbook. The culture has moved beyond that and is well into the realm of real-time knowledge available to everyone. Our students need to know how to tap into these resources, as do we.

MOONSHOT TOOLS

AGoogleADay.com
A daily trivia game that encourages students to use a search engine to find the answers to short, engaging questions.

PowerSearchingWithGoogle.com
An online class that's always available for students of research methods. It's specifically aimed at teaching tactical search skills on Google, but it goes into some more advanced research strategies near the end. This is really a MOOC that is offered as a "live" class (that is, with thousands of students taking the class simultaneously) several times each year. But the content is always available for use year-round.

Google Search Education
A large collection of content for teaching search and research skills at beginning / intermediate / advanced levels (including links to downloadable lesson plans and activities, links to video content, schedules of upcoming training events, etc.).

Google Education
Learning resources from Google covering everything from Search Education through coding and training opportunities.

Videos on How to Search from Dan Russell and Sal Khan, founder of the Khan Academy

"Search by Image" (5 minutes):
http://www.youtube.com/watch?v=v0kGEP-0Ttw

"Recycling in Mumbai" (8 minutes):
http://www.youtube.com/watch?v=UG9hjtAXufg

"Finding the shortest president" (4 minutes):
http://www.youtube.com/watch?v=3m7j-JCW8wU

"Population growth rate of India and the US" (12 minutes):
http://www.youtube.com/watch?v=FGQlniksGlo

Articles on Teaching Research Skills

"Powerful literacies: Why and how vast knowledge matters more than ever" See http://dmrussell.net/presentations/Powerful-literacies-Why-vasty-knowledge-matters-Jan-2014.pdf.

Google in Education—Napa Valley Institute
See http://napainstitute2014.sched.org/.

"What does it mean to be literate in the Age of Google?" Association of Computer Technology Educators of Maine, Augusta, Maine, October 11, 2013
See http://lectures.princeton.edu/2012/daniel-m-russell/

"Digging In with Google" Investigative Reporters and Editors IRE Conference, San Antonio, Texas, June 22, 2013
See http://ire.org/conferences/ire-2013/sessions/.

Advanced Power Searching Skills for Business Journalists Arizona State University, Phoenix, Arizona, March 19, 2013
See https://www.youtube.com/watch?v=YhXQ7QmEbtY.

Mindtools: What it Means to be Literate Now
Google Apps for Education Summit,
Honolulu, Hawaii, January 8, 2013
http://dmrussell.net/papers/Mindtools-talk-Jan-2013.pdf

150K+ Students per Class: What it takes to design, operate, and run a MOOC at scale Future of Information Alliance presentation, Washington, D.C., November 12, 2012

Classes on Search

Lesson Plans for Teaching Search
Search education lesson plans–sixteen different lessons on how to search at basic, intermediate, and advanced levels of difficulty
http://www.google.com/insidesearch/searcheducation/lessons.html.

Basic Class
Become a Super Internet Searcher
Covers basic web architecture and basic search techniques
http://dmrussell.googlepages.com/BecomingaSuperInternetSearcher.pdf.

Intermediate Internet Search Skills
Covers topics between basic and advanced
https://sites.google.com/site/dmrussell/Home/intermediate-search.

Advanced Class
Offers a good problem set; research literacy; overview of different Google content types; assessing web-page credibility
See https://sites.google.com/site/dmrussell/presentations-1/Becoming-a-super-internet-searcher-practicum.pdf?attredirects=0.

Practicum Class
Advanced problem set; review of CSEs, Alerts, search web history, Toolbar
https://sites.google.com/site/dmrussell/presentations-1/Becoming-a-super-internet-searcher-practicum.pdf?attredirects=0.

Teacher's Class
A two-hour hands-on tutorial on search intended for teachers. Covers keyword choice, query refinement, other kinds of media, advanced operators, credibility assessment. All in two hours.
See http://dmrussell.googlepages.com/Google-search-for-teachers-complete.ppt.

Web Credibility
How do you learn to tell if something is credible or not. A two-hour hands-on class for teachers.
https://sites.google.com/site/dmrussell/Home/Credibilityclass.pdf?attredirects=0.

Search for Librarians
Top 12 Things You Need to Know. Covers twelve short lessons on different methods for search. One-hour class. Posted: October 14, 2009
https://sites.google.com/site/dmrussell/presentations/Top-12-things-you-should-know.pdf?attredirects=0.

GET INSPIRED: REAL-LIFE EXAMPLES OF MOONSHOTS IN EDUCATION

BY ESTHER WOJCICKI

6

Educators know that no two classrooms, teachers, or students are the same. So what might work best for you and your students might not be ideal for the teacher across the hall, let alone one in another district, state, or country. With that in mind, the aim of this chapter is to describe a wide range of interesting methods that have worked well in a diverse array of school settings. Instead of considering any of these examples as a strict blueprint for your own classroom, we challenge you to think outside the box: How might some of the best practices from your past experiences be applied in new ways? Perhaps you will find some inspiration from one or more of the following profiles from schools that have taken innovative approaches to teaching and learning. We invite you to think about how some of these scenarios might play out in your own classroom.

Some things to keep in mind as you read this chapter includes the particular constraints of your school or district. We understand that individual teachers do not always have a lot of flexibility or choice when it comes to hardware or software. Some teachers might not have the infrastructure in their school to access reliable Internet service, and others may not have enough (or any) devices to run desirable programs. We want to be clear that we do not believe that "moonshot thinking" is contingent upon having the newest software or top-of-the-line gadgets. We believe in maximizing what you have, and we are confident that with a bit of creativity and resourcefulness, your moonshot is actually much closer than you think, even if your district is not especially high-tech or well off.

A More Detailed Look at Blended Learning

In Chapter 1 we quoted the definition of blended learning given by Michael Horn of the Innosight Institute, now known as the Clayton Christensen Institute for Disruptive Innovation. In 2011, Innosight published a free book, *The Rise of K–12 Blended Learning*. It is an excellent book outlining forty schools and districts that are using this approach. In the three years since it was published, blended learning has grown tremendously, but it is still a long way from being universal.

> The definition of blended learning is a formal education program in which "a student learns at least in part at a supervised brick and mortar location away from home and at least in part through online delivery with some elements of student control over time, place, path and/or pace. In addition, the modalities along each student's learning path within a course or subject are connected to provide an integrated learning experience."

There are four blended-learning models given by the Christensen Institute:

1. The Rotation Model
2. The Flex Model
3. The a-la-Carte Model
4. The Enriched Virtual Model

1. The Rotation Model

There are four different rotation models in which students rotate between lecture, group work, homework, and online learning on a fixed schedule or at the teacher's discretion. The proportion of online learning to classroom learning can change in each of the four models as the teacher finds appropriate.

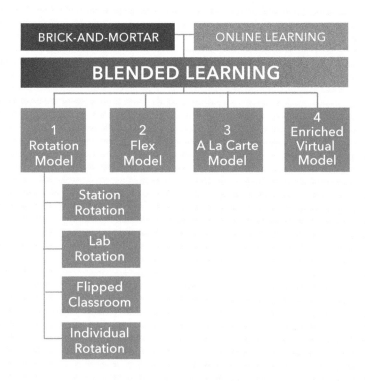

Source: http://www.christenseninstitute.org/wp-content/uploads/2013/04/ blended-learning-taxonomy1.jpg

Station rotation

The student rotates between lecture, group work, projects, and online learning within the classroom.

Lab rotation

The student rotates between the classroom and a computer lab or other locations on campus.

Flipped classroom

The teacher records videos of himself or herself using QuickTime or Camtasia, and then students watch the lectures at home. They come to school ready to do the exercises or hands-on work that used to be the homework. Hence, it is called the "flipped classroom," because the classwork and homework have flipped places.

Individual rotation

The student rotates on an individual basis among learning modalities, one of which is online learning.

2. The Flex Model

In this program, the majority of instruction is online, combined with small-group instruction, group projects, and face-to-face instruction.

3. The a-la-Carte Model

This is a program in which students take one or more courses entirely online with an online teacher of record and at the same time continue to have brick-and-mortar educational experiences. This is a course-by-course model. Students may take the online courses either on the brick-and-mortar campus or off-site. This differs from full-time online learning and from the Enriched Virtual Model because it is not a whole-school experience.

4. The Enriched Virtual Model

This is a *whole-school experience* in which students divide their time between attending a brick-and-mortar campus and learning remotely using online delivery of content and instruction. Many Enriched Virtual programs began as full-time online schools and then developed blended programs to provide students with brick-and-mortar school experiences. The Enriched Virtual Model differs from the flipped classroom because in Enriched Virtual programs, students do not usually attend the brick-and-mortar campus every weekday. It differs from the a-la-Carte Model because it is a whole-school experience, not a course-by-course model.

One common misconception is that blended learning can be simply equated to technology-enabled or online learning. Blended learning does typically include some online instruction, though a more important component of a blended experience—indeed an essential one—is that the student can control his or her own pace, allowing for personalization of both content and timing of curriculum to an individual's needs without a strict time limit. Ideally, a student can feel empowered to review a particular concept for as long as it takes until he or she feels that it has been mastered. Another component of blended learning is classroom instruction of the more traditional sort, led by a teacher in a brick-and-mortar location away from a student's home. Online and offline learning are integrated to create an environment that promotes mastery-based learning and emphasizes the students' ownership over their own educational experiences.

Now, this description might sound familiar to you, but you may not have heard it referred to as "blended learning." Perhaps you have heard of similar programs described as "deeper learning," "project-based learning," or even "twenty-first-century learning." Again, blended learning does not have one strict pattern, but it is centered on the empowerment of students to take ownership of their own learning, and on development of the 4 Cs for twenty-first-century learning.

Real-Life Examples from the Classroom

Flipped Classroom: Los Altos School District

As mentioned above, in the flipped classroom, homework and in-classroom work are flipped. Instead of being introduced to a topic through a teacher's lecture in the classroom, students learn the basics of a concept as homework. For example, in a flipped math class, the homework assignment might include a Khan Academy video, which the students watch at home, that walks them step by step through the procedure of how to divide fractions. The next day, their in-school experience might involve interactive exercises or projects about fractions, personalized to each student's learning needs. Some activities might include using adaptive math software in a computer lab or tablet learning games.

In one flipped-classroom model, the Los Altos School District, in Los Altos, California, has partnered with the non-profit Khan Academy since 2010. During this time, Los Altos has used Khan's videos and software in a blended-learning initiative in math, rolling the program out across grades five through eight. The "flip" in the Los Altos math classrooms has evolved quite a bit beyond simply viewing video content at home and doing corresponding math exercises at school. Khan Academy's software not only allows teachers to see the problems their students are answering correctly and incorrectly; it also provides a dashboard of data ranging from the amount of time students spent on a particular exercise, to the exact concepts that students rewind and rewatch in their videos.

Los Altos teachers use this information to provide the most timely and appropriate support possible to each student. With knowledge of each student's specific challenges, teachers can maximize their classroom time by providing tailored one-on-one instruction, supplementing learning with additional interactive offline activities, or allowing students to work collaboratively on group projects. Khan

Academy has also benefited greatly from partnering with Los Altos. Data insights from classroom usage help its developers determine the features that provide the best support for both students and teachers. For example, student data indicate the types of exercises and feedback that lead to the most meaningful learning gains, and help shape the analytics dashboard to provide the highest-quality insights for teachers.

● MOONSHOT TOOLS

How to Flip your Classroom

Interested in implementing a "flip" in your own classroom? If you, like many teachers, are accustomed to spending a majority of teaching time standing in front of your students lecturing, you might want to experiment with assigning your lecture content as homework. If textbooks are your typical source for content delivery, you might consider supplementing them with other media, or asking your students to find or create their own content, inspired by their interests.

You might be pleasantly surprised by just how creative they can be! In later chapters of this book, we will provide more specific suggestions based on grade level and subject that we hope will spark some ideas on how to maximize your classroom time to bring out the innovator both in you and in each one of your students.

Los Altos illustrates that blended learning can be personalized to both the student *and* the teacher. It truly can be what you make of it, and what works best for you and your students. While it is understandable that implementing a brand-new system is daunting at first, you might find, as teachers in Los Altos and other districts have, that you are now able to provide more meaningful guidance to each student, as well as greater collaboration within the classroom. Keep in mind that you can tweak the methods you use over time, and that it might not be obvious right away whether your changes are working. Our advice is to be patient and use your best judgment. You will be able to tell if your students are responding well.

Rotation Models: Gilroy Prep and KIPP Comienza

Does your school have computer labs, laptop carts, or access to tablets? If so, a rotation model of blended learning might yield positive results for your students. In a *lab rotation*, students rotate between a computer lab, where they focus on individualized online learning, and a classroom (and/or other locations) where they work on offline activities, which may include group projects, hands-on activities, or more traditional teacher-led instruction. As with the flipped classroom, a rotation model is highly customizable, and activities both in the lab and in the classroom can be tailored to each student at the discretion of the teacher. In one successful implementation of the rotation model, students at Gilroy Prep, a Navigator charter school in Gilroy, California, use lab time to work on math and reading skills, with online assessments to keep teachers abreast of each student's progress.

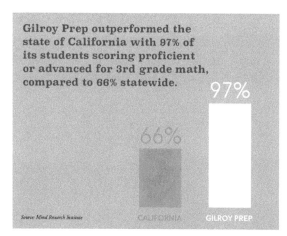

Gilroy Prep outperformed the state of California with 97% of its students scoring proficient or advanced for 3rd grade math, compared to 66% statewide.

97%

66%

Source: Mind Research Institute

CALIFORNIA   GILROY PREP

In just three years, Gilroy Prep has leveraged a combination of technology, innovative teaching methods, and interventions to close the achievement gap, reaching 97 percent proficiency in third-grade math, compared to the state average of 66 percent.

During an eight-hour school day, students spend about one hundred minutes using computers. Class time is designed to promote mastery, and involves high-energy activities such as songs and chants to help children connect to and better understand concepts.

With touchscreen computers and iPads available, student progress is carefully monitored during computer time using SuccessMaker, an adaptive digital curriculum that provides a customized learning path and scaffolded feedback based on student performance. Teachers are also trained to use ST Math (ST is short for "Spatial-Temporal"), a software program developed by the MIND Research Institute. Developed on the basis of research findings in neuroscience and mastery-based learning, the program introduces math concepts through game-based visual learning, and has improved standardized math scores across eight states in just one to two years. Gilroy Prep has integrated ST Math into its blended-learning model not only by assigning it during computer lab time, but also by sending its teachers to a professional-development program geared toward ST Math, carefully monitoring student progress, and implementing interventions when needed.

If computer labs aren't available in your school, don't fret—a *station rotation* blended-learning model can be implemented in a single classroom. This might involve small groups of students rotating between stations, one of which might include use of computers or tablets. At KIPP Comienza Community Prep School in Los Angeles, Google Chromebooks and tablets are rotated among over three hundred students so that everyone gets a turn.

With no more than fifteen students at each station at a time, students using computers are assessed via adaptive software in reading, writing, math, and science. Programs include the Common Core Standards–aligned DreamBox Learning for math, and Accelerated Reader for reading practice. These technologies allow review of challenging concepts and give students the ability to move more quickly through material that they already understand. Insights generated from these software packages are provided to the teacher in real-time reports, allowing offline small-group instruction time to be customized for each student. If you have a limited number of computers or tablets available to you, experimenting with small groups in a station-rotation model might be a way to provide more differentiated instruction to your students. In addition to the tools and programs we have already mentioned, Chapter 6 provides a breakdown of many more resources that you might want to try in your classroom.

Flex Model: Summit Public Schools

At Summit Public Schools (grades 6–12) in Sunnyvale, California, a unique approach to blended learning has shown measurable results in a school environment in which 67 percent of students are learning English as a second language. In a great example that shows how blended learning can encompass many different teaching methods and environments, Summit's flex model adapts to each student and takes an innovative approach akin to that of an early-stage high-tech startup in Silicon Valley. Online-learning time at Summit includes a cus-

tomized content "playlist" for each student, which he or she completes at his or her own pace, using a school-provided Chromebook. Face-to-face interactions with teachers are flexible, and adapted to the current needs of the student. Summit believes that project-based learning is critical for college and "real world" success, and dedicates much of its classroom time (one hundred hours per subject per school year) to small-group projects. With possibilities ranging from domain-specific presentations like science experiments to interdisciplinary projects covering multiple subject areas, teachers help facilitate and pace student groups, who have autonomy in the methods and tools they use to complete their work.

With the goal of building a culture of innovation, Summit Public Schools utilizes "lean startup" methodology, subscribing to the mantra popularized by Eric Ries: "Build, measure, learn." In order to determine what the best course of action is for each student, Summit relies on and highly values student feedback. Students are encouraged to speak up with their opinions on all aspects of the learning process. If and when something is not having the desired result, teachers work with students to try to devise and implement a different course of action.

● MOONSHOT TOOLS

To read more about Summit Public Schools' flex model of blended learning and to spark some new ideas of your own, check out their profile on the Christensen Institute's website. http://www.christenseninstitute.org/summit-public-schools/

This flexible, adaptive culture has led to Summit's development of its six-point core "flex model" of blended learning. Not only do teachers facilitate group projects and personalized learning for their students, they also act as mentors—supporting growth both in and outside of the academic setting. Teachers are each assigned ten to fifteen student mentees, and meet with each of them once a week to discuss their personal learning goals. Summit students also focus two hours a week on reading-comprehension skills using an eReader software called Curriculet (formerly Gobstopper), which allows teachers to embed quizzes and other assessments within text to quickly assess the best ways to support each student's reading skills. Students are also encouraged to be active in their communities, and they meet weekly in groups to discuss issues that are important to them. Summit also dedicates eight weeks of the school year to "expeditions," where students can elect to take courses in extracurricular areas of interest or pursue internships or "passion projects." These expeditions allow students the unique opportunity to consider their long-term career goals by applying skills learned in school to real-world settings.

Project-Based Learning: Acton Academy

Acton Academy, in Austin, Texas—currently serving grades 1 to 9, with plans to open a high school for the 2015–16 school year—stands out with its project-based curriculum and its mission of supporting each student on his or her unique path in life. Acton Academy's curriculum aims to help students "learn to know," "learn to do," and "learn to be." As part of the "learn to know" portion of the curriculum, students spend ninety minutes in the morning and ninety min-

utes in the afternoon on computer-based learning. During this personal work time, they may choose from one of four online programs to supplement their learning. These consist of software that reinforces skills in reading (Learning Today), math (DreamBox), spelling (ClickNKids), and foreign languages (Rosetta Stone). Other programs used at Acton include Khan Academy, Manga High, GoodReads, and NoRedInk. Since students are allowed to choose the software and games that support their reading, writing, and math skills, they feel empowered to take control of their learning and create their own personalized experience.

Hands-on science projects—part of the "learn to do" in Acton's curriculum—allow students to participate directly in the process of scientific inquiry. Each Tuesday, students receive a new challenge. For example, one week they were tasked with determining which model of a paper airplane could fly the farthest. After receiving the challenge, students are given time to tackle it on their own. Then a lesson and discussion follow on the scientific principles underlying the challenge. Finally, they return to the initial question with newly acquired knowledge they can apply to solve the problem.

Beyond the use of software and projects in this blended-learning approach, Acton Academy encourages critical thinking and mastery learning through a combination of Montessori and Socratic pedagogy. But Acton does not focus only on the academic success of its students. It is also committed to helping them build interpersonal skills with real-world applications that will benefit them long after they graduate from Acton. This is the "learn to be" portion of the curriculum. In the fifth grade, students participate in a leadership-training program where they serve as mentors to their classmates and complete a series of challenges to ease their transition into middle school. Each student earns an "independent learner" badge upon successful completion of the leadership program. Ambitious twelve- and thirteen-year-olds are also invited to apply to become Acton Guides, a teaching apprenticeship program where Guides help develop and deliver blended-learning experiences to younger students (ages six to ten). Students also keep one another accountable through "running partner" relationships. Meeting regularly in pairs, the partners check in on each other's progress and goals, and support each other by providing constructive feedback and affirmation.

● MOONSHOT TOOLS

Inspired by the story of Acton Academy? What are some aspects of its Learn to Know, Learn to Do, and Learn to Be curriculum that you might be able to implement in your own classroom? Perhaps you might institute hands-on challenges in your science class, or allow students to choose the tools or apps that might best supplement their learning in reading, math, or writing. Even if your school does not have an organized system to develop student leadership skills, you might be able to make just a few simple changes that could result in meaningful growth in your students' academic and personal lives.

From Teacher-Centered to Student-Centered: Blended Learning at Eastside College Prep

Suney Park is a sixth-grade teacher at Eastside College Preparatory School in East Palo Alto, California. Eastside College Prep is an independent school for grades 6 through 12, with the mission of serving historically underrepresented students. Ninety-eight percent of students at Eastside are first-generation college bound. Suney's sixth-grade class at Eastside is self-contained: She teaches all subjects, including math, science, language arts, reading, and social studies. In 2011, Suney and a colleague, (Eastside Prep's seventh- and eighth-grade math teacher) were approached to pilot Khan Academy in their math classes. Although the idea of adding a brand-new, unfamiliar component to the curriculum was daunting, Suney's principal and vice principal were incredibly supportive, even attending initial meetings between Khan Academy and Eastside Prep. During the pilot year, Suney met weekly with a Khan Academy representative to discuss implementation in their classrooms. The first year was devoted to developing materials such as concept maps, unit outlines, and assessments. The two Eastside teachers shared and developed curricular materials together, and leaned on each other for support.

During the first semester of the pilot program, Suney used Khan Academy as a supplement to her existing math curriculum, using it twice a week for forty-five minutes at a time. According to Suney, this was a way she could begin to cautiously try a new way of teaching while keeping it very much "on the side" and not letting it encroach upon her existing methods. By the following semester, she was ready to take the next step in fully integrating Khan Academy into her math curriculum. Despite her creativity in lesson planning and her concerted efforts to help each student reach his or her fullest potential, she felt that something needed to change in order to support the growth of each individual student based on his or her own needs. She felt that she needed to step outside her comfort zone and see if Khan Academy could be a gateway to differentiating and customizing each student's math learning experience.

Fast-forward three years. Suney's sixth-graders now use Khan Academy as a core component of their math curriculum. Students work with Khan math videos and exercises three times a week, for ninety minutes at a time. Suney makes recommendations to each of the students based on individual progress. They choose the order in which they follow these recommendations, and they have the freedom to choose other activities if they have completed what she recommended, or if they simply need a break. Half of their Khan Academy time is designated as independent study, and the remainder is spent working with fellow students, or with Suney one-on-one or in a small group for concepts that require additional support. The independent-study time, as Suney emphasizes, helps students develop autonomy, and helps them understand that struggle is part of the learning process. She teaches her students the concept of "No pain, no gain" and feels that it is a critical part of the learning process.

> " Suney's students greatly appreciate being in control of their own learning, and are empowered by helping one another. "

Suney's students greatly appreciate being in control of their own learning, and are empowered by helping one another. Not only have they improved academically—there are fewer students failing unit tests now than before the Khan Academy pilot—but they have also developed skills like empathy, patience, and communication. When surveyed about their experiences using Khan Academy, students reported growth in self-esteem, self-concept, self-awareness, and mindfulness. Despite her initial trepidation, Suney is now thrilled to use blended learning in all subject areas that she teaches, from math to science to social studies to language arts. She finds it satisfying that students can work to the best of their own ability, with resources that are customized to their needs.

The biggest challenge Suney faced was letting go of some control of her classroom. As she describes it, her approach shifted from being teacher-centered—focused on the content she delivered—to student-centered—shaped around how to craft each child's learning experience to maximize his or her potential. With a strong philosophy of community-building through communication and respect, Suney trusted her students to be able to learn on their own and learn from each other. When asked if she had any advice for teachers who feel that the status quo is not working for their students, Suney empathizes with those who are intimidated by the idea of completely overhauling their curriculum. But she then paraphrases some advice she once heard from Bill Gates at a Khan Academy event: Success equals innovation. Once you stop innovating, you're missing out, and someone is going to beat you to it. If you're a teacher who is interested in change, start small, she advises. Give your students something to try on their own, and go from there. "They can do much more than you ever imagined," she says. "It's not all about you. Think about what kind of teacher you want to be, and who the center of your teaching is."

The iCAN Model: Whittemore Park Middle School, Horry County, South Carolina

Horry County Schools in South Carolina serve approximately 39,000 students. The district is the third-largest in South Carolina, and is rolling out a district-wide personalized-learning initiative powered by technology. This model is focused on a core blended-learning curriculum and supported by personalized digital content to ensure college and career readiness for all students. Jennifer Janes is a sixth-grade English Language Arts teacher at Whittemore Park Middle School in Horry County, where approximately 83 percent of students are served by the free and reduced-price lunch program. She defines blended learning as an instructional model to provide true differentiated instruction. In her classroom, this is made possible by rigorous targeted instruction paired with adaptive technology, which allows each student to develop his or her own learning path.

At Whittemore Park, a rotational blended-learning model is being implemented. Students rotate between teacher-directed learning, personalized adaptive learning, and digital-content creation during hundred-minute blocks. Jennifer and her fellow teachers team-teach these rotations, and work together collaboratively to refine their model constantly. According to Jennifer, blended learning could not be implemented without support from both her administration and her peers. Her middle school is partnering with Education Elements as its learning-management system, which allows students and teachers access with a single sign-on to its dashboard. The company is collaborating with Whittemore Park to develop an implementation plan and to provide training to its staff. Other digital content includes ALEKS, iReady, Achieve3000, Discovery Education, IXL, and USA Test Prep.

Like Suney Park, Jennifer was taken out of her comfort zone when she first began implementing blended learning in her classroom. She now loves the blended-learning model, and reports that students seem more engaged. The biggest challenge for her was to accept that the model takes time to perfect, and to learn to adapt to challenges along the way. Incorporating blended learning at Whittemore Park has taught her to be reflective about her teaching, and she would advise teachers starting out to be willing to take risks and to accept a new way of teaching.

Beyond Buzzwords: Student-Centered Science at Thomas Russell Middle School

Joyce Tang invokes a classic proverb when she talks about blended learning in her classroom. "Regardless of subject discipline, new teachers should focus on the core value of 'teaching students how to fish' and the development of self-reliance," she says. A recent winner of the STEM Teacher of the Year award, Joyce is a science teacher and technology lead at Thomas Russell Middle School in Milpitas,

California. Early in her career, she wondered if there were more effective ways to teach science than staying at school until 6 P.M. every evening to prepare the next day's lab. Looking back, she reports that the switch from a "top-down" teacher-centered classroom to a student-centered one allowed her to empower both herself and her students.

Science instruction, according to Joyce, lends itself to student-centered learning. "Why spend hours 'talking' science to students when they can experiment themselves?" she asks. Giving the example of a lesson on pH, Joyce compares a "teacher-centered" approach—a fill-in-the-blanks worksheet and a cookbook-recipe-like "lab" instruction—with a "student-empowered" one—where the teacher might place a few unknown chemicals in front of the students and challenge them to figure out a reproducible recipe to achieve a solution with a pH of 7, with a possible variation to minimize the amount of chemicals used.

"In the latter example," Joyce explains, "students must demonstrate the ability to 1) think through and understand the question, 2) know the basic science of pH, acidity, basicity, 3) know how to use and read pH paper, and 4) know how to use a textbook or online resources to assist in accomplishing the task. The teacher suddenly becomes the facilitator and not the sole instructor, because the students are now instructing themselves! But this teacher's responsibility has not decreased: The teacher now must be addressing at least four different aspects of learning at any given time during the lesson, because each student works at different pace. The teacher must also be knowledgeable in the chemical properties of the substances, knowing that no poisonous gas or toxic precipitation will be chemically produced at any time in this experiment. The teacher, finally, must have great rapport with the students, because the students know to respect the freedom given and the trust placed in them to handle chemicals freely. Undeniably, student-centered learning places more rigorous demands on this teacher than the same teacher running a teacher-centered classroom."

Joyce also finds that group work and technology have supported her efforts to encourage twenty-first-century skills like collaboration and communication in her science classroom. However, she feels that the efficiency of group work increases when it is combined with independent work. "Students must equip themselves with the necessary knowledge prior to grouping to make the group time productive. I find the efficiency of group work increases when students—choosing their own group or being assigned to a group—have been given independent learning time prior to grouping. Most students enjoy their independent work time, a time when they can learn science on their own and ponder what they have learned," she says. Joyce also notes that the addition of Chromebooks at Russell Middle School, beginning in 2012, has streamlined the discovery of science concepts by having the web at students' fingertips. "Before the Chromebook era, computer labs were for word processing and science enrichment such as interactive games and tutorials. With the arrival of Chromebooks and, suddenly, fast connectivity and mobility, my third eye has opened. Some examples would include taking pictures of a flower using Chromebook and directly uploading them to Google's search-by-image to identify the species' scientific name, using Google Calendar to teach stages of human pregnancy/fetal development, and using Google Map Engine to draw a map of fungus found on campus."

Being an innovative teacher is an ongoing growth process, and Joyce is always thinking outside the box and trying new things. In the spring of 2014, she incorporated 3D printing into her classroom for the first time, to help students better understand continental drift. Using free online resources for computer-aided 3D modeling and design (i.e., tinkercad.com and blender.org), Joyce's students played paleontologist as they used the technology to turn a 2D sketch of bones to 3D printed models. After models of human, dinosaur (lystrosaurus), and other vertebrate bones were printed, students "excavated" them from a sandbox in order to identify and compare bones and reconstruct a lystrosaurus skeleton. In a reflection about the experience, Joyce notes that while seeing and touching the end product was greatly satisfying, leading to a round of applause and a number of selfies taken, the printing and reconstruction of the bones took a level of patience and perseverance that not all of her middle-schoolers were willing to put forth. All in all, Joyce sees the experiment as a positive step in the challenge of making the field of science more real and relevant to her young students.

"What one person might view as failures," she says, "I see as opportunities to improve. Failure in education is when students are leaving the classroom grumpy, upset, bored, unchallenged. Failure in teaching is when students cannot translate and apply what they have learned in the classroom to real life. There is no failing in a lesson; there is only failing to recognize the need to improve." When asked if she has any advice for new teachers, Joyce feels that they "should remember that great teaching cannot happen without a competent and caring teacher. It will not be the worksheet or the activity that the students remember about their subject; it will always be the teacher's profound interpersonal impact that students found memorable. Buzzwords—blended learning, flipped classrooms, standardized testing, holistic teaching—are nothing but buzzwords. Strengthen your subject-matter competency and classroom management, and you can excel in any paradigm."

Pt England School: How Google Apps Improved Literacy and Student Engagement

Pt England School in Auckland, New Zealand, operates on a motto of "strive to succeed." But in a neighborhood where most families are of low socioeconomic status, among surrounding wealth and affluence, the road to success has not been without challenge and hard work. Ninety percent of Pt England's primary-school students are of Maori or Pasifika descent, a demographic that is often found in the lowest-achieving cohort in New Zealand. With a government initiative to help this demographic achieve academically, Pt England has spent the past several years focusing on student engagement through collaboration and integration of digital platforms.

In 2008, Pt England began training its staff in the use of Google Apps for Education. Not long after they integrated the apps into their teaching, improvements in student engagement began to emerge. Around the same time, Pt England began to work with several neighboring schools to form the Manaiakalani Cluster—a group focused on raising student literacy. With a renewed focus on digital learning and literacy, student confidence and use of technology improved. After Pt England incorporated Hapara's Teacher Dashboard, test scores showed significant progress in literacy in just three years.

All students at Pt England have their own personal blog to share their learning and to showcase their work in an online student portfolio. In the Manaiakalani School Cluster, there are over two thousand blogs, and the number is growing each year. Professional development is taken very seriously at Pt England, and it is done through both online and offline events. The school hosts a Digital Immersion site to train new teachers how to incorporate technology in 1:1 Chromebook classes, and a Digital Teacher Academy in partnership with Google to train new teachers.

According to Dorothy Burt, Professional Development Leader at Pt England School, students feel a sense of pride in their academic achievements and are gratified to receive positive feedback on their blogs. Teachers report a renewed sense of engagement with their classrooms after integrating Teacher Dashboard and Google Apps. Overall, Burt feels that using Google tools has leveled the playing field for Pt England's students, who now feel successful in their own right and proud of their hometown.

● MOONSHOT TOOLS

Visit Dorothy Burt's blog post: Google Apps for Education helps Pt England School raise achievement levels at http://googleenterprise.blogspot.com.au/2012/06/google-apps-for-education-helps-pt.html
Also check out this video: Pt England School has Gone Google https://www.youtube.com/watch?v=iz_s0lr1eu0

Moonshots in Education Around the World: Shanghai's Results on PISA

It has been well documented that there are vast cultural differences between the educational systems of the United States and those of other nations. One of the most often cited is the comparison between the U.S. and East Asian countries and, in particular, China. Historically, Chinese schools have been considered more rigorous than American ones, with more and longer school days, and more focus on testing and memorization through repetition.

Shanghai, China's largest city, first participated in an international standardized test in 2009. The Program for International Student Assessment (PISA) is a worldwide study on student literacy in mathematics, science, and reading. First conducted in 2000, the test is administered every three years to fifteen-year-old students. The 2012 edition was taken in sixty-five countries by approximately 510,000 students between the ages of fifteen years, three months and sixteen years, two months. The definition of "literacy," according to PISA, goes above and beyond content knowledge (e.g., how to convert fractions into decimals). In each domain, PISA asks students to apply what they have learned. For example, in math, students should be able to solve problems with real-world applications, understanding concepts like rates of change across time and space. They should also understand the processes of the scientific method, including formulating questions, testing hypotheses, and evaluating evidence. In reading, students are expected to be able to understand, interpret, and reflect upon written texts.

To summarize, PISA is a carefully constructed assessment that requires knowledge beyond what can be acquired through rote memorization. Because of this, many experts were surprised when Shanghai scored at the top of all three PISA domains—math, science, and reading—out of the sixty-five countries participating, in 2009, its first year taking the test. In comparison, the United States scored 23rd in science, 17th in reading, and 32nd in math in 2009. Shanghai continued to rank at the top in the 2012 PISA, whereas the United States scored only slightly better than in 2009, ranking 21st in science, 17th in reading, and 26th in math.

There are obviously many factors that might play into a score on an international standardized test, and whether a direct comparison between Shanghai and the United States is a fair one is a topic of debate. For our purposes, we found very interesting the disparity between the stereotype of traditional Chinese education—heavy on rote learning and memorization—and Shanghai's success on PISA, which focuses on application of knowledge. Af-ter investigating further into the current state of Shanghai schools, we ourselves were surprised at the rapid change of schooling practices in Shanghai. It started with curriculum reform in 1988, and inaugurated a second substantial reform effort in 1998 (Tan, 2012). The "Second Curriculum Reform" was piloted in 2002 and eventually rolled out to all Shanghai schools over the next ten years. This large-scale reform was based on a move towards an information-technology-powered "knowledge economy," a significant shift away from traditional transmission of knowledge from teacher to pupil. With updated goals, including cultivating innovation, building students' character, and seeking an ultimate outcome of "quality-oriented education"—as opposed to "exam-oriented education"—Shanghai's overhaul of its education system can be analogized to a move from the 3 Rs methods of the past to the 4 Cs approach of the twenty-first century.

Post-reform Curriculum in Shanghai
One of the key areas of focus in the Shanghai reform is to "change the learning style" from the traditional Chinese methods of repetition and rote memorization to one where students are active learners rather than passive sponges for information (OECD, 2009). With the goals of increasing participation and equipping students to acquire knowledge to solve real-world problems, the students are encouraged

to come up with their own research questions to test by experimentation and by exchanging ideas with their peers. Whereas previous editions of the national Chinese curricula were highly centralized and virtually identical throughout the nation, schools are now more autonomous. Approximately one-third of the curriculum is now open for schools to localize their curricula to take into account the individual needs of members of their communities, including customized student electives and inquiry-based independent research. Assessments have also been redesigned to be more formative and holistic; multiple-choice questions have been minimized, with examination questions covering information that may not have been directly covered in class, in order to challenge students to apply knowledge to new problems.

> **" As the curriculum in Shanghai has changed to engage students in active learning processes, the role of the teacher has also evolved from lecturer to facilitator. "**

The Role of Teachers in Shanghai
As the curriculum in Shanghai has changed to engage students in active learning processes, the role of the teacher has also evolved from lecturer to facilitator. Previously, teachers were as seen as the dispensers of knowledge. Since the reform, the slogan for teaching practice is to "return class time to students," with the teacher becoming

a "co-learner." Whereas previous teacher evaluations focused exclusively on the presentation of lectures, teachers are now evaluated on how well they integrate student participation and collaborative activities into their lessons. Another mantra of the current pedagogy is that "To every question there must be more than a single answer."

It is also notable that teaching is considered a preferred occupation in China—one that comes with a stable income that has improved over the years, along with relative job security. Professional development and mentorship is ongoing throughout one's teaching career. Teachers often work in groups to study and improve, and are often reviewed by their peers as well as by mentees and supervisors. Universities with teacher-training programs tend to attract high-quality applicants because of a policy that student-teaching candidates are given priority admission.

Lessons from Shanghai and other Success Stories
We have learned a great deal from profiling blended-learning success stories here in the U.S. and around the world, and we have found that across all of them, a number of common themes emerged. First, traditional teacher-led instruction has been replaced by a student-centered experience. This can look very different from classroom to classroom. However, regardless of whether your classroom implements a lab rotation, a project-based curriculum, a Khan Academy–driven math curriculum, or other tools and techniques, the greatest challenge lies in stepping outside your comfort zone, trusting yourself and your students, and being open to experimentation. This is where the true moonshot lies. Your first effort may not work, but small changes can add up and have a huge impact.

MOONSHOTS IN MUSIC THEORY

WITH MAYA KITAYAMA

Maya Kitayama is Co-Editor in Chief of The Campanile, *Palo Alto High School. This article is presented as an example of the work of a blended-learning student.* —E.W.

Tall, outgoing Michael Najar, resident choir and AP Music Theory teacher at Palo Alto High School (Paly) of California, greets me at the door of his choir room, asking for five minutes before he sits down with me. He then walks back to his office and closes the door, conversing with a student of his. I wait with a couple of kids who regularly reside in the classroom during lunch, all of whom seem perfectly content spending their lunchtime with the choir teacher.

Najar, finally available to chat, sits down with me in his tiny office, complete with a computer, recording equipment and rows upon rows of music theory books. With his open and friendly persona—what one might expect of a music teacher—he begins the interview with explaining his interest in the intersection between music and technology, which first developed in college. As a student, Najar gained access to various online music tools, enabling him to learn music more effectively. As he left college and eventually found himself teaching, the variety of tools available to coach skills like ear training, sight training and general composition began to expand.

Najar is known as an innovator within this high school, an impressive feat considering the school's location within the heart of innovation—the Silicon Valley. He teaches the AP Music Theory course, an elected advanced placement class complete with an AP test that takes place during the month of May. However, Najar teaches the course through an erupting style of teaching commonly referred to as "blended learning," a style that encompasses both technology and the typical classroom, incorporating them into a hybrid system. Students who elect to take the course are entering either their junior or senior year of high school. It is recommended that they have "previous experience with music" along with either "own[ing] or hav[ing] access to a computer on a regular basis," according to the Paly Course Catalogue.

During the first semester, AP Music Theory students meet once a week during sixth period to discuss and complete homework, similar to the model of the "flipped classroom." The rest of the time, all content, learning and assessments are available through Najar's online programs, tests and video tutorials. Students often have larger summative assessments in class, but they also take a fair amount of assessments online. This model, Najar believes, actually raises the achievement levels for all students. He acknowledges that within most classes, students fall into three different levels of understanding: A third of the class is bored with the material, a third of the class is at the expected level of comprehension, and a third of the class is left behind without understanding the material. Through the freedom that blended learning allows, that 33 percent of the students who are seriously struggling in comprehension are asked to come in and get personal help from Najar himself.

Considering the apparent success this course is already experiencing, Najar initially believed that the course is "particular to Music Theory." Furthermore, as the course is an elective, there are fewer risks involved through taking a chance with blended learning. Within Paly specifically, there is a reduced amount of weight put on an elective AP course. In other words, "No one cares if an AP Music Theory class doesn't do well on the tests," Najar quips.

However, the lack of risks in teaching a blended-learning course has not led to a letdown in student performance. Najar's "Aha!" moment came early on in the first semester, when he was still getting the course together. "After a week of not seeing [the AP Music Theory students], they came in and we were able to discuss [the content]," Najar said. "They all participated."

This class discussion proved to Najar that this model carried immense potential for success, and he has not been disappointed as the year progresses. Obviously, Najar has observed some of his students slipping into the role of typical "slacker" students, a trend he believes is bound to happen regardless of the teaching method. "If you're not a good student in class, you're not going to be a good student online," Najar explains.

❝ Through blended learning, the AP Music Theory students have more choice, a privilege that in turn empowers them to go farther in their learning. ❞

However, according to Najar, the students' test scores and overall performances align with those of students of years past. But the current students also have more independence and access to more tools. Through blended learning, the AP Music Theory students have more choice, a privilege that in turn empowers them to go farther in their learning.

In order to offer a course taught in such a way, Najar had to essentially recreate the course, and without the help of the Palo Alto Unified School District. When asked about the administration support he received when creating the content, he pulls out an elementary-looking certificate with a chuckle, telling me briefly about the "certification" class he took through the Santa Clara Office of Education. Without any actual assistance from the district, Najar turned to online resources to help him craft his course before the start of the school year. What he discovered, much to his benefit, was an online world of people connecting and collaborating through different social media platforms like Twitter, Facebook and Schoology. Connecting through these online sites allowed him access to different ideas, rubrics and general support from a community of teachers and educators pioneering this new and upcoming world of blended learning.

The AP Music Theory course runs with the assistance of various online music programs, namely Sonic Fit and Note Flight, two programs that function as assessment-based practice where students can practice and establish their skills. Najar also utilizes many different technological tools like Google Forms, Quizlet and YouTube. Much of the content and actual "teaching" part of the class is performed through video tutorials that Najar makes and posts onto the Music Theory site. He has experimented with more complex programs for screen capture recording, such as Screenium, but has found that he can simply use the recording tool in QuickTime to make simple video tutorials for his students. Furthermore, Najar has discovered he can aggregate all kinds of different resources and tools and embed them into one place.

"I did a unit on [Google] Forms," Najar says. "I embed every part of the unit in one place, everything from a Quizlet to a Form, videos, assignments, formative and summative tools in one place."

The initial drawbacks came from Najar's lack of experience using such programs. Before the year began, he had little knowledge of Google Forms or Google Sites, nor did he have any experience creating the video tutorials that are now so essential to the continuation of the course. Najar recognizes that his biggest failure thus far mainly pertains to preparation. Getting acclimated to all the new technology and resources presented a challenge for him, and he needed to undertake a fair amount of experimenting and learning in order to prepare the course.

The biggest realization for Najar came from the shift he experienced while teaching this course. He no longer believes teachers are supposed to just provide content, especially considering the increasing ability of students to figure things out for themselves.

"Classes with more breadth are going to actually find online learning is better," Najar says. "If all you need is content, why not find it off your phone or computer? What we're looking to do is expand depth, and I certainly have not perfected it. But my goal for the next couple of years is that it'll make the class deeper, because you can put the content in the students' hands, and we the teachers become facilitators of deep learning."

Najar is persistent in emphasizing the changing roles of both students and teachers, noting that this shift may be hardest for teachers, who are slowly coming to understand their changing role in the classroom. "[School] cannot be content driven, there is no reason for it," Najar says. "Students are so empowered now, [teachers] who are having the most trouble are the ones who are fighting the fact that they're not the content providers anymore."

Furthermore, Najar notes that the situation with regard to student success in blended learning is similar to that with regard to teacher success. "If you're a bad teacher in a regular classroom, you're going to be a bad teacher online," Najar says. "All the challenges I have as a teacher are the same ones that exist online."

There is still the argument that a morphing education system that moves away from the traditional classroom also moves away from the community and social aspect that stems from students learning in a classroom together. Najar is quick to reveal that he does not disagree, and is a big proponent for expanding community within the classroom. However, through experience, he has found that his relationship with his students has not suffered any negative effects while undergoing the blended learning switch. "Human connections are important, I don't think we've lost that in our switch over," he says.

In fact, Najar believes he now experiences a wonderful connection with his students via social media. More so with his choir class—comprising over 80 students—as opposed to AP Music Theory, he connects with his students in Facebook groups to both inform students of choir-related announcements and to keep up with them on a different interface.

"I never friend students, but they're part of my Facebook groups," Najar says. "I know who they're with, what they're doing, who they ask to Prom that weekend because they post pictures. I feel it's a very vibrant community. I'm constantly keeping up with them."

As the bell for sixth period rings, AP Music Theory students trickle into the choir room, pulling up black chairs, arranging themselves in a sort of semicircle, facing Najar, who is seated in a chair similar to the students', typing away into his Macbook Pro. The final bell rings, and the conversational buzz among the students slowly diminishes, as Najar shifts his focus from his laptop to his students. He welcomes the class and starts off a discussion regarding the course, blended learning, and what the students really think.

> " You can do [the learning] on your own time, at your own pace, back up the video, skip something if you already know it... "

After a short survey of raised hands, it is concluded that this course is the first experience for all of these students in taking a blended learning class. Aside from a sprinkling of students who've taken entirely online courses through the local community college in subjects like Java and Linear Algebra, no other students have any experience working in an environment that strays away from the traditional classroom.

Najar asks the students for their true opinions, and one student raises her hand and speaks of the independence and responsibility a blended learning course requires. "I thought it was pretty informative, it's just that this method of learning requires a little bit more self-discipline, where I have to recognize I need help and I have to come to you," the student explains.

Another student raises a hand in agreement. "We don't discuss assignments during class, so we have to figure it out on our own," the student says. "If you totally don't understand something, it takes more time to get help because you have to go in during a certain time during the week."

Najar agrees that this format does bring up different challenges, but several other students chime in, offering the positive side to the same format.

"You can do [the learning] on your own time, at your own pace, back up the video, skip something if you already know it," one student offers.

"It makes the days a lot less stressful; if we need help we can just come in," another student agrees. "Just allows more time."

Others begin to join in, adding that the course feels "more like a college course," with a lot more flexibility built in, the ability to cater to different learning speeds, and so many additional resources to supplement understanding.

Yet another student brings up an interesting point regarding the potential success of blended learning functioning in core curriculum classes. "I've had a lot of teachers that aren't technologically competent, so it wouldn't work out," the student explains.

Najar acknowledges the interesting point brought up, and asks an additional question. "Don't you think that's a problem? Don't you think technological competency should be a part of how teachers teach?" The class murmurs in apparent agreement.

One girl sitting in the back, pencil and paper resting in her lap, raises her hand in response to Najar's inquiries. She agrees with a previous comment suggesting that blended learning will only work for classes that are self-elected. "It wouldn't work for like math, or the core classes in general," she says.

Najar prods her for more. "But why?"

"It requires hands-on explanation," she replies in a slightly quieter tone, possibly taken aback by his push for further explanation.

Again, he pushes her. "Why?"

She attempts to carry out the thought she's trying to get across. "Say you're learning a proof, if you're doing a difficult problem, you can't just look up the answer," she tries. "Or . . . I guess you *can* look up the answer."

Najar smiles, as he watches realization dawn on her face. "Yes, you can, you do it all the time," he finishes.

The class of AP Music Theory students—20-some adolescents who have just spent the last 12 or 13 years in the industrialized education system that hasn't changed since its inception—is silent.

"You guys think the way school works now is the way school should work," Najar continues. "Breaking down the walls a little bit more won't hurt you."

STEM SUCCESS: PROGRAMMING "OUTSIDE THE BOX" IN AP COMPUTER SCIENCE

BY ESTHER WOJCICKI

Looking more like a college campus than a high school, Palo Alto's Gunn High School has some of the best teachers and courses around. It is one of the top public high schools in the nation, ranked as number 17 by *U.S. News and World Report* in 2014. It is in this top school that Joshua Paley, a computer-science teacher at Gunn High School in Palo Alto, stands out as a true educational innovator. He came up with the idea for blended learning in his high-school computer-science courses long before anyone else thought to do it at the high-school level. That was back in 2002, when he set up his own website for the class at the cost of less than $100 per year. He first got interested in blended learning because, as he says, "I wanted to survive. I am not the most organized person, and putting the content online was a good way to communicate with students and parents while keeping myself sane."

He had originally encountered this type of teaching when he was a graduate student at UC Berkeley with Professor Brian Harvey. Professor Harvey thought people learn best when they are working together, and he encouraged his students to work collaboratively. So, when Josh started teaching at Gunn, it was only natural for him to try out what he had experienced as a grad student at Berkeley. The only problem is that it had never been tried anywhere and certainly not at Gunn High School. At that time students were penalized for working together. Collaborating on homework was tantamount to cheating. Collaborating on homework was even considered cheating and unethical as late as 2012 when Harvard students were caught "cheating."[1]

Nonetheless, Josh got administrative support for this style of teaching from his department chair, Tom Saults, and nobody objected to his creating a website, and so he was launched. It took more than a decade for other teachers to start creating websites, he says. Josh adds, "I have no idea how they managed before that." As for his peers, he says they found his approach a matter of curiosity. E-mailing was not common at that time; leaving a note or contacting someone directly by phone or in person was the way people interacted. His journey along the way was not easy, especially after Tom Saults left. One of Josh's later supervisors tried to fire him for his unconventional teaching style. Fortunately, the supervisor wasn't able to make the firing stick.

Josh uses multiple tools to support his teaching: programming environments, browsers, and computers. His classroom has a desktop computer for each student. His website is a one-stop shop for students: It tells them what the assignments are, when the tests are, and what is expected.

● MOONSHOT TOOLS

For more information on Daniel Pink and Sir Ken Robinson, please visit YouTube.

In the fall of 2013, Josh had 330 students signed up for computer science, the largest enrollment for computer science in the Palo Alto School District, and probably the largest enrollment in any California school. He now has other teachers helping with the program. His method of teaching is hands-on and project-based; it correlates with the philosophy of Sir Ken Robinson and Daniel Pink.

The Gunn High computer-science program involves three hours of class time per week, during which time Josh lectures for about forty-five minutes total for the week (about fifteen minutes per class). The rest of the time, except for tests, is allotted to group work. Students choose their own extra-credit projects and get very involved in them. Josh believes that "doing projects is more valuable than scores on tests." Many of his students have gone on to have their own startups and develop websites like OpenGov.com, and GetAround.com.

He strongly believes that the social component of learning is so important that without it students do not learn effectively. "Just giving students access to computers is insufficient. The culture of the classroom and the social component is key," he says. Giving students ownership of their learning is an important part of his methodology. The Gunn High School computer-science courses consist of the following:

> Introduction to Computer Science
> Functional Programming
> Object-Oriented Programming
> Programming Mobile Devices
> AP Computer Science

The school has four designated tracks: Mechanical Engineering Emphasis, Electrical Engineering and Computer Science Emphasis, Computer Software Emphasis, and Computer Graphics Emphasis. All the classes use the blended-learning approach.

JOURNALISM AND MEDIA STUDIES: TEACHING THROUGH FREEDOM, RELEVANCE, AND RESPECT

BY ESTHER WOJCICKI

9

One of the areas in which blended-learning programs are most effective in middle school and high school is journalism—or media studies, as this field is known today. The Wikipedia definition of media studies is "a discipline and field of study that deals with the content, history and effects of various media; in particular, the 'mass media.'" However, this historical definition does not include a large part of what many consider media studies today, and this is study involving the use of electronic devices to facilitate communication. These can be computers, cameras, video devices, phones, or tablets. The result is communication twenty-first-century style. The definition also includes historical media such as newspapers, magazines, radio, and television. But the twenty-first century is the century of media. Today virtually all students, even in low-income areas, have some kind of electronic device, and they are connected to the Internet. The Internet has changed our world, and cell phones enable us to carry an entire library in our pockets.

Media studies can easily be incorporated into multiple subject areas, including language arts, science, English, and social studies. There is no need for additional equipment, personnel, or training.

Media studies includes student-created websites, blogs, videos, photographs, newspapers, magazines, and television. It can incorporate all aspects of blended learning.

There are compelling reasons to incorporate media models into all writing instruction in the high-school curriculum, not least because assignments involving these very skills are in the new Common Core State Standards.

Stanford professor of education Linda Darling-Hammond emphasizes the new expectations for students today, which include the abilities to do the following:

Communicate
Adapt to change
Work in teams
Solve problems
Reflect on and improve performance
Analyze and conceptualize
Manage oneself
Innovate and criticize
Learn new things all the time
Cross specialist borders

These are skills included in Common Core. Perhaps even more compelling, employers today want employees who can think, collaborate, and communicate effectively, not employees who are good at filling in boxes on multiple-choice tests. They want employees who have Internet skills, computer skills, and *thinking* skills, and who know how to use popular software programs. In short, they want employees with journalism experience. Writing is thinking. Thomas Friedman of the *New York Times* wrote a column on April 20, 2014, in which he explains what it takes to get a job at Google. Friedman interviewed Laszlo Bock, a Google recruiter. Friedman writes, "The first thing Google looks for 'is general cognitive ability—the ability to learn things and solve problems.'" But in fact,

Google is representative of all desirable workplaces: Most employers are looking for employees who can think and solve problems, and that is why the high-school curriculum should help prepare students to exercise these abilities.

Here is one example of a school curriculum that does just that: train kids to solve problems. It is the Palo Alto High School Media Arts program, where I teach. It is the largest program of its kind in the nation. More than six hundred students out of a student body of nineteen hundred are electing to take media studies in the new 22,000-square-foot Media Arts Center, which opened October 2014. It is great to have a wonderful facility like that, but in fact the program can be done in a portable classroom like the one I was in for twenty years. The program has consistently won awards from the Columbia Scholastic Press Association and the National Scholastic Press Association. The program studies a variety of media and platforms: newspapers, television, magazines, tablets (Flipboard publications), and mobile phones.

The Media Arts program has seven websites all connected to programs at the school, two broadcast-television classes (which produce the program *INfocus*), a news magazine (*Verde*), a sports magazine (*The Viking*), a literary magazine (*Calliope*), a foreign-affairs magazine (*Agora*), a photography magazine (*Proof*), an arts-and-entertainment magazine (*C Magazine*), a newspaper (*Campanile*), video production classes, and a yearbook (*Madrono*).

WEBSITES

http://voice.paly.net
http://www.palycampanile.org/
http://verdemagazine.com/
http://infocusnews.tv/
http://vimeo.com/palyvideoproductions/
http://www.vikingsportsmag.com/
http://issuu.com/c_magazine

Palo Alto High School Journalism Program

NAME	LINK	YEAR-FOUNDED
Central Website	http://voice.paly.net	1998
The Viking	http://www.vikingsportsmag.com/	2007
Verde	http://verdemagazine.com/	2000
The Campanile	http://palycampanile.net	1918
Television	http://www.palyinfocus.com/	1999
Video production	no online presence	1998
Agora	http://palyagora.com/	2011
Madrono	no online presence	1918
C Magazine	http://www.palycampanile.org/the-c-magazine	2012
Calliope	no online presence	1960s

The main attractions of the program are *freedom* and *relevance—freedom* for students to write about issues that are *relevant* to their concerns. They are trusted to pick partners they can work with instead of being assigned partners; one thing most kids like about school is being with their friends. Teachers can make suggestions, but, in order to succeed, students need to feel in control of their learning; they have to be given the freedom to learn independently, and this is greatly facilitated by the use of computers. Alan November uses his Digital Learning Farm model to show teachers how technology allows students to take ownership of their learning, create their own learning tools, and participate in work that has meaning to them and to others.

Just as important as freedom and relevance is *respect*. Students have to feel respected by their teachers and their peers in order to carry out the collaboration that is required. In our program, student journalists are treated with respect on a daily basis—as individuals, as collaborators, as researchers, as writers.

The Palo Alto program also teaches *grit*—an important skill for today, as we saw in Chapter 4. Friedman also addresses this in his column, when he says the number-one character trait employers are looking for is grit. Paul Tough, in his best-selling book *How Children Succeed: Grit, Curiosity, and the Hidden Power of Character* (2013), gives multiple examples of the importance of grit. It isn't easy on a high-school campus to publish a full-sized twenty-eight-page, three-section newspaper every three weeks, especially when the responsibility falls squarely on the students. Students learn to think quickly, write to the point, work in teams, rely on each other, and stick it out until the publication meets its deadline. It is an opportunity to learn grit in a controlled environment.

Of course, the students don't sign up for a course in grit. They sign up because they hear that they are given the big three: *trust*, *respect*, and *freedom*. (And by the way, they think it is also fun, and that is because they are working collaboratively with their friends.) Everyone, no matter what age, wants trust, respect, and freedom. As I've said earlier in this book, most classes in K–12 give students little of any of those. In fact, everything is controlled so that teachers can prepare their students to pass the high-stakes tests that are now ubiquitous.

Respect

So how do we let students know they are respected? The number-one way in Palo Alto's Media Arts program is by honoring their First Amendment rights—giving them the freedom to pick their own story ideas and investigate and write about topics of interest to them. While that might seem clichéd or simple, in fact, students in most states of the U.S. do not enjoy First Amendment rights. This is due to the 1988 Supreme Court decision in *Hazelwood v. Kuhlmeier*, which gave teachers and principals the right of censorship of the student press to teachers and principals. Only eight states have passed laws guaranteeing that all student publications have the right to publish freely. These states are Arkansas, California, Colorado, Iowa, Kansas,

Kentucky, Massachusetts, and Oregon. More states should take steps to allow students this freedom.

Respect also entails trust, and in the program students share the responsibility for learning with the teacher. While the teacher comes up with the curriculum, students implement it and practice real-world skills.

When students are told what to write about, they are, unsurprisingly, not excited about writing. In fact, there is a lot of cheating and plagiarism. Take the infamous five-paragraph essay, still assigned in most schools' English classes nationwide. Students hate it. It's stale and inauthentic—a form that does not exist outside of the classroom. It's little wonder that there's a thriving online essay market. Giving these fusty writing assignments is not the best way for students to learn or to get them excited about learning. But when students have an opportunity to write about issues of importance to them, they become interested in writing.

Here is one other important reason students take the program: Students like learning to write in a variety of genres that can be used on the web, including news, features, reviews, opinion, and sports. This kind of writing is a world away It gives them a break from the five paragraph expository essay that students learn in English classes nationwide.

Schedule

Getting down to details, this is how the program works. At the beginning of every production cycle for each publication, the students brainstorm story ideas for all the sections: news, features, arts and entertainment, opinion, and sports. The students working on the website have to do this daily, even several times a day; the students working on television do it daily; and the newspaper and magazine students brainstorm ideas every week or two, since the publications have a longer cycle. Students love this process, because they are the ones who come up with the ideas for stories, and since the ideas are theirs, they want to write them. This ties to the blended-learning model and its promotion of students' ownership of their learning.

As you can imagine, brainstorming sessions can be very lively, and the process encourages students to be aware of the world around them so they can suggest interesting topics. The general rule they follow is that a good story idea is the key to an interesting article. They are taught that if they are not interested in writing the article, no one will be interested in reading it, so they had better come up with an idea they *like*.

At the end of the story-ideas session, students filter out any outlandish proposals in their quest to make sure the publication maintains its ethical standing and is treated with respect by readers. The collaborative process fosters the development of good judgment—and if it doesn't, then the teacher needs to step in gently and remind students about the ethics of the media program. Their ideas come from reading other publications, reading websites, talking to people, and being aware of what is going on in the world. Imagine how powerful those skills are for lifelong learning habits. Students learn to pay attention to what is going on in the world around them.

Instead of the teacher being in charge, it is teenagers collaborating with other teenagers, and it works. Putting them in charge is an act of trust and respect on the part of the teacher. Of course, the teacher is still there, but as a guide off to the side. Even so, that role is still significant. In all the media programs, the editors run the class every day, with coaching from the teacher before and after class. Each student has a role, and they work together as a team. There are editors, section editors, senior reporters, reporters, photographers, business managers, advertising managers, circulation managers. This process teaches students about teamwork, collaboration, problem-solving, and self-control—all skills that are in demand in the job market.

One important aspect of the program is high expectations. The adults in charge expect students to measure up to the high expectations that the program has established. This is not busy work, but rather a series of challenging assignments that have a beginning, a middle, and an end—and at the end is a tangible, authentic work product, something that others can and will read, listen to, or see.

Standards are high, and students rise to meet them. Teachers need to expect high-quality, well-researched stories, turned in on time. I expect my students to read the articles I send to their e-mail or Facebook accounts every night. I expect them to work together and learn to get along. My standards are high, and I find that my students always rise to meet them. And not just in my own estimation: For many years, they have been recognized for their excellence with awards from the Columbia Scholastic Press Association and the National Scholastic Press Association. You don't need to enter national competitions, but you could recognize students who write good articles by having some kind of ceremony at the end of every month. Kids love being recognized and getting a piece of paper to acknowledge it.

A second critical aspect of the program is accountability. Even though students are in control of their learning, there is still accountability. All work is turned in on Google Docs and edited on Google Docs. This makes it very easy for the teacher to see when the work was turned in, the revisions that were made to the work, and what the writer's peers did in the way of editing. The editors edit the stories under the guidance of the teacher, and this is facilitated by the ease of use of Google Docs. Students can work anytime, from any computer. Also, the program is free. Google now also has Google Classroom which makes organizing the student work easier. However, one of the drawbacks is that when the student turns in the work, it then belongs to the teacher and no additional edits can be made until the teacher returns the work to the student. While this may work well in some classes, it can be a block in classes where student collaboration editing take place without the teacher having the time to review and return the work

Districts might want to invest in Hapara, an excellent program that has a feature called "Teacher Dashboard," enabling teachers to see exactly what students are doing in real time. It features a way to organize student work so that it is much easier to find and track, making it easier to grade. Hapara also has a way to analyze student progress and provides easy-to-understand data tied to the Common

Core State Standards, helping the teacher to analyze students' progress. The ownership of the work does not transfer to the teacher in Hapara when the student submits the work.

A third critical aspect to the program is allowing the students to have freedom, respect and trust. It is really not surprising that students are attracted to programs like Palo Alto High School's Media Arts program. Adults want to work for organizations that give them respect and freedom. Teenagers, too, gravitate to opportunities that make them feel good about themselves.

Freedom, respect, trust, and high expectations: these are the ingredients of a thriving blended learning environment, and they are inherent in school media arts programs.

Journalism Programs

These programs are the epitome of effective blended learning in language arts and also in project-based learning. Students work more than 50 percent of the time using computers in collaborative projects on articles they have chosen themselves. Project-based learning instruction has been shown to be the most engaging and effective method of instruction. The teacher does not need to be an entertainer to get the students' attention. He/she just needs to feed into the students' natural drive to have some control over their learning and to work on projects of interest to them.

There are three reasons why it works well, and they all are embedded in journalism programs:

1. The projects can be chosen according to the student's personal interest in the topic, as opposed to assigning the same worksheets or book reports to a whole class.
2. They involve student ownership of the work.
3. They provide opportunities for genuine peer collaboration.

Here is an example: The first assignment students get at the beginning of the year is writing a personality profile. It can be about anyone they want—a classmate, a close friend, a parent. They get pretty excited about this assignment because they like writing about the people in their lives; they also like the idea that the final product may be published, even on a blog. They read multiple models of personality profiles, then write their own. You can put them together in a book or on a website. Super-easy to do. This year at Palo Alto High School, all 9th and 10th grade teachers participated in an experiment where the first assignment of the school year was to write a personality profile. Both the students and teachers loved the assignment and said it was one of the best ways they have found to introduce students to each other, get a writing sample, and get kids excited about writing. It was a win-win-win assignment.

In writing the personality profile, the students learn a specific style of writing as well as broadly applicable writing skills like word usage, mechanics, selectivity, and organization. These skills are not taught independently but embedded in the assignment. Students do not even realize they are learning them, because the focus is on the assignment, not on a worksheet. Additional assignments are in the same vein: reviews of movies and restaurants, opinion pieces, features, sports stories, and news stories. Journalistic writing gets kids excited about writing.

Another assignment, which can be done in a journalism class or an English class, is walking to a nearby frozen-yogurt place, for example, tasting all the different flavors, and then comparing them with the flavors of gelato from a store nearby. Not surprisingly, students are engaged and passionate about their reviews—and passion is key to learning. English, history, and humanities teachers should try replacing traditional expository assignments with more authentic and journalistic ones.

Students can publish their work online in blogs or websites, or they can publish in hardcopy using printers like aPrintis, a printer specializing in school publications, or local printing shops for newspapers and magazines. Examples of blogging sites are Blogger, Tumblr, and WordPress. There are many companies that help students make websites, including Google Sites.

Media studies is probably the most effective project-based, blended-learning curriculum in high school. It trains students for the job market and makes them into productive citizens of the Internet world.

The goal of the program is to have high-school students learn to work independently, do intelligent research, and collaborate effectively in person as well as on the Internet. I am confident that John Dewey, one of the founders of progressive education, would enthusiastically support media-arts programs. They empower students to do, not just talk about doing, or watch someone else do. What could be more genuine than that?

SUGGESTED ASSIGNMENTS

Below are blended-learning journalism assignments for any subject area. Any of these ideas can be adapted to film or photos as well as the traditional written format.

Personality Feature or Personality Profile

This is the best way to encourage students to get to know one another at the beginning of the school year. Have them interview one another and then post their interviews to a class blog that they can all access. There are multiple advantages: Students get to know one another, and they learn interviewing skills, writing skills, and publishing skills in the process. Have students peer-edit the work. The teacher can look over the peer edits and make additional comments. This is so easy with Google Docs, since teachers can see who edited what and when.

Feature

Students can read features in magazines and then imitate the style. Feature topics could be anything from local beaches to skateboards to the local museum. Basically, kids can pick anything they find interesting; the role of the teacher is to help narrow the topic so they can actually do it. For example, instead of writing about photography, kids can write about a specific photographer in the school or community.

Review

Students love doing reviews. They love to express their opinion about anything and everything. Even in science classes, for example, students can review websites that explain concepts in science. But for English and journalism classes, some more common types would be:

Movie review: This is different from a movie report. The students need to evaluate the plot, the acting, the setting, the cinematography, and the overall effect. So they need to know something about each of these categories.

Product review: Students can review any product from ice cream to software. The idea is to get them to write about something they care about.

Website review: Students are constantly on the web, so it is a simple thing to have them review a website of their choice. The hidden agenda is that they have to give reasons supporting their choice.

Game or App review: Students play computer games all the time, more than most parents and teachers would like—so why not let them review a game or App they like or dislike? Again, they need to support their choice.

Restaurant review: This is by far the students' favorite review. They are assigned to go to a restaurant together—any restaurant, even a fast-food one. They are to review the atmosphere, the service, the food, and the cost. I suggest reviews online from the local newspaper's website and from the *New York Times* website to use as models. Also, they can search for published reviews on their own. The hidden agenda here is to have them collect information, analyze it, and write it up in a logical order (putting the most important things first), with correct spelling, punctuation, and grammar.

Opinion Article

National and international issues: Every day there is another issue, another crisis somewhere in the world. Have students pick an issue (this requires them to search the web) and then write about it and express their opinion, supporting their position. Students can work in groups. For social-studies classes, this is a perfect fit. For English classes, the teacher can tie an article to an issue students are reading about in fiction. For example, in Fitzgerald's *The Great Gatsby*, there are themes of overindulgence, overconsumption, materialism. These problems exist today in the real world. Have students locate articles about such issues and write about them.

Local issues: Most communities have a website with local news. It would be good to locate that website and have students read the stories. That way, they can find issues that are of interest to them and then write opinion pieces about those issues. It sounds really simple, and it is. Students are usually more easily engaged in local issues that affect them directly than they are in dramatic issues happening on another continent.

News Stories

Writing a news story is one of the hardest assignments for students because they have to decide what is most important—unlike traditional writing assignments in most schools, where they are used to just regurgitating what they have been told and not used to making a decision. That is the beauty of news writing for Palo Alto's Media Arts program: Kids need to think. There are six important facts they need to present—who, what, when, where, how, and why—and they need to write it up in the inverted-pyramid style (most important first).

Sports

Students who participate in sports or are regular spectators—which means most students—love to write about them. First, have the students read some sports stories online. Let them pick out the best ones and share them with their classmates. Then have them write a story about their school's sports or athletes. It is fun for them, fun for the person being written about, and, in the process, they learn how to write.

PARTNERSHIP FOR 21ST CENTURY LEARNING

Journalism studies also teach the essential skills listed by Partnership for 21st Century Learning, a collaboration of education and business leaders. These are skills that the business leaders want to see in all employees, and that the Common Core State Standards require. See the chart below and compare. The primary difference is that journalism provides even more. See the course outline that follows the chart.

Important skills students need for the twenty-first century

COMMON CORE STATE STANDARDS	EMPLOYERS WANT	JOURNALISM TRAINING PROVIDES	TRADITIONAL TEACHING METHODS PROVIDE
Access and evaluate information	YES	YES	LIMITED
Use and manage information	YES	YES	LIMITED
Analyze media	YES	YES	NO
Create media products	YES	YES	NO
Apply technology effectively	YES	YES	NO
Be adaptable to change	YES	YES	NO
Be flexible	YES	YES	NO
Manage goals and time well	YES	YES	NO
Work independently	YES	YES	NO
Be self-directed learners	YES	YES	NO
Work effectively with others	YES	YES	NO
Manage projects	YES	YES	NO
Produce results	YES	YES	LIMITED
Guide and lead others	YES	YES	NO
Be responsible to others	YES	YES	NO
Be good digital citizens	YES	YES	NO

Here is the handout given to students entering Advanced Journalism at Palo Alto High School as an example of the skills students learn and the effectiveness of journalism as a curriculum for the digital age. As you can see, most of these skills are vital for performing well in nearly any workplace today. These skills make people more likely to succeed, regardless of what job they have.

COURSE OUTLINE

INTRODUCTION TO ADVANCED JOURNALISM

Goals of the Program for Students
Improve your writing skills and Internet communication skills
Learn how to write effectively UNDER PRESSURE
Improve your computer and desktop publishing skills
Learn how to work effectively together as a team with all kinds of
    people under a variety of situations (without losing your cool)
Improve your oral communication skills
Improve your ability to think critically and quickly
Make you more aware of local, national and international news
Learn how to work effectively both as a team player and as a leader
Learn how to accept responsibility and follow through on a project
Learn how to work effectively under stress
Learn how to work effectively with all types of people.
Develop your entrepreneurial skills

Qualities of a High-Performing Student
Turns in all stories on time
Does high quality research
Reads the paper on a daily basis
Takes initiative
Responsible
Dependable
Consistent
Can handle criticism
Can handle setbacks
Can be a leader and a team player
Proofreads and edits own work
Plans ahead (yes!!!)
Interviews several sources
Participates in class discussions
Does not talk when others are talking
Sensitive to the needs of others
Attends production meetings and works with editor group
Asks questions if does not understand
Consistent attendance in class
Gets requisite ads ($400 per year)

The Production Cycle (a.k.a. how it all works)

1. Story Ideas

Everyone must fill out a sheet of story ideas for each newspaper cycle. This includes news, opinion, features, arts and entertainment (A&E), sports, and any Spotlight/Verbatim/1 in 1900 ideas. This is a VERY IMPORTANT step of the production cycle. Without good story ideas we will not have good stories. Everyone is expected to participate in class when we brainstorm story ideas. After we have created a large list of possible story ideas, you will submit your top five choices of stories you would like to write. We will make every possible effort to assign you stories that you are interested in, although we cannot guarantee it.

2. Writing/Editing Stories

After we have brainstormed story ideas, you will be assigned one or more stories to write. You will be given a deadline for the first draft, and this draft will be edited by the Theeds. (Theeds=the editors) You will make all necessary edits and share a second draft with the Theeds.

NOTE: The Section Editor for your stories will also be editing your second drafts. After you have completed the second round of edits by Section Editors you will submit a final draft.

3. Production

On the first day of production, you will be assigned a page partner (or two), with whom you will be working. You and your page partner(s) will be assigned one page of the newspaper (along with the stories that must go in it) to design. You are responsible for creating an interesting and visually appealing page, complete with edited photos, captions and any graphics that need to be created on Photoshop.

In order to ensure that your pages are as outstanding as they can possibly be, you are responsible for getting a *Design Check*, a *Section Editor Check* and three *Editor Checks*. To get a Design Check, you must sketch a layout of the page design you have in mind and have it approved by a Theed. Afterwards, you will use the InDesign software to execute that design. Once you have completed placing all text and images, print your page for your Seed to check. He/She will make edits to both the text and the design, and you must make those edits and give the improved page back to the Seed for more edits. This process will continue until the Seed is satisfied with the page, at which point they will give you a Section Editor Check. You must continue this process with three Editors (Seeds = Section Editors)

NOTE: you may NOT simultaneously ask two or more editors for a check. You must obtain one Editor Check before you can proceed to the next. Also, a Section Editor Check is necessary before any Editor Checks.

If you have an ad placed on your page, you will need to obtain an *Ad Check* from one of the Ad Managers, who will ensure that the ads are properly placed and formatted.

4. Distribution

At the brunch following the final day of production, everyone must come to the classroom to pick up and distribute newspapers around the school. Roll will be taken and we will be marking down cutters, so you must remember to do this! We don't want anyone at Paly deprived of a Campy edition. That would be horrible for all parties involved.

Requirements of the Class

1. Write one story per edition or two stories for a minimum of 600 words per edition. Everyone must write even if your story is not published. If your story is not printed in the paper it will go on *The Campanile* website and Voice Your Story must be uploaded to Voice to get credit.

2. All stories must be turned in to Google Docs and labeled properly: Last name, first name: kind of story, name of story.

Example: Brown, John: feature, Skateboarding

3. Turn all of your stories in on time. *Do not turn in late stories;* students who turn in *more than two consecutive late stories* will be asked to drop the class. Even if your story is not complete, do the best that you can and turn in what you have so that you can meet each deadline. Extensions will only be given for legitimate problems, not because you forgot or had too much homework. Send extension requests to xxxx@googlegroups.com.

4. You need to learn to use Twitter and Google+ since every advertiser will have the option of having you promote their company.

5. You should regularly read online the *New York Times, San Jose Mercury News, Wall Street Journal, Time,* and *Palo Alto Weekly* to get story ideas.

6. Do the readings for the class sent to you via Google Groups (will be every few days).

Grades

Everyone in the class *should* get an A. If you are not getting an A, it means that you are not working as an effective member of the team to produce the best paper ever. It means you are writing poor quality stories, not turning in stories on time or not getting your ads. If you fail to turn in stories on time or fail to do the necessary research, you will be asked to choose another class instead of *Campanile.*

Your grade should not be the first thing you think about in *Campanile.* It should be being part of the *Campanile* team effort. In fact, to make you relax, everyone will start with an A grade. The only way you can get lower than an A grade is to fail to do what is required for the class (see above requirements). As long as you write your stories, turn them in on time, get your ads, and participate in class and production you will get an A. It's that easy!

To get an A make sure you do the following:

a. Turn in your stories on time in class and to Google Docs and name them correctly.
b. Upload your story to Voice after every issue
c. Produce good quality stories that are well researched and supported
d. Do good work on production week
e. Contribute to story ideas
f. Contribute to paper critique
g. Be helpful all the time
h. Be enthusiastic
i. Get your ads
j. Clean up after yourself and make sure our room looks nice

Blocks to Implementing a Media Arts Program

If these skills are easily taught in blended-learning programs, including journalism, and are required by the Common Core State Standards, then why aren't all schools adopting this approach?

There are four major reasons why this type of education is not being more quickly adopted.

Reason #1

While students involved in blended learning tend to score higher on tests, administrators are worried that if teachers do not teach directly to the tests, students will do poorly. High stakes testing is test targeting the Common Core State standards tests and the PISA test (Programme for International Student Assessment). While both of these tests target language skills, teachers and administrators want subject matter that directly targets the test, including worksheets and practice sessions. They don't realize that journalism embeds all the language arts skills being tested and that students learn and remember when they are engaged.

Perhaps we should re-evaluate why we as a nation are focusing on testing instead of projects. we can definitely continue to test since so many government agencies are requiring it, but we should also offer alternative types of testing including projects.

Teachers and administrators feel compelled to teach to the Common Core State Standards and administer the PISA test so that they can get and keep funding. Since teachers' salaries are tied to test scores, they feel a need to be in control. As a result of the testing, much creativity and innovation disappear from the classroom.

Reason #2

Teachers still think of their role in the classroom as the "sage on the stage," and schools of education are still training teachers to be the sage of the twentieth century.

Teachers need to see their role as collaborators and facilitators rather than lecturers; however, this is a difficult transition for many teachers to make. They are used to being in control, and they find it hard to relinquish that control. It is difficult to break the cycle, which is why pedagogy has remained largely unchanged for centuries. The school as a whole is seen as a place where students have little input. One important example, discussed near the beginning of this section, is the 1988 Supreme Court *Hazelwood* decision, which gives principals and advisers the right to censor the student press. The censorship of the student press in the U.S. is worse than in China. Only eight states have passed laws guaranteeing that student newspapers have First Amendment rights. These states are Arkansas, California, Colorado, Iowa, Kansas, Kentucky, Massachusetts, and Oregon.

Reason #3

The administration feels that students need to be constantly monitored to achieve the desired goals. It would be good if there were special courses for administrators in blended learning.

It is hard to teach independence when students have no freedom. Administrations need to abandon programs that monitor every student's computer screen to ensure that he or she is on task; this invades students' privacy, destroys independence, and demonstrates a lack of trust between student and teacher and administration. Also, in many school districts search engines are blocked because administrators are afraid of what students will find. Administrators are afraid to lose their e-rate funding which is the affordable rate funding for Internet access for schools and libraries provided by the Federal Communications Commission. As a result, they follow the motto: "When in doubt, cut it out." The federal government has to do a better job of explaining the ramifications of the Children's Online Privacy Protection Act (COPPA) and the Children's Internet Protection Act (CIPA) so that school districts will not be so fearful. We don't stop teaching kids to drive just because we are afraid of accidents.

Reason #4

It is hard to find teachers with journalism experience. Perhaps we should train all teachers to read media and write a blog.

Most teachers have no experience teaching journalism, and most English teachers are not familiar with assignments other than response to literature essays. Also, we have a young and highly inexperienced teaching corps. More than 50 percent of teachers leave the profession after five years. It is hard to be innovative as a teacher. Policymakers think that new teachers entering the profession would be the most tech savvy and innovative, but, in fact, the opposite is true. While they know tech tools for personal use, they don't know how to use them in the classroom. Also, lecturing is a more familiar model to teachers who just spent two years in lectures in schools of education.

Blended learning can help teachers be more effective in all situations. If all teachers, no matter what the subject area, expected students to do some collaborative writing for the web about subject areas students are studying and personally find interesting, then the problem would be on the way to be solved.

One example of a student publication.

Here are a couple of pages from the Palo Alto High School sports magazine, *The Viking*.

http://www.vikingsportsmag.com/

From a recent issue of the arts-and-entertainment magazine, called *C Magazine*.

The C Magazine //
Edition 13 //

The C Magazine //
Edition 10 //

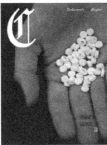

The C Magazine //
Edition 12 //

The C Magazine //
Edition 8 //

From the website for *The Viking.*

THE MAGIC OF MOTIVATION

BY PAUL KANDELL
Media Arts Teacher at Palo Alto High,
adviser for Verde and Voice

⑩

"It's the *motivation*," Aleksandar told me after his first week as a "journalist-in-residence" observing classes in the new Media Arts Center (MAC) at Palo Alto High School. A Macedonian government journalist and youth media activist who came to us through an international exchange program, Aleksandar had made relatively few connections with our students in his time with us so far. But I liked him. He understood the magic of journalism education and wanted to build a program in his home country. Also, he was observant and I valued him as a kind of contemporary Alexis de Tocqueville dissecting our culture with outside eyes. "Your students are *so motivated*," he said, looking both awed and deflated after a day spent wandering around the MAC a bit like the owl-eyed man taking in Gatsby's mansion. "I'm not sure I can make that happen back home."

In one sense, Aleksandar is right. The most distinguishing trait of the program I have led with my colleague Esther Wojcicki for the past 15 years (she was here another 15 before then!), is that students are very, very motivated. They come to class early and stay late (often well into the night). They revise and revise again. They eat meals together and develop a tribal loyalty to their publication staffs.

They develop and deliver presentations about how to improve their products, and they experiment endlessly with new ways to get their messages out. Often they vie for leadership positions, and sometimes they just attach themselves to a media arts class as the only thing that keeps them coming to school. They care about their work, passionately.

Sometimes it feels as though the program ought to have its own moon or at least an orbiting space station. Students come to us seeking something-other-than-traditional-school by the hundreds. With roughly 200 advanced journalism students on half a dozen publications, 100 more students in beginning journalism each year, and a few hundred more in photography and video production classes (not to mention the hundreds of students in English classes taught there), the MAC is an enormous undertaking.

While we don't have any planetoids circling the MAC, we do have something most cities don't have—a competitive media marketplace with students from different publications trying to scoop each other, competing for Twitter followers and Facebook likes, boasting who can deploy the latest app or service. We have new publications sprouting all the time. Last week a girl came to me with a plan to create an online magazine for "academically minded" students "How can I help?" I said. And there is our nascent Paly Radio Club, a fledgling effort that wants to be the school's version of "This American Life."—bring it on.

We breathe this air daily, so much so that sometimes we don't appreciate where it comes from. But the good news for Aleksandar and everybody else who wants to emulate our success is that there's no great secret about the motivation magic practiced at Paly by Esther for the past three decades. The curricular ingredients—audience, ownership, project-based learning, learning communities, and access to technology—are known by most teachers even if few seem to understand how to unleash their power the way journalism teachers do.

Audience

Simply put, students care about their work in our classes because they're not publishing for their teachers. They're publishing for a community of readers comprised of 2000 students and their families in print, and, many more on the Web and via social media. If they do it right, they can make a positive impact. If they screw up, thousands of people will know. They have power, and they know it and they are interested in learning how to channel it responsibly and professionally.

Ownership

Ownership in journalism class is not hypothetical or vague. It is ensconced in California Ed. Code 48907, the most powerful student press law in the country (and possibly the world), which gives student editors control over editorial content. I give a lot of advice in my publications classes, but students are free to accept or discard it as they will. Want to replicate our success? Start by having your state pass a similar law—as half a dozen states have done. Want to keep your students in mental lockdown? Stick with the standard espoused in U.S. Supreme Court's 1988 *Hazelwood* v. *Kuhlmeier* decision, which gives principals overly broad rights to censor student expression.

Project-Based Learning

The magic is in the mission. We don't demean students with breaking every objective down into a thousand tiny pieces, never letting them take a shot at the whole. Rather, we put them in teams and give them truly substantial objectives (again, of their own choosing): design a newspaper center-spread exploring aspects of the school's new policy on cheating; write a staff editorial—ideally supported by a unanimous vote—commending or supporting the way the administration enforces the school dress code; publish a 48-page sports magazine that does for your campus what *Sports Illustrated* does for the nation of sports lovers; build and maintain a website that provides your community with round-the-clock news coverage they won't find elsewhere. We do teach the small stuff, too, but only in the context of the large. Students know that when they are successful at these tasks they have an achievement worth noting.

Community

Adolescents want to experience a sense of *belonging*, and we provide a community that fulfills that need. We eat meals together and celebrate birthdays. At Back-to-School Night, I see parents smiling most when I talk about the "family" atmosphere in my classroom. Well, students want to be on teams; they crave being on teams. Why not facilitate that?

Access to technology

A classroom should not be a cage. Rather than restrict the use of cell phones and other technology in the classroom, in the MAC we encourage their responsible use. Is there a startup in the neighborhood that is offering a new app? Bring in the creators to invite students to take it for a spin. Got a new tool? Put it in students' hands and let them try it on for size. You want 21st century skills? You need to provide 21st century tools built on the principles of promoting community, collaboration, innovation, and multi-platform publishing, the Paly MAC is designed in many ways as an anti-cage.

Some will say that unleashing these forces is harder in non-journalism classes, and I agree to an extent. But Esther and I have done so in our English classes, and we have seen others do so, too, with predictably terrific results. It takes an awareness of the principals at the core of this book—and energy and discipline in applying them.

That's true whether you're in Peoria or Palo Alto—or Macedonia.

APPS AND TOOLS FOR TEACHERS

BY ESTHER WOJCICKI

This chapter is dedicated to delving a bit deeper into some of the applications and tools that have worked consistently well in a variety of blended-learning settings. But before we get to the specifics on products to try, we'd like to clear up some misconceptions about technology in education.

Busting the Myths

One myth that we want to bust is the idea that online learning or the use of educational technology is making teachers obsolete.

The twenty-first century has already given us some amazing innovations that would have seemed virtually impossible just three or four decades ago. From smartphones to robot vacuum cleaners and self-driving cars, advances in technology have certainly changed our lives. But, while you might no longer need to memorize phone numbers or vacuum your own living room, we firmly believe that skilled teachers will always be in high demand. If anything, the development of "edtech" tools has helped teachers become more creative and effective in the classroom—making their roles all the *more* important to student learning. Time-consuming tasks like taking attendance or keeping track of homework assignments can be done with the click of a mouse or the touch of a screen, allowing more class time for group projects or one-on-one student mentoring.

Another myth is expressed by the old saying, "You can't teach an old dog new tricks." If completely overhauling your teaching methods seems overwhelming, we understand! However, we also believe that making small changes can yield significant benefits over time. If there is even just one specific area of your students' classroom experience that you'd like to improve, perhaps you might try experimenting with a new tool or two over the course of the next term with a specific goal in mind (for example, the encouragement of more teamwork in class). If the new methods work well, you can continue to use them. If not, you can try something else. Even seemingly minor changes can have an impact, and if something ends up not working—well, that feedback is also valuable. Think positively—you might find something that you and your students both really enjoy and learn from, and overcoming any feeling that change is overwhelming will feel quite satisfying. And who knows? You might just pick up some new tricks.

Hardware

As an individual teacher, you might not have much say in what technology is available for use in your school or district. With that in mind, we will attempt to provide a wide variety of options that can work everywhere from schools that are equipped with a single computer lab or laptop cart all the way up to those with 1:1 tablet or Chromebook programs. For those of you who have the luxury of choosing hardware for your classroom, the decision will likely be influenced by the grade level of your students and the types of activities that will be performed on the devices.

For instance, if you are an elementary-school teacher whose pedagogy typically involves many hands-on projects, iPad apps and games might be a great way to supplement your curriculum with engaging activities. But if you are a middle-school or high-school teacher and your students are writing papers and using online resources to conduct research, Chromebooks[1] are a cost-effective way to introduce many web-based tools in your classroom. Chromebooks are the most reasonably priced laptops and are available from a variety of manufacturers, including Samsung, Dell, and HP. Check on the web for all the latest producers of Chromebooks.

Finding out what will work best for you and your students may take a bit of trial and error. This might mean trying out one method for a while, and making small changes until you see substantive improvements in student engagement and learning. If you're in a 1:1 tablet classroom, you might want to introduce several supplementary apps and allow students to choose which they find most interesting, fun, and useful. If this is your first time experimenting with a blended-learning scenario, try to remember that there is no wrong answer. You are empowered to make decisions and changes as you see fit, and we trust that you will know what is working for you and your class. The addition of tech tools to teaching is no silver bullet—what is and will always be most important is the quality of the human interactions that underlie the use of technology in education. Like the original quest to go to the moon, your Moonshot in education might take considerable effort before you reach your ultimate goal. And that is 100 percent okay.

Blended Learning 101

Silicon Schools[2] and the Clayton Christensen Institute for Disruptive Innovation[3] have teamed up with Khan Academy[4] to provide a free Blended Learning 101[5] course. Whether you're new to blended learning or you just want to review the basics of personalizing learning for K–12 students, this is a great introduction. The course covers the basic models of blended learning, the roles of teachers, students, and administrators, and examples of how different schools have implemented models that have worked for them. The five-part course is free, and includes over forty videos and guides that you can review completely on your own schedule.

The Learning Accelerator is a non-profit organization that believes blended learning has the potential to transform American education. Its mission is to mobilize $100 million over the next five years to establish and implement scalable solutions in school districts that wish to adopt blended learning. To learn more about its solutions, and for general resources on blended learning, check out its website at learningaccelerator.org.

Professional Development

Although much of blended learning focuses on personalized learning experiences for students, we would be remiss if we did not discuss some of the new tools available for personalized professional development for teachers. EdSurge[6] has put together a great guide[7] to resources and tools that teachers and schools are using to "remix" the traditional professional-development experience.

Tools for Teachers

According to many teachers we've spoken with, one of the biggest advantages of integrating technology into classroom practices is the amount of time it saves. There are many tools that can help improve your organization and productivity, as well as your communication with students and parents.

GOOGLE APPS FOR EDUCATION

Google Apps for Education[8] is a suite of free web tools that are accessible from any web-enabled device. From e-mail to spreadsheets, from word processing to calendars, everything is automatically and securely backed up to the cloud. What's more, Google Apps are built to be shared and worked on collaboratively. Team members can contribute to a project simultaneously or comment on one another's work if they are working at different times from different locations. If you have your students turn in papers using Google Docs and Drive, you can type inline comments, link to references, or even record voice comments,[9] In May 2014, Google introduced Classroom,[10] a tool for teachers to create and organize assignments, provide feedback, and communicate with their students through Google Apps for Education.

We've dedicated an entire section to more detailed descriptions of Google Apps for Education. Check it out in Chapter 12.

HAPARA

Hapara[11] is a company "powering Google Apps for educators." With its Teacher Dashboard, you can have a bird's-eye view of all of your students' current activity within Google Apps. Which documents have they recently worked on? Whom have they shared documents with? How much time did they spend on that paper assignment? Beyond getting the answers to questions like these, you can also quickly create folders to organize students by course or section, and easily open files and reset passwords. Hapara's Remote Control product allows you to quickly set each student's browser to a designated URL. And in the event that you catch a student's eyes wandering, you can close the window in question with a quick click of the mouse. Hapara is used by teachers in over thirty countries, and has been found to be a great time-saver for classrooms that use Google Apps.

THE ANSWER PAD

The Answer Pad[12] is a real-time assessment tool for teachers. Free for up to two hundred students and eight groups, The Answer Pad is accessible via any web-enabled device, and also has a free iPad app called TAPit. When you are ready to assess student knowledge, save time by using The Answer Pad to administer and score tests, and create detailed reports on student skills. Even open-ended questions are supported by the platform, which includes templates for eight different types of answers: number wheel for numeric responses, fill-in-the-blank, pie-shaped or rectangle shade-in for graphs, coordinate plane, multiple-choice, yes/no, true/false, and five-answer choice. Students can show their work on the "scratch pad," and The Answer Pad offers item analyses by skill, class, and student.

Exit Ticket[13] is a student-response system that can be used with multiple devices and is designed to accelerate student learning. The free plan has the assessment editor (Launch, Practice, Exit, and Quicket), modules (Teacher, Projector, and Reporting), heatmaps, and basic functionality you need to use Exit Ticket all by itself. Teachers can add on functionality with optional purchased applications; they can customize their plan à la carte and just pay for what they need.

MASTERY CONNECT

MasteryConnect[14] is a platform that provides evaluation tools for teachers to support mastery learning in the classroom. It includes real-time assessment tools with instant data and reporting, discussion and collaboration tools, curriculum maps, and resources for state and Common Core Standards alignment.

Tools for Administrators

PROJECT 24

Project 24,[15] presented by the Alliance for Excellent Education,[16] helps districts address key concepts having to do with the effective use of technology and digital learning. With the goal of achieving college and career readiness for all students, the Project 24 framework provides planning tools, advice, and ideas for district leaders from experienced educators and organizations. The seven core components are academic supports; budget and resources; curriculum and instruction; data and assessments; professional learning; technology and infrastructure; and use of time. To participate, sign up at Project 24, assemble a team, and take the free self-assessment on digital readiness. A confidential customized report will be sent to you with recommendations on resources for your district.

Video Resources

Video can be a great medium from which students can learn concepts. And you can introduce new concepts to your students via video without reinventing the wheel, or even having to operate a camcorder yourself. The web is full of fantastic resources to supplement your curriculum, and creating your own content is much simpler than it may seem. YouTube EDU is a channel curated by YouTube that allows you to discover, create, and share educational videos. The channel includes over 700,000 high-quality videos made by YouTube partners like Khan Academy, Stanford University, and TED-Ed[17]. Categorized by subject area and grade level, this rich library might very well contain the perfect video to get your students thinking about a topic in a whole new way. YouTube for Teachers provides helpful hints on how to integrate YouTube into the classroom, and it organizes videos according to the Common Core Standards. And to keep students on task while viewing YouTube videos, the YouTube for Schools network is available to allow just YouTube EDU content, while limiting access to non-educational material.

If you are ready to create and share your own video content, starting a YouTube channel is very simple. If you have a Google account, you can begin recording videos right away. Tools like Camtasia[18] can record content directly from your computer screen and can upload it right to YouTube with the click of a button. Still looking for great video content to add to your repertoire? Check out Lynda.com for tutorials on software, business, and creative skills, or Coursera,[19] EdX,[20] and Udacity[21] for top university-quality lectures and course content. Here are a few more suggested sites to easily create videos.

WE VIDEO

WeVideo (www.wevideo.com) is a collaborative online video creation tool that allows users to upload their own media clips or use stock media clips to produce their own video. It has a video editor which provides tools for editing the video easily. One of the things that makes WeVideo so great is the collaboration aspect. You can invite other people to create and edit which is great for the collaborative classroom.

CREAZA EDUCATION

(www.creazaeducation.com)

Another Video creation suite of tools is Creaza Education, one of Europe's 20 fastest growing and most innovative learning companies. It is easy to use because the video and audio edition tools are web based; no need for downloads. It is easy to mix and edit a project. It also has a built-in soundtrack editor and a built-in storyboarding tool.

STUPEFLIX

https://studio.stupeflix.com/en/

Stupeflix allows users to make amazing videos in seconds. It is hard to believe, but true. This is the kind of app that students love. They can use their favorite photos and audio clips and drag and drop their images into a sequence to create the video. It is super fun for kids starting in elementary school.

MASHER

www.masher.com

Masher allows users to create video mash-ups and offers clips from BBC's Motion Gallery and Rip Curl videos. Student can add their own images and video clips as well. It is simple to use and allows students to drag and drop.

ANIMOTO

http://animoto.com/

Animoto makes it possible to quickly create a video using still images, music, and text. If you can make a slideshow presentation, you can make a video using Animoto. Animoto's free service limits you to 30 second videos. You can create longer videos if you apply for an education account.

Tools for Communication and Feedback

There have been quite a few articles recently about the decline of e-mail use by today's youth. As you may well know, tweens and teens these days are more likely to send text and instant messages to their friends. If you use e-mail as your main line of communication with your students, your messages might be ignored, or even go completely unseen.

EDMODO

Edmodo[22] is a free social network that boasts a user base of over 33 million teachers and students around the world. It provides a secure network for teachers to communicate and collaborate with their students. Discussions on Edmodo have the feel of conversations on popular social networks like Facebook and Tumblr. You can ask open-ended questions, conduct quick surveys, or share assignments and interesting links. Edmodo's Gradebook features easy views of student progress over time, and allows for quick analysis of student performance. Badges can be awarded for performance or behavior based on benchmarks that you define, and Edmodo's Analytics can help you zone in on which topics students might need additional help with. Edmodo also hosts, on its own App Store, over five hundred educational apps that are integrated in its network. These apps range from flashcard creators to help students study to creative storytelling tools and standards-aligned math activities to supplement your curriculum. If you're looking for a new way to engage your students while keeping track of their progress, Edmodo is free and available for web and mobile (iOS and Android).

CLASS DOJO

With over 20 million registered users, ClassDojo[23] is a behavior-management system that incentivizes positive behaviors and provides customized feedback and communication between teacher, students, and parents. For teachers, who in traditional classrooms can spend more than half of class time monitoring and managing student behavior, ClassDojo has been found to be both engaging and effective in positive behavior change over time. With consistent reinforcement of good behavior through simple clicks on any smartphone, laptop, or tablet, the system helps students become intrinsically motivated to be good citizens, which can be a significant contributor to positive learning outcomes. ClassDojo's behavioral-change system is rooted in immediate, fun feedback. Students can create and customize a brightly colored alien-like avatar, which will represent them on the service. Teachers then assign feedback based on the types of behaviors they would like to encourage in class (e.g., hand raising, teamwork, thoughtful question asking), and notifications are sent immediately as points are given or subtracted. With no need for teachers to manually enter data, ClassDojo's analytics include detailed reports that can be accessed and shared with parents and administrators with just a few clicks or taps. With these rich profiles of behavioral change in your students available at your fingertips, time previously spent on classroom management can be reallocated to more substantive activities—namely teaching and learning!

CLASSBADGES

ClassBadges[24] is a free, easy-to-use online tool with which teachers can award badges to students for accomplishments or academic mastery. Through your teacher account, you can award badges customized for your classroom or school. Badges can easily be aligned to academic goals or associated with existing school awards.

Tablet Tools

Whether you are just getting started with tablets in your school, or you're looking to supplement your curriculum with some new tablet apps, these next few tools have been created to ease your transition.

GOOGLE PLAY FOR EDUCATION

Google Play for Education[25] is a curated app store created especially for schools. If your school is equipped with Android tablets, Google Play for Education can be easily searched for content categorized by grade level, subject, and Common Core Standard. The app store contains thousands of teacher-approved apps, K–12-appropriate e-books that range from classic literature to current textbooks, and YouTube EDU's library of videos to provide additional explanation of complex concepts that students might get stuck on. Google Play for Education also makes it easy to set up multiple tablets for instant distribution to an entire classroom, school, or district.

The Apple App Store's Education category is updated frequently with collections for students by grade level and subject. With over 65,000 apps designed for the iPad, Apple's education library includes everything from textbooks to interactive science activities to basic grammar lessons made into engaging, bite-sized games. Mobile Device Management[26] for iPad allows configurations of settings for multiple devices and accounts. Teachers can also temporarily limit all devices in their classroom to the use of a single app in order to avoid distraction, or to ensure security during testing.

NEARPOD

Nearpod[27] is an app that allows teachers to create original presentations or curate content from existing multimedia libraries. Presentations can then be shared to all student devices, and synchronized so that all students are viewing the same material at the same time. Questions and responses can be submitted in real time, and teachers can quickly assess and monitor results for individual students and entire sections through Nearpod's analytics dashboard. The app can be accessed across many platforms: Android tablets, iPads, Windows 8.1 Devices, Nooks, Chromebooks, PCs, and Macs.

Content Creation Tools

AVER TABCAM

Aver Tabcam[28] is a wireless camera that captures live or recorded video and allows teachers to project and manipulate content from a computer or tablet. Live video can be presented from anywhere in the classroom and annotated in real time. The wireless camera allows you to be mobile to interact with students even if you are presenting from the other side of the room. Supporting content like images and other video resources can also be added. Recorded lessons can be instantly shared for flipped classroom settings, future study, or to help absent students or substitute teachers stay up to date with the curriculum.

ZAPTION

Zaption[29] is a web-based video-editing tool that lets teachers add images, quizzes, and discussions to instructional videos. Starting with original content, or with videos from YouTube or Vimeo, you can quickly add images, text, quizzes, and discussions to turn video from a passive viewing experience to an active learning experience. Zaption's analytics platform allows instructors immediate feedback to gauge student understanding and engagement with key concepts.

Curricular Resources

EDUCADE

Educade[30] is an online portal for teachers that focuses on combining traditional teaching methods with twenty-first-century skills. Its existing library includes lesson plans from teachers spanning all grades K–12 and all subject areas. For inspiration, current lesson plans—including interactive apps, game-based learning, and creative hands-on projects—are searchable and downloadable. You can also create your own and share with the community.

PINTEREST FOR TEACHERS

You have probably heard of Pinterest, but have you heard of Pinterest for Teachers?[31] The company paid attention when it noticed many teachers creating boards for ideas ranging from classroom decor to creative projects and Common Core–aligned curriculum. The Pinterest for Teachers site now consists of thirty boards that hold ideas for preschoolers through high-schoolers, classroom management tips, and tech tools.

TEACHERS PAY TEACHERS

Teachers Pay Teachers[32] is an open marketplace and community where teachers can offer their original curricular materials to other educators. These can include lesson plans, assessments, worksheets, and project guides. According to the site, teachers have earned over $15 million on Teachers Pay Teachers since its launch in 2006. The site is searchable by grade level, subject, price, and resource type. As with other marketplace sites, ratings and reviews are publicly given for each item and seller.

Curation and Presentation

BLENDSPACE

Blendspace[33] is a free tool for teachers that allows simple and elegant organization of web resources to create and share lesson plans with just one URL. If you have ever planned a presentation that involves slides, videos, text, and graphics, you know that switching back and forth between applications and files on your desktop can be frustrating and time-consuming. With Blendspace, all of your links, videos, and materials are collected in one place and arranged in a clean tiled format in any order you choose. No more desktop clutter and windows lost behind others! What's more, you can build quizzes into your presentations, and collect real-time responses from students to measure their understanding. This can help you adapt as you teach by letting you know which concepts are proving to be more challenging than others. Blendspace is available on any web-enabled device via its browser, and it also has built a native app available for iPad.

Language Arts

ACHIEVE 3000

Achieve 3000[34] is a system that offers individualized, differentiated online instruction to support the development of literacy and science skills. Its literacy system first assesses a student's baseline reading level, and then continues to assess and to increase complexity of texts to support fluency, comprehension, vocabulary, writing, and critical thinking. Programs are available for grades 2–12 with Common Core alignment. There are also versions for English Language Learners, as well as for adults and teachers.

HEADSPROUT

Headsprout, formerly known as MimioSprout,[35] develops products to support reading in grades K–5. Headsprout Early Reading is a K–2 supplemental program that provides individualized instruction through eighty online lessons and printed stories with built-in assessments and performance reports. Headsprout Reading Comprehension, for grades 3–5, helps students comprehend and apply knowledge of texts through fifty thirty-minute online adaptive lessons. Some lessons include making inferences, identifying main ideas, and learning vocabulary in context.

MINDSNACKS

Popular mobile-learning-game developer MindSnacks[36] has released two apps to sharpen students' vocabulary and conversation skills. MindSnacks Kids' Vocab features nine games for kids ages seven through twelve (grades 2–7) to help them learn the spelling, proper usage, and pronunciation of 350 words and phrases through twenty-five lessons designed by experts. For those preparing for the SAT, MindSnacks SAT Vocab helps students learn, practice, and master five hundred words to build essential PSAT, SAT, and GRE vocabulary. Beyond definitions and pronunciation, the app features lessons covering key SAT elements, including antonyms, context, and spelling. The company's latest offering, Elevate,[37] offers fourteen beautifully designed games that train attention and memory while strengthening skills in listening, reading comprehension, writing, and communication. Elevate is available on the Apple App Store, Google Play, and the Amazon App Store.

NEWSELA

Newsela[38] is a new company focused on improving reading comprehension through the development of non-fiction literacy. The website, used by tens of thousands of schools in all fifty states and seventy countries, offers current news stories written by professional journalists at five different reading levels for grades 3–12. Covering topics from science to money to the arts, Newsela publishes new articles daily.

Common Core–aligned quizzes accompany the articles and help assess development of reading fluency and critical thinking skills. Teachers and students can also comment and hold online discussions on articles via the site. Subscribers to the service can also quickly access a dashboard view of student progress at the individual and classroom level.

NOREDINK

Created by a former high-school English teacher, NoRedInk[39] helps students improve their grammar through engaging material and immediate feedback. With content based on each student's favorite hobbies, celebrities, and other interests, NoRedInk's grammar assessments aim to give students authentic learning experiences. Instead of multiple-choice tests, students are given editing tasks that assess their knowledge of sentence structure, punctuation, and capitalization. Each experience is tailored to the student by allowing independent practice at the student's own pace and tutorials on concepts that he or she gets stuck on. The service—which is free for teachers—boasts tens of thousands of users; over 40 million grammar questions have been answered to date.

SHMOOP

Shmoop[40] offers free learning guides, online courses, college readiness prep, and test prep in an approachable, teen-friendly voice to make academic content relevant and enjoyable to students. Shmoop's English-literature catalogue includes Shakespeare, best-sellers, and even Dr. Seuss. For teachers, the site also offers ideas for Common Core–aligned assignments, activities, and assessments.

TOONTASTIC

Toontastic[41] for iPad is a creative storytelling app made for kids ages five and up that guides them through the development of a narrative arc in the creation of an original cartoon. The app provides support in defining story scenes, including Setup, Conflict, Challenge, Climax, and Resolution. Each scene can be customized and animated with characters, backgrounds, and music. Cartoons can be saved and shared securely on the ToonTube network. Launchpad Toys, the creators of Toontastic, have also curated Common Core–aligned lesson plans from teachers who have used the app across K–12 grades in many subject areas, including language arts, math, science, and social studies.

Math

ALEKS MATH

ALEKS Math[42] (Assessment and LEarning in Knowledge Spaces) is a web-based assessment and learning system for K–12 math, originally developed by a team of cognitive scientists and software engineers at the University of California, Irvine, with funding from the National Science Foundation. ALEKS is based on research in mathematical cognitive science known as Knowledge Space Theory. Through adaptive questioning, ALEKS accurately assesses a student's level of knowledge and then delivers targeted instruction on the exact topics the student is most ready to learn. As the student works through a course, ALEKS keeps track of learning and mastery of topics. It boasts an "average historical student learning rate" of about 90 percent.

DRAGONBOX

DragonBox,[43] a multi-platform math game that teaches algebra, was conceived in the belief that human beings are hardwired to learn extremely complicated concepts. Designed by a math teacher and a cognitive scientist, DragonBox uses pictures instead of numbers or variables to introduce mathematical rules through discovery. With two levels of difficulty (ages five through twelve, and ages nine and up), DragonBox is a series of learning tools for algebraic concepts through an interactive, engaging game. Learning resources for teachers and a seven-day trial of the game are available via the DragonBox website.

DREAMBOX LEARNING

DreamBox Learning[44] is an online elementary math program that provides personalized learning experiences for students with integrated assessments and alignment to the standards of U.S. states and Canadian provinces, as well as Common Core. Lessons are built around the development of conceptual understanding and fluency, and the program adapts lessons on the basis of real-time student performance. DreamBox's adaptive framework can adjust difficulty, scaffolding, hints, and sequencing of lessons to allow students to progress at a personalized pace. Teachers are provided with current student progress data based on concepts as well as standards alignment.

EQUATIA

Equatia,[45] developed by the Stanford School of Education's Learning, Design, and Technology program and built by Luckybird Games, is an open-world, role-playing adventure game focused on helping elementary-school students develop arithmetic fluency. Equatia has been used in Rocketship and SPARK blended-learning schools.

MANGA HIGH

Manga High[46] is a game-based learning site, built by mathematicians and game specialists, where students learn mathematics via casual games aligned to Common Core standards. Four principles underlie the games on Manga High:

Adaptivity: Each game is designed to adapt to the student's ability level and to adjust so as to make it not too easy and not too hard.

Automaticity: A simple game mechanic is overlaid on the core learning concept of each game, and is repeated until the concept is learned and becomes an automatic cognitive process.

Discipline and self-learning: Because Manga High engages students through games, motivation can be higher than through traditional pedagogy.

Application of theory: Each game is developed to be applicable to a "real world" concept to further encourage student interest both within and outside of the classroom.

SOKIKOM

Sokikom[47] is a Common Core–aligned math program used in over 15,000 schools and 1,000 districts in all fifty U.S. states and in over sixty countries. Developed around positive reinforcement, social learning, and personalization to engage students in math instruction, Sokikom also helps teachers to streamline classroom management. The online math program is adaptive, and starts with a diagnostic assessment to begin the student's personalized learning experience. Activities are designed to be fun, and include instructional video hints for times when students get stuck. You can sign up for a free trial on Sokikom's website.

KHAN ACADEMY

Khan Academy[48] is a commonly used tool in the blended-learning classroom. The website features thousands of free educational resources, including a personalized learning analytics dashboard, over 100,000 math practice exercises, and over 5,000 video tutorials stored on YouTube, which teach mathematics, computer science, economics, medicine, and many other subjects. Khan Academy reaches about 10 million students per month and has delivered over 300 million lessons. You can learn more about Khan Academy and its mission and philosophy from founder Salman Khan's book, *The One World Schoolhouse*, in which he describes and promotes blended learning and project-based learning.

MATHALICIOUS

Mathalicious[49] is a subscription-based site that offers project-based lessons exploring the math behind real-world topics. Each project takes about two to three days to complete and revolves around a general guiding question involving a familiar topic like ordering pizza. Teachers can download lesson overviews, student objectives, a list of aligned Common Core Standards, handouts, and lesson guides. After a project has been completed, feedback and experiences can be shared with Mathalicious teachers around the world.

MOTION MATH

Motion Math[50] creates games for iOS and Android that teach the building blocks of mathematics while overcoming intellectual challenges. Its suite of eight games makes difficult concepts like fractions and number-line estimation fun for elementary-school students. Its latest game, Pizza, lets kids apply their skills to a real-world situation: running their own pizza restaurant. Motion Math offers volume discounts for schools, and boasts over 600,000 users per month. Its Fractions, Zoom, Hungry Fish, Wings, Match, and Questimate games are available as a bundle on the Apple App Store. Its Motion Math: Fractions! and Hungry Fish games are also available on Google Play for Android users.

ST MATH

Created by MIND Research Institute, ST Math[51] is game-based instructional software for K–5 and secondary classes and is designed to boost math comprehension and proficiency through visual learning. Integrating with classroom instruction, ST Math incorporates the latest research in learning and the brain and promotes mastery-based learning and mathematical understanding. The ST Math software games use interactive, graphically rich animations that visually represent mathematical concepts to improve conceptual understanding and problem-solving skills.

TENMARKS

TenMarks[52] (from Amazon) is a web-based adaptive K–12 math program closely aligned to the Common Core that aims to deliver deep conceptual understanding and mastery. Used in over 25,000 schools, its problems are created to engage students in problem solving, and to provide them with scaffolding and feedback that support them and help build a strong foundation in mathematical skills. When a student needs an intervention, the adaptive engine takes them through a step-by-step instructional session.

Science

CK12

CK12[53] provides open-source content and technology tools to help teachers globally. Free access to high-quality, customizable educational content in multiple modalities suited to multiple student learning styles and levels allows teachers, students, and others to innovate and experiment with new models of learning. CK12 helps students and teachers alike by enabling rapid customization and experimentation with teaching and learning styles. CK12's goal is to provide tools that can help increase student learning through engagement, and to provide more universal access to learning and content, irrespective of educational resources otherwise available for a school or region.

MONSTER PHYSICS

Monster Physics[54] (iOS), created by the maker of Stack the States and Stack the Countries, is a game where you complete missions by designing contraptions with a wide variety of parts to navigate your monster toward a goal. Missions are completed by using basic physics on parts like wheels, ropes, and propellers. Basic physics terms are defined in a "learn" section at the beginning of the play experience, and are demonstrated throughout completion of the mission.

SCIENCE 360

Science 360[55] is a video library sponsored by the National Science Foundation that shares the latest scientific breakthroughs with the general public. Its collection of videos is created by scientists, colleges and universities, and science and engineering centers around the world; each video is embeddable to put on websites, blogs, and social-networking pages.

SCIENCE FUSION

Science Fusion[56] is an inquiry-based science program from Houghton Mifflin Harcourt. It is an interactive curriculum with simulations, animations, videos, virtual labs, and assessments that can be accessed at home or in the classroom on any web-enabled device. Its digital curriculum includes hands-on activities and video-based projects that help encourage scientific thinking.

VIDEO SCIENCE

Video Science[57] (iOS) is a growing library of over eighty hands-on science lessons that are great for home and the classroom. These short videos demonstrate inexpensive and easy-to-reproduce experiments that are designed to inspire and excite kids of all ages.

NATIONAL GEOGRAPHIC

National Geographic[58] is a website with videos, photos, and stories from around the world that can be used to supplement home and classroom learning. With an extensive library, and a separate website built just for kids, National Geographic used as a supplement in your blended-learning classroom can provide kids the opportunity to explore places and things that they otherwise might not be able to experience.

STUDENT CPR

Student CPR[59] is an online program designed to incorporate CPR into a high-school blended-learning curriculum. It replaces a conventional classroom-based course with an online course, and allows students to learn on their own schedules and at their own pace from home or a computer lab. Each school also has the option to provide hands-on training by a skilled evaluator using a manikin.

STEM

FIRST ROBOTICS

FIRST Robotics[60'] mission is to inspire young people to be science and technology leaders, by engaging them in exciting mentor-based programs that build science, engineering, and technology skills, that inspire innovation, and that foster characteristics for a well-round-ed life such as self-confidence, communication, and leadership. Parents and community members serve as volunteers, and the programs take place after school and on the weekends.

THE LEGO MINDSTORMS

The Lego Mindstorms[61] robotics set can command five different models of robots with WiFi, Bluetooth, or smartphone. The programming capabilities are endless. Lego Mindstorms are toolkits that allow students to make programmable robots (software and hardware included). This is the third-generation Mindstorms series. The programmable brick is an ARM9-based processor that runs Linux, with 16MB FLASH memory, and 64MB RAM. The five different models you can build are Ev3storm, Track3r, Gripp3r, R3ptar, and Spik3r.

WONDER WORKSHOP

Wonder Workshop[62] (formerly Play-i) is the creator of Dash and Dot, two programmable, tablet-controlled robots that encourage computational thinking in children ages five and up. Young children with no programming experience at all can learn basic coding principles through a drag-and-drop icon-based interface. The possibilities are limitless, as more skilled coders can scale up to Blockly[63], or even Java and Objective-C. The first shipment of Wonder Workshop robots will be available in Fall 2014; they are available for pre-order at makewonder.com.

SCRATCH

Scratch[64] is a multimedia programming tool that can be used by students, scholars, teachers, and parents for a range of educational and entertainment purposes for math and science projects, including simulations and visualizations of experiments, recorded lectures with animated presentations, animated stories in social sciences, and interactive art and music. Simple games may be made with Scratch as well. You can view the existing projects available on the Scratch website, or modify and test any modification without saving it, without online registration. Scratch allows you to use event-driven programming with multiple active objects called "sprites." Sprites can be drawn—as either vector or bitmap graphics—from scratch in a simple editor that is part of the website, or they can be imported from external sources, including webcam.

MIT APP INVENTOR

MIT App Inventor[65] is a simple-to-use but very powerful app that enables students to build and store data in a database. Students can create a make-a-quiz app, and teachers can save questions in a quiz for their students to answer. Because App Inventor provides access to a GPS location sensor, students can build an app to help them remember where they parked their car; an app that shows the location of their friends at a concert or conference; or an app that gives their own custom tour of their school, their workplace, or a museum.

Students can write apps that use the phone features of an Android phone; they can write an app that periodically texts "Missing you" to their loved ones, or an app, "No Text While Driving," that responds to all texts automatically with "Sorry, I'm driving and will contact you later." Students can even have the app read the incoming texts aloud to them. Students can use App Inventor to communicate with the web, writing Android apps that talk to their favorite web sites, such as Amazon and Twitter. The App Inventor book is a free online download that offers video tutorials, a concept map, and more. The endnote has a link to the App Inventor Curricula.[66]

VIRTUAL NERD

Virtual Nerd[67] (developed by an expert tutor and a designer, and acquired by Pearson Education) is a free library of over 1,500 video tutorials for middle- and high-school math. Virtual Nerd is a supplemental learning resource and instructional platform. Lessons are designed to build solid foundations in core concepts prior to moving on to more complex ones. Math topics are categorized by alignment to the Common Core State Standards, the SAT, and ACT.

Foreign Languages

DUOLINGO

Duolingo[68] is a free service that allows users to learn a new language while translating the web. Through simple game activities, even the most novice second-language learners can contribute to the company's mission. For beginners, basic words and phrases are introduced, and guidance is always available from the translations of others in the global community. The system supports learning of vocabulary, grammar, spelling, and pronunciation. Feedback is provided immediately, and progress is shown with fun badges. Available on iOS and Android, the award-winning Duolingo supports Spanish, French, German, Portuguese, Italian, and English learners.

MINDSNACKS

If you're looking for a fun way to supplement your foreign-language teaching (or learning!), MindSnacks[69] offers bite-sized games to learn Spanish, French, German, Mandarin Chinese, Portuguese, and Japanese. Available for iPhone and iPad (with Android versions in the works), each language app includes eight or more unique games and fifty lessons to learn over a thousand words and phrases. Lessons range from basic vocabulary to spelling, grammar, and conversation, and they include audio clips recorded by native speakers. Thoughtfully developed to customize each learner's experience, the apps adapt using a personalized algorithm, and provide enhanced review of content based on need.

ROSETTA STONE

Rosetta Stone[70] offers multiple solutions for K–12 language learning. Covering thirty languages and stressing skills like speaking, writing, reading, and listening, Rosetta Stone can be used in English- and foreign-language classrooms, and for college and career readiness. Its TOTALe PRO platform is flexible enough for blended-learning scenarios from a flipped classroom to BYOD (bring your own device). Through this program, students can interact with online coaches, work at their own pace through adaptive software, and access contact through both web and mobile devices.

Social Sciences

MINDSNACKS

From the creators of the popular language-learning apps, MindSnacks U.S. Geography[71] (iOS) has eight educational games covering all fifty states for beginning and intermediate geography students, and for trivia buffs and travelers. The programs go far beyond state capitals; they offer sophisticated and content-rich material including famous citizens, major landmarks, and state mottos. Addictive games and fun graphics provide an engaging learning experience.

STACK THE STATES

Stack the States[72]/Stack the Countries[73] (iOS). These complementary geography games have been voted "Best Kids Apps for iPad" and "Best Educational Game App Ever." Each costs only 99 cents, and kids love the engaging animations and sounds. The object of the game is to create a stack of states or countries. You are asked various questions about the states and countries, including capitals, shapes, abbreviations, nicknames, and location.

US GEOGRAPHY BY DISCOVERY EDUCATION

US Geography by Discovery Education[74] (iOS) is a fact-filled app that teaches and tests facts about geography and culture for different regions of the United States. Kids read information and watch videos about each region and then complete activities and challenges. Activities aren't timed, but challenges are. The app keeps track of kids' progress, giving them the option to post scores on a parent's Facebook account. In addition, the app provides access to recent and timely Discovery news stories and video segments. News-story categories include Earth, dinosaurs, and archeology, and the videos show a wide variety of topics; each video is a minute or two long. The app also awards kids a medallion each day they answer enough activity questions. An iPad-only edition is also available.

In Khan Academy Better Money Habits,[75] Bank of America and Khan Academy joined forces to create a free platform to improve financial literacy. The platform explains financial concepts in a simple and conversational way and is completely free of advertising. In addition, Khan Academy provides videos on financial subjects with no editorial control from Bank of America, reflecting a shared goal of providing information in an unbiased environment.

Fine Arts

ADOBE CREATIVE CLOUD

Adobe Creative Cloud[76] brings together everything teachers and students need to access Photoshop, Illustrator, InDesign, and more. It allows students to build and publish websites, mobile apps, iPad publications, and content for any medium or device.

GOOGLE ART PROJECT

Google Art Project[77] has more than 30,000 great works from multiple real-world collections like the Art Institute of Chicago and the Tate, and presents them in virtual galleries. Kids can browse artworks either on the webpage or by exploring a map (like Google's Street View) of the museum itself. High-resolution images mean you can get a closer look at these paintings than if you went to the museum itself. It is a great way for teachers to take their students on virtual visits to museums worldwide.

IWORK

iWork[78] is an office suite of applications created by Apple Inc. for its OS X and iOS operating systems. It is now a free download for all Macs and has some interesting applications, including Keynote, a presentation program; Pages, a word-processing program; and Numbers, a spreadsheet application.

MOMA ART LAB

MoMA Art Lab[79] is a great drawing/creative app for the iPad, and it is easy to use because there is an excellent tutorial. It works for all ages. Younger kids can finger-draw lines and shapes and choose colors. Older kids can draw with scissors, make a line design, collaborate on a group drawing, create a shape poem, make a collage, or create a sound composition. There is an audio guide to help non-readers.

PAPER

Paper[80] is a creation tool for all grade levels, available for the iPad. To start creating, students just tap it or pinch on an open book, and the page fills the screen and becomes editable. Paper comes with two free tools: Draw (a fountain pen) and Erase. Additional tools are available for $1.99 each via in-app purchase and include Sketch (a pencil), Outline (a marker), Write (a pen), and Color (a water-color brush).

Multiple Subjects

APEX LEARNING

Apex Learning[81] is an interactive digital curriculum developed in order to close the achievement gap, reduce the dropout rate, and improve student outcomes. Its standards-based curriculum covers middle- and high-school math, science, English, social studies, world languages, and Advanced Placement courses. It is adaptive and can be used for differentiated instruction in both remediation and advanced course work.

FUEL EDUCATION

Fuel Education[82], formerly Aventa Learning, is a full virtual pre-K–12 curriculum that includes courses, content, and assessments. The catalogue includes over five hundred courses and over 100,000 hours of instructional content that can be integrated into blended-learning classrooms or used in distance learning. High-school courses cover standard, honors, and AP tracks, and all curricula are mapped to state and national standards.

BRAINPOP

BrainPop[83] supports individual, team, and whole-class learning in traditional, blended, and flipped learning settings. At school and in informal learning environments, the characters help introduce new topics and illustrate complex concepts. Through the newly launched My BrainPOP, teachers and students can keep a record of learning accomplishments through quizzes, game play, and activities. My BrainPOP includes teachers' access to the Mixer, which lets them tailor assessments to meet each student's needs. A great fit for mobile learning and BYOD classrooms, BrainPOP's educational apps have been downloaded millions of times and lauded in countless reviews.

COMPASS LEARNING ODYSSEY

Compass Learning Odyssey[84] is a suite of learning solutions for primary and secondary grades across all subjects. It provides personalized instruction for students, and informative assessments and data analytics for teachers in real time. Parents can also log in to the system to monitor their child's progress and achievement.

K12

K12[85] provides online instruction for K–12 grades for distance learning, and individual online courses can be purchased for home schooling and blended classrooms. With content covering all grades and subjects, K12 provides many options for personalized learning, and remediation as well as advanced coursework.

SHMOOP

We met Shmoop[86] before under Language Arts, but it also offers educational materials to help teens understand a variety of other topics, including biology, U.S. history, algebra, and calculus. The site's literature section covers classics, but users can also access in-depth information on characters and themes in modern works like *The Hunger Games*. The site's real strength, though, is in its presentation. Instead of just offering endless pages of content, Shmoop breaks subjects down in fun ways. Character profiles give zany accounts of mythological figures (Agamemnon laments that he "was married to Clytemnestra, but then she killed me . . . so yeah"). Virtual flashcards help students memorize AP Spanish terms, and a lengthy DMV section weaves humor into its state-by-state rules of the road. And the site's learning resources are legit: the conversational content is peppered with pop-culture references, but much of it is written by Ph.D. and Masters students from schools like Stanford and Harvard. A separate section for educators—available for a fee—includes resources for teaching civics, literature, and other topics.

Other Resources

Open Educational Resources (OER) are freely accessible articles, books, courseware, and other media that are supported by Creative Commons licensing— www.creativecommons.org. Here are some examples of OER:

> Khan Academy
>
> OER Commons[87]
>
> OER University[88]
>
> PhET Interactive Simulations[89]
>
> Global Lives Project[90]
>
> Project Guttenberg
>
> Gooru
>
> CK12
>
> WikiEducator
>
> EngageNY

If you are looking for more blended-learning resources (and there are infinitely more), check out these two websites to start:

> 21stcenturylit.org
>
> Blended Learning Tool Kit http://blended.online.ucf.edu/
>
> Blend My Learning http://www.blendmylearning.com/
>
> Blended Learning, The Clayton Christensen Institute for Disruptive Innovation
>
> Blended Learning Implementation Guide, from Digital Learning Now!
>
> Blended Learning on Edsurge
>
> Blended Learning on Getting Smart
>
> International Association for K-12 Online Learning (iNACOL)
>
> This is Blended Learning, from Cities for Education
>
> Entrepreneurship Trust (CEE-Trust)

Please keep in mind that our list is by no means exhaustive, and by the time this book goes to print, there are likely to be a number of new entries. In creating this list, however, our goal was to share some go-to resources that we know have worked well in many classrooms, including some of our own and our colleagues'.

This is where the fun begins: when you're ready, pick out a few to try out with your students, and try to stick with them for at least a week or two. Some will work better than others in terms of engagement, and some will yield more interesting learning outcomes than others. We'd love to hear about the experiments, successes, and, yes, even failures in your classroom. We'll be adding additional resources at moonshotsineducation.com, and we invite you to join us in continuing the conversation there.

In other chapters, we will be discussing additional ways to grow your personal learning network and to keep up with the latest developments in education technology and blended learning.

GOOGLE APPS FOR EDUCATION

BY ESTHER WOJCICKI

12

It is pretty amazing to see the amount of support Google Apps for Education gives to teachers and to blended learning. The tools Google offers teachers and students consist of the following: Gmail, Calendar, Drive, Docs, Sheets, Slides, Sites, and Google+. In August 2014, Google added Classroom, a tool to integrate Google Drive, Docs, and Gmail to support teachers in creating assignments, providing feedback, and communicating with students. Google Apps for Education is free for schools, it contains no ads, and its services do not collect or use student data for advertising purposes or to create advertising profiles. Additionally, K–12 Google Apps for Education users do not see ads when they use Google Search so long as they are signed in to their Apps for Education accounts.

● MOONSHOT TOOLS

There are many presentations online at the Google Training Center (www.google.com/edu/training) that any teacher can use for a staff-development presentation or just individually to see the many ways Google Apps can be used in the classroom.

Google Teacher Academy

The Google Teacher Academy (GTA) is a free professional-development program designed to help primary- and secondary-school educators from around the globe get the most from innovative technologies. Each GTA is an intensive, two-day event during which participants get hands-on experience with Google tools, learn about innovative instructional strategies, receive resources to share with colleagues, and immerse themselves in a supportive community of fellow educators.

Approximately fifty innovative educators from around the world are selected to attend each GTA session. Applicants include classroom teachers, curriculum specialists, technology advocates, librarians, administrators, professional trainers, and other education professionals who actively serve the world's primary- and secondary-school teachers and students.

Participants are selected on the basis of their professional experience, their passion for teaching and learning, and their successful use of technology in school settings. GTA is particularly interested in educators who actively provide mentoring or training for other teachers. GTA is designed to create a strong professional community of educators who support each other over the course of a year.

● MOONSHOT TOOLS

Google Summits

Google Summits are held all over the world many times a year, providing hundreds of ideas for using Google products and blended learning in the classroom. The speakers are teachers who volunteer to share what they are doing in the classroom using Google tools. This is particularly effective because the model is teachers teaching teachers. Each Summit takes up to eight hundred teachers, and they are usually sold out. Prices are minimal and include lunch.

The web address is www.gafesummit.com.

The presentations are posted online once the Summit is over; they can be accessed on the website under "Resources." Check them out by going to www.edtechteam.com/summit.

Teachers can also watch videos online for free at this address: http://www.google.com/edu/training/tools/.

And here are stories about how Google tools work in the classroom: http://www.google.com/edu/stories/.

The rest of this chapter will give specific information for using Gmail, Calendar, Drive, Docs, Sheets, Slides, Sites, Google+, and Classroom.

Google Drive

Google Drive lets you store and share all your stuff, including documents, videos, images, and other files. You can sync, store, and access your files anywhere—on the web, on your hard drive, or on the go. Google Drive has a number of components that can be used for document editing anytime, anywhere.

> Google Docs is an online word processor that lets you create and format text documents and collaborate with other people in real time.
>
> Google Sheets is an online spreadsheet application that lets you create and format spreadsheets and collaborate with other people in real time.
>
> Google Slides is an online presentations app that allows you to show off your work in a visual way.
>
> Google Forms is a special extension of Google Sheets. With Forms, users can create a form document to publish to the web that will accept data and populate a spreadsheet behind the scenes.
>
> Google Drawings lets you easily create, edit, and share drawings online. The tool includes all the sharing and visibility features of other Google Drive products, along with the ability to create shapes and layout guides, organize graphics, and much more.

How Teachers Use Google Drive

Storage: Google Drive lets you store and access your files anywhere—on the web, on your hard drive, on the go. Your files and productivity tools are hosted in the cloud and allow for flexible and collaborative work anytime, anywhere.

Collaboration: Help students collaborate and be able to track their contributions. They will learn to set up a Google account, create Google documents, collaborate inside a document, and track the changes made, including who made each improvement. The real-time collaboration feature of Docs in Google Drive makes it ideal for group assignments, revision cycles, and shared notes, all of which helps create a more efficient classroom. Built-in tools like autosave, revision history, comments, and an equation editor are useful for students and teachers alike.

Some examples of how teachers are using Google Drive include:
- Collaborate with other teachers and share lesson/curriculum plans
- Consolidate notes for department or faculty meetings
- Create a simple webpage with Docs publishing
- Share and collect assignments without printing
- Provide instant feedback to students
- Track instructional interventions

Some examples of how students can use online documents:
- Improve writing skills through peer editing and feedback
- Access documents in class or at home
- Work on reports, research, or papers together with peers, who may be in different classes, schools, or even countries
- Keep a continuous, running log of assignments such as journal entries or writing samples

Understanding Drive Filing, Folders, and Sharing

Google Drive allows you to save any document, spreadsheet, presentation, drawing, or form as a template for others to use. Templates are available in the template gallery, linked in Docs, and can be found by searching, browsing categories, or clicking directly to the template preview.

With Google Apps for Education, you can create templates specifically for use at your school's apps domain. This domain has its own template gallery, which is separate from the general public gallery. You cannot submit a template to the public gallery with your school's apps account—just to the gallery for your school. If you want to submit a template, first sign in to your personal Google account.

When you use a template, you create your own copy, so it doesn't matter if the template owner changes or deletes the original template; your copy remains unchanged.

Classes often have several common formats that can take advantage of shared templates for any student or teacher to use. For example, a teacher could allow students to easily create a predetermined format for bibliographies, book reports, research papers, or presentations, or for any other type of assignment, like storyboards. A student government could create common documents for club budgets or newsletters.

Administrators could create a standard format for reporting attendance, grades, or behavior logs. If there's a document format that can be used by many people, it may be helpful to save it as a template.

Better, faster teaching and classroom management with Docs

Google Docs provides many ways to improve everyday teaching and help you manage your class. For example: Sharing/grading assignments in Google Docs and Power commenting in Google Docs for teachers.

Creating Google Spreadsheets (Sheets)

Sheets in Google Drive allows teachers and students to easily aggregate, organize and analyze information in one place. With advanced tools for sorting, formatting, visualizing information with charts and pivot tables, and entering formulas, online spreadsheets can be used in a variety of settings.

Some examples of how teachers can use online spreadsheets:
- Create a seating chart
- Record grades with an organized grade book
- Track attendance and reports on missing assignments and on behavior
- Store a database of contact information for students and parents
- Use a word cloud gadget to visualize written responses
- Use an Apps Script to automatically send feedback to students.

Some examples of how students can use online spreadsheets:
- Collect data from across the web for research
- Create interactive flashcards with a spreadsheet gadget
- Format a weekly class schedule.

Easy, Fast Ways to Build Slides

With Google Slides, you can easily create, share and edit online presentations. Here are some things you can do:
- Share presentations with your students and co-workers
- Upload and convert existing presentations to Google Drive format
- Download your presentations as .pdf, .pptx, or .txt files
- Insert images and videos, and format your slides
- Publish and embed your presentations in a website, allowing access to a wide audience
- Draw organizational charts, flowcharts, design diagrams, and much more within a presentation
- Add slide transitions, animations, and themes to create show-stopping presentations.

Google Drive Slides also allows you to collaborate with others to build a compelling story that will captivate your audience. Creating presentations together is easy because you can:

- See exactly what others are working on with colorful presence markers
- Edit a presentation with other people simultaneously from different locations
- Use revision history to see who made changes or to revert to earlier versions
- Say hello, start a conversation, or share new ideas using built-in chat
- Use the comments feature to provide asynchronous feedback on slides.

Easy, Fast Ways to Build Forms

With Google Drive, you can quickly create a form or survey and then send it to students, parents, teachers, or staff. Their answers will be tracked in one spreadsheet. Because forms are filled out online, there's no need to enter results manually. Responses are collected and displayed immediately in a corresponding Google Drive Sheet, which allows you to sort, analyze, and visualize the information.

You can send forms to anyone—even people outside of your school apps domain. Respondents can access the form via e-mail, a published web page, or a site where it is embedded. Forms also generates an automatic summary with charts, graphs, and statistics about your form responses and can notify you when new responses are submitted.

Here are some live examples of forms you can preview and try:

- Collecting mailing addresses
- U.S. History pop quiz for grade school
- Student group welcome form
- Club event requests

And here are some other tasks that could be performed using Forms:
- Structured peer editing and feedback
- Assignment checklist and submissions
- Applications for positions in clubs, students, government.

How to use Google Drawings

With Google Drawings, you can create and collaborate on flow charts, design diagrams, and create other types of drawings. You can also chat with other editors from within Google Drawings, publish drawings as images, comment on images, and download drawings to your computer.

Real-Life Examples of How Google Drive Is Used in Schools

Dan Maas, chief information officer of Littleton Public Schools in Colorado, talks with an interviewer about the example of Mrs. Katie Christie's fifth-grade class: "I'm inspired by literally hundreds of class-rooms in our district and how they're using technology to help their students learn. Mrs. Christie's 5th grade class at Runyon Elementary School, for example, is using Apps in a particularly impressive way as part of the 'Inspired Writing' initiative. The curriculum revolves around a Google Site that houses learning objectives, resources and videos, assignments, student and teacher work. Mrs. Christie posts assignments daily on a Google Calendar, which is embedded into the class's Google Site and can even be added to a student or parent's personal Google account. Google Docs lets students do different kinds of creative homework, including using Google Drawings to creating flowcharts for a book report and relying on Presentations to collectively create and speak to a deck about astronomy." [1, 2]

Mike Hathorn, a teacher at Hartford High School in Vermont, explains that with Google Docs, the students in the Digital History class are not only more engaged in the class, but are also interacting and collaborating more with each other, their teachers, and the community. In one example, Hathorn asked students researching the Olympics to debate on the topic of whether or not gold medals should be revoked in certain cases. Half the class collaborated on an essay arguing that the medals should be taken away, and the other half argued against it. Hathorn shared his student's final essays with one of the English teachers, who said they were some of the best essays he had ever seen. Senior Patrick Roberts says, "Having nine people work on the same thing at the same time was a totally unique experience. It has transformed the way we learn."[3]

Wendy Gorton, an educator in Portland, Oregon, who has worked in schools around the world, used a publicly shared Google Doc to gather a list of schools that wanted to partner with schools in a different country for World Read Aloud Day. With the live Document, Wendy was able to gather interest, and with Calendar she was able to match people up with ease.

Andi Kornowski, a teacher at Kettle Moraine High School in Wisconsin, finds a way of connecting with her students to build meaningful relationships with them using Google Forms. Some people think that technology makes things more impersonal, but Ms. Kornowski shows how Google Forms has helped her grow closer to all her many students.[4]

Lucie deLaBruere, a teacher in St. Albans, Vermont, writes: "One of the first times that these tools helped provide a game-changing learning experience was when we conducted the 'City Lights' project a few years ago. Our 7th and 8th graders used GPS devices, Google Apps for Education, Google Maps, and Google Earth to map locations of every streetlight in the city, then researched the link between crime and the lack of lights. The students then used Google Docs and Slides to gather their research and present it to the St. Albans City Council. They were able to experience civic engagement first-hand, and see the role their recommendations played in the design of the city."

Kevin Brookhauser, who teaches Humanities and Digital Citizenship in California, uses Docs to create an open climate in his classroom. He says, "The number one recommendation I have for teachers who assign projects using Docs and Drive is to turn the hand-in process upside-down. Rather than having students turn in their work at the end of the assignment cycle, have them turn it in at the beginning. The first step in any class project is to have students create their document, presentation, or spreadsheet, and have them share it with you as the teacher immediately. This allows teachers to monitor and support students through the entire process."

Gmail

Gmail gives you a custom e-mail @your_school.edu address and tools to get things done from anywhere. You can access Gmail from any computer, phone, or tablet, and it works online and offline. Gmail is free and without ads for schools.

You can search your inbox and stay organized with labels and filters. Gmail is mobile, so students and faculty can be productive from anywhere. Students and teachers can see who is online and connect instantly with Hangouts text, voice, and video calls. The administrator can limit access to chat or e-mailing outside of the domain.

How Teachers Use Gmail

Send, receive and search your mail: Gmail has many of the standard features of the most popular e-mail applications and services around today. In addition to the essentials of writing, sharing, and receiving e-mails, learn more about Gmail's latest additions to save you time teaching and managing your class and curriculum.

Create filters and labels: Gmail doesn't use folders. Instead, to help you organize your mail more effectively, Gmail uses "labels." Basically, labels do all the work folders do and give you an extra bonus: You can add more than one to a message. There is no limit to how many labels you can apply to an e-mail. And, because Gmail aggregates all related e-mail messages into "conversations," when you label one message in the conversation, you automatically apply the label to all the messages in the conversation.

Filters are an automatic organization system that let you tell Gmail how to handle your e-mail based on the sender, the recipient, or the subject or message content. Filters analyze e-mails as they receive them and perform certain actions on the messages such as labeling, archiving, deleting, starring, or forwarding. Filters even keep messages you want out of spam. Once you set up a filter, Gmail does this all automatically based on a combination of keywords, sender, recipient, and more.

You can decide to label e-mails from distribution lists, label e-mails from certain individuals, and star e-mails with attachments. Please note: You can create an unlimited number of filters, but only twenty filters can forward to other addresses. You can maximize your filtered forwarding by combining filters that send to the same address.

Use Tasks to manage your To-Do list: Tasks is the part of Gmail designed to help you keep track of the things you need to do, without needing to leave your inbox. You can create lists of items, set due dates, add details or notes, and even add e-mail messages from your Gmail account directly to Tasks. As with a written to do list, you can check items off your list (with great satisfaction). Even better, you can view a history of your completed tasks and the date you crossed them off.

Oftentimes, you will receive an e-mail that adds a new task to your to-do list. With the integration of Gmail, you can actually add a related e-mail directly to your task list and have the ability to click and recall the e-mail referenced.

Manage contact information for colleagues, parents, and students: Like an online address book, the Contact Manager in Gmail gives you easy access to the people you want to reach. All your e-mail contacts are stored here—just click Contacts from the mail menu along the left side of any Gmail page to access and edit your contacts' information.

Contacts make it easy to compose e-mail because Gmail will auto-complete for e-mail addresses in your Contact Manager. You can also store more information than just a name and e-mail address. For example, you can include title, phone numbers, addresses, instant-message accounts, websites, notes, and even birthdays. You can add custom fields like "Parents' Names" or "Graduation Year."

Use text, voice, and video chat anytime, anywhere: Google Chat lets you send and receive text, voice, and video messages to and from teachers, students, and other people at your school or district, right in your inbox. Your chats also behave like e-mail. Gmail can save your chats so you can search them later, you can reply to an e-mail with a chat (if the person is available) and have Gmail save the conversation as well.

Sometimes explaining yourself in person is quicker than typing out an idea and waiting for a response. So, you can now use voice and video capabilities or Google Hangouts in your Gmail chat. From within Gmail, have an actual conversation with someone or even chat face-to-face over video.

This can be great in the classroom for one-on-one conferences with colleagues or parents (provided that the parents have a regular Gmail account with video chat enabled). You can also save on mobile-phone minutes and save time looking for phone numbers.

Create groups to differentiate between different classes and work groups: It's easy to create a group for your school or district. Use a group as a mailing list to send e-mail messages to your class or meeting invitations to all teachers at once, using the group's single e-mail address. Or, use a group to quickly share Google documents, sites, videos, or calendars with multiple colleagues or with parents using a single address.

With user-managed groups, you can allow teachers and students to set up their own groups, without the need to have the domain administrator set up and manage the group.

Use Google Translate within Gmail to foster global pen pals: Did you ever dream about a future when your students could easily overcome language barriers and develop global pen pals? Well, that day is a lot closer. Back when Google launched automatic message translation in Gmail Labs, lots of users and educators were curious to see how people would use it. Some people just wanted to set up Gmail to translate everything into their native language, thus saving countless explanatory phone calls. But others started using it to help them learn other languages.

Because message translation was one of the most popular Labs, Google decided it was time to graduate and move it into the real world. Now, parents, teachers, and students worldwide can use Gmail and simply click Translate in the header at the top of the message.

Real-Life Examples of How Gmail Is Used in Schools

Savings: Henry Thiele, Assistant Superintendent for Technology & Learning at Maine Township High School District 207 in Illinois, says that with the switch to Google Apps for Education, "We've saved more than $784,000 over six years."[5]

Security: Ellen Puffe, Associate Editor and Communications & Advancement Specialist at the Office of Information Technology, reports on the University of Minnesota's switch to Google Apps. "The features and functionality of Google Apps for Education are far superior to the services previously offered by the University of Minnesota. Additionally, Google's architecture, data center infrastructure, and security policies are unparalleled in the industry." [6]

Google Sites

Google Sites allows you to create customized websites and webpages without using HTML or other complex coding languages. It works in a web browser on all computers, so teachers, students, and parents don't need to buy or download software.

Students and teachers can build class and project websites without writing a single line of code. It's as easy as writing a document. And, to save even more time, you can provide your students with hundreds of pre-built templates. Administrators can manage site-sharing permissions across the school, and authors can share and revoke file access at any time.

How Teachers Use Google Sites

Create and update your own personal, class, or school site: Google Sites allows you to display a variety of information in one place, including videos, curriculum, calendars, student activities, attachments, and text. It also allows you to share it for viewing or editing with a project team, an entire school, or a large district. You always control who has access to your site.

Here's what you can do with Google Sites:
Customize your site
Create sub-pages to keep your content organized
Choose page types: webpage, announcements, or file cabinet
Have a central location for your web content and offline files
Keep your site as private or public as you want
Search across your site's content with Google Search

Customize your site layout: There are several ways to simply change your site layout, page order, navigation, fonts, etc. Whether you use Sites as a one-stop location for class schedules or links to valuable content, you'll have plenty of ways to customize.

Embed YouTube videos, calendars, and forms for very cool instruction: In addition to adding gadgets, there are basic needs such as inserting calendars. Use other Google Apps, such as Forms, to build highly engaging instruction. You also can include instructional videos from YouTube to create more robust lesson plans or enhance any course subject.

Real-Life Examples of How Google Sites Is Used in Schools

Clemson University in South Carolina requires all students to create a Google Site. You can read the overview and see examples at www.clemson.edu.

Mike Hathorn of Hartford High School has his students research a topic of their choice—from Hurricane Irene to wars to infomercials—then create a Google Site based on what they have learned from reading, conducting interviews, and gathering relevant information from various resources. Once the websites are completed, they are all made public through Hathorn's Creating a Digital History Site, so students learn how to work to obtain the appropriate permissions, and to ensure accuracy and authenticity. As a testament to the thoroughness and legitimacy of the content, the sites created about Hurricane Irene were used as a resource by the local media and the Hartford community on the first anniversary of the hurricane in 2012.[7]

Kern Kelly, a Google Certified Teacher at Nokomis Regional High School in central Maine, reports that in his district they decided to buy all high-schoolers a domain so that they can take their eportfolio with them when they graduate, carrying with them their digital footprint.

Google Calendar

Google Calendar—which is free for schools—helps you keep track of life's important events, all in one place. Calendars can be shared school-wide or with select colleagues. Scheduling has never been easier, since you can overlay multiple calendars to find a time that works for everyone. You can schedule school events, send out invitations, and let Google Calendar handle the RSVPs for you. Students can easily find time to meet up for school projects by utilizing shared calendars.

Calendar is integrated with other Google Apps, like Gmail, Hangouts, and Drive. Reply to invites right from your inbox without visiting Calendar. Include a Hangout link in calendar events, and join the Hangout from the web or your phone. Attach a Drive file to an event so everyone has the agenda, or knows what files to review.

How Educators Use Calendar

Use Calendar to increase teacher productivity and efficiency: Google Calendar is an outstanding tool in your role as an educator or school administrator. It lets you add student assignments, copy assignments, attach class or project files, and create work folders.

While your Google Apps school account automatically creates a primary calendar for you, it can be useful to have several additional calendars to help organize the different parts of your life. The primary calendar that comes with your Google Apps account will be associated with the name and e-mail address of your account. However, you can create as many secondary calendars as you like. For example, you might want to have a school/work calendar that has all the events and appointments related to school (staff meetings, school events, conferences). In addition, you may want to have a separate personal calendar for keeping track of events and appointments outside of work (a doctor appointment, dinner with a friend, exercise class).

These different calendars not only allow you to see different information on your calendars (you can choose one color for school and a different color for personal), but also let you set different privacy settings for different calendars. This allows everyone at your school to see your school/work calendar, while not allowing anyone to have access to your personal calendar.

Share Google Calendar with colleagues and students: Besides creating a personal calendar to help organize your own activities and priorities, it can be useful to create calendars to share information across groups of people. Here are some examples of group calendars that could be used at your school:

- Class calendar for events such as activities, class meeting times, testing schedules, and lesson objectives
- Homework calendar with detailed descriptions of homework assignments, links to relevant materials, and due dates
- Schoolwide academic schedule, with in-service days, holidays and other scheduling anomalies
- Group-project deadlines and milestones for a group or team to track workload
- School sporting-event schedules that can be shared with the entire school

Use Google Calendar for your school schedule: A calendar can be created with Google Calendar to mirror the information usually printed in a school academic calendar. This could include events such as:

- First/last days of classes
- School vacations
- Finals/mid-term weeks
- Teacher in-service days

Use Google Calendar for class projects: Sometimes it can be helpful to separate long-term project assignments from the general class schedule. For example, if there is an end-of-year research paper and presentation, it might be helpful for your students to have a separate "Research Project" calendar that has all the due dates and milestones for the project. Then the project calendar can be viewed on its own.

It is easy to find the information because it won't get lost in all the events scheduled in the class calendar.

You could also have your students use a special-project calendar when working on a group project. Group members can collaborate and share a calendar together so everyone can have access to the project meeting times, project deadlines and milestones, and other project-related activities (going out to do a survey/market research, conducting an interview, etc).

Create and use lesson plans using Calendar: Planning and organizing your curriculum on a semesterly, monthly, or even daily basis can be a hassle. Yet staying on schedule with your class(es) and related lesson plans can lead to dramatic increases in student learning and your efficiency as a teacher. Many educators are now using Google Calendar to:

- Plan curriculum for each class, subject, and semester
- Organize student activities such as reading assignments and group or team reviews and projects
- Guide new or temporary educators
- Provide access to administrators, peers, and parents so everyone can see how the children's tasks are being planned.

A Real-Life Example of How Calendar Is Used in Schools

Google+ Hangouts

Hangouts bring conversations to life with photos, emoji, and even group video calls. Connect with friends across computers, Androids, and Apple devices. Hangouts are simple to use. Educators can join simply by setting up a Google+ page and signing up for the Hangout feature, which is free.

Real-Life Examples of How Google+ Hangouts Are Used in Schools

Ms. Nunez, a teacher in Arizona, had to miss class to have surgery. With Google+ Hangouts she was still able to join her class every day during her recovery, helping her students prepare for their end-of-term exams and showing how much she cared.[8]

Tools like Google+ Hangouts help teachers deliver learning beyond the classroom walls. For example, Vida Fernandez, a Special Education ninth-grade English teacher in Passaic, New Jersey., taught a lesson on Frankenstein using Hangouts to connect with another class in Germany. The two classes represented the prosecution and defense in a "trial" of Dr. Frankenstein, and both developed a sophisticated understanding of the narrative and characters of the book.

Kern Kelley at Nokomis Regional High has a student club called Tech Sherpas. They felt they could do the most good by providing live technical support to whoever wants it. So, please ask us a question and we'll do our best to answer it on the spot, or do the research and provide the answer the following week.[9]

Here are some ideas for using Hangouts in the classroom. Some of them come from Andrew Marcinek, teacher of digital and information literacy in Groton, Massachusetts.

> **Broadcast and archive live sessions.** Students can develop a presentation and broadcast it live to a conference that they would have liked to attend but could not afford to travel to. They can then archive the presentation and share it with others afterward.

> **Share screens and create collaborative demonstrations.** Students can share a YouTube video on Hangouts and then archive the interaction on a dedicated YouTube account.

> **Create live shows and talks for broadcast.** Students create scripts, configure sets, and then film their show live via a Hangout.

> **Create a two-way conversation in digital format.** Hangouts is a good alternative to Skype or Facetime.

> **Develop online portfolios.** Hangouts allow users to save and archive their online interactions; they thus serve as a good online portfolio tool.

Use the application for professional development. Professional-development sessions are made easier and more accessible.

● MOONSHOT TOOLS

Teachers can find more ideas at
https://sites.google.com/site/gpluseduhangouts/ideas

Classroom

Classroom, which was released in August 2014, is the latest addition to the Google Apps for Education suite. This tool is designed to help teachers efficiently create, organize, and distribute assignments across Google Docs, Drive, and Gmail. Classroom automatically creates folders in Google Drive for each student and assignment and allows teachers to quickly monitor student progress. Classroom also allows teachers to make announcements, provide feedback, and answer questions from students in real time, and it lets students organize their work, complete and turn it in, and communicate directly with their teachers and peers.

Here are some of the benefits of Classroom:

> **Easy to set up.** Teachers can add students directly or share a code with their class, allowing students to join individually. It takes just minutes to set up.

> **Saves time.** The simple, paperless workflow allows teachers to create, review, and grade assignments quickly, all in one place.

> **Improves organization.** Students can see all of their assignments on an assignments page, and all class materials are automatically filed into folders in Google Drive.

Enhances communication. Classroom allows teachers to send announcements and start class discussions instantly. Since students can post to the stream, they can help out their classmates.

Affordable and secure. Like all Google Apps for Education, Classroom is free for schools, contains no ads, and does not use data or content from students or teachers for advertising.

Within Classroom, teachers can create an assignment, use it in multiple classes, and choose how students will complete the assignment (for example, whether each student receives an individual copy or all students work in the same copy of the assignment). The teacher can track who has completed the assignment and who hasn't, and provide feedback to individual students. Here's an example of the assignment flow with a Google Doc between a teacher and a student:

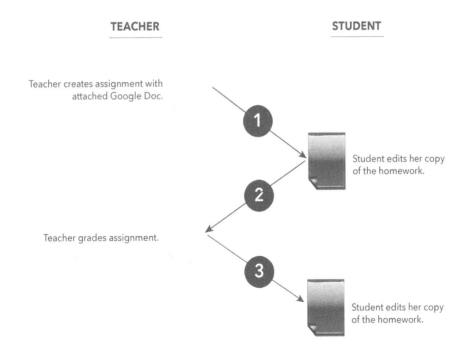

TEACHER	STUDENT

Teacher creates assignment with attached Google Doc.

1

Student edits her copy of the homework.

2

Teacher grades assignment.

3

Student edits her copy of the homework.

1. Teacher selects the option to create a copy of the Google Doc for each student and sends assignment to class.

2. When the student turns in his or her assignment, he or she loses edit access to the Google Doc but remains a viewer.

3. When the teacher grades the assignment, he or she has edit access to the Google Doc. When the student receives the graded assignment back, he or she becomes the editor and the teacher has view/comment access.

Both the teacher and the students can see a list of pending and completed class assignments. The teacher can see all the grades for the assignment, and the students can see their own grades for completed assignments.

Add a Class

As a teacher, one of the first things you will do is create a class in Classroom for each of the classes you teach. In a class, you can add students, create assignments, post announcements, return reviewed assignments, and send messages to students.

Classes are interactive for students, too. They can comment on announcements that you make, share a post with classmates, or return an assignment.

To add a class:

1. Sign in to Classroom at classroom.google.com.
2. Click the + icon in the top right corner of the page.
3. Enter the class name in the first text box.
4. Enter a short description in the second text box, such as section, grade level, or class time.
5. Click the *Create* button.

Once you've created your class, you can choose which image is displayed for the class in the stream. To change the image from the default:

1. Place your mouse over the top banner image in the class stream.
2. Click *Change Photo* in the bottom right corner of the image.
3. From the gallery, select the image you want to use for your class.
4. Click the *Pick Course Image* button to add it to your class stream.

Note: At this time, only the teacher of a class can change the image in the class stream.

You can also choose to display a profile photo next to your name both in the class stream and on the class card on the home screen. Classroom uses your Gmail picture as your Classroom profile photo. See Selecting your Gmail picture for instructions on adding a photo.

From the home screen, you can rename or delete a class using the menu icon (three dots arranged vertically) in the upper-right corner of the class card:

To rename a class, click the menu icon and select *Rename.*

To delete a class, click the menu icon and select *Delete.*
Warning: You will no longer have access to any posts or comments that have been added to this class, although documents will still be accessible through Google Drive. There is no way to undo this action.

Add Students to a Class

A teacher can add students to a class directly or give students a code to add themselves. To add students directly:

1. Sign in to Classroom at classroom.google.com.
2. Click the class where you want to add the student.
3. At the top of the page, click *Students.*
4. Click the *Add students* button to add students. Click the *My contacts* drop-down list to see your contact list and domain directory.
5. Select the students you want to add.
6. If you can't find a student you're looking for, enter the student's name or e-mail address in the search box.
7. Click the *Add students* button.

To add students by giving them the class code:

1. Sign in to Classroom at classroom.google.com.
2. Go to the class page. The class code is on the left of the stream.
3. Send an e-mail to students with the class code or write it on the board in your classroom.
4. Tell students to go to classroom.google.com and enter the class code.

You have the option of resetting the code or disabling it by clicking the code itself to access the drop-down menu.

Create an Assignment

You can create an assignment in your class stream, attach materials to it, assign it to one or more classes, and grade and return it to students.
To create an assignment:

1. Sign in to Classroom at classroom.google.com.
2. Select a class.
3. Click *Assignment* at the top of the stream.
4. Enter the title of the assignment.
5. Enter a description of the assignment or any additional instructions, if needed.

6. Click the date under the description to set the date for students to turn in the assignment. By default, assignments are due the next day.
7. If you want the assignment turned in before midnight on the due date, click *Add time*, click into the time, and enter a time or select one from the drop-down list.
8. To attach a Google Drive item, a YouTube video, a link, or a file from your computer to the assignment, click the appropriate icon.
9. Locate and select the relevant item. When you add the item, it appears in the assignment form.
10. If you attach a Google Drive item, you'll have a few options on how the student will interact with the item:
    Click *Students can view file* if you want all students to read, but not change, the same item.
    Click *Students can edit file* if you want all students to make changes in the same item.
    Click *Make a copy for each student* to provide a unique copy for each student.
11. If you want to give the assignment to another class, click the name of the class at the bottom of the window. You'll see a list of all your classes. Select which ones should receive this assignment.
12. Click *Assign* to send the assignment to students.

Post an Announcement

You can post an announcement in your class stream at any time.
1. Sign in to Classroom at classroom.google.com.
2. Select the class to open the stream.
3. Click *Announcement* or just click in the text box at the top of the class stream.
4. Enter your announcement.
5. You can attach a file from your computer, a Google Drive item, a YouTube video, or a hyperlink to the announcement using the icons next to the *Post* button.
6. Click *Post* when you're done.

Anyone in the class can add a comment by clicking in the *Add a comment* box and entering text. All comments are visible under the announcement in the stream. As the teacher of the class, you can delete any inappropriate comments or posts from students.

To edit an announcement, click the menu icon (three dots arranged vertically) in the top right corner of the announcement and select *Edit message.*

To delete an announcement, click the menu icon (three dots arranged vertically) in the top right corner of the announcement and select *Delete message.*

E-mail a Student

To e-mail a student:

1. Sign in to Classroom at classroom.google.com.
2. Click a class that the student is in.
3. At the top of the class stream, click the *Students* tab.
4. To the right of the student's name, click the envelope icon. If you want to send a message to multiple students, check the box next to each student's name and click the *Send email* button at the top of the page.
5. A new e-mail message box opens. Enter a subject and message and click *Send.*

Note: You can also send a private message to a student when providing feedback on an assignment. For instructions, please see Grade and return an assignment.

Grade and Return an Assignment

To access students' completed assignments:

1. Sign in to Classroom at classroom.google.com.
2. Open the class and click the assignment in the class stream to see the student submissions page.
3. Click next to the name of a student whose assignment you want to review.
4. To view all work turned in by the students for this assignment, click the *folder* button which will open the Google Drive folder where all of the work is stored. Click any attachment they have turned in to review their work.

Remember, you can edit or comment right in any document on Google Drive. Simply make any comments and close the document. Your comments are automatically saved and ready for the student to review when you return the assignment.

To grade and return an assignment to a student:

1. Sign in to Classroom at classroom.google.com.
2. Open the class and click the assignment in the class stream.
3. Find the student and click *No grade* in the same row. The words turn into a box where you enter the grade.
4. The default point value for an assignment is 100. To change this, click the *Points* drop-down list on the right above the list of students and select the point value for the assignment or click the number and enter a new number. Only whole number grades are supported at this time. You cannot enter a letter grade or a decimal point.
5. Enter the grade in the box.
6. Enter grades for any additional students.
   Warning: The grades that you enter on this page will not be saved unless you return the assignments to the students.
7. Check the box next to the student or students whose grades you want to return.

8. If you want to return an assignment without assigning a grade, skip the grading steps above and just check the box next to the student or students.

9. Click the *Return* button.

10. Enter any additional feedback in the box and click *Return Assignment*. After you click *Return Assignment,* the student receives an e-mail message letting him or her hem know that you've returned the grade. Also, the student regains edit access to any Drive items that were part of the assignment.

To change a grade:

1. Sign in to Classroom at classroom.google.com.

2. Open the class and click the assignment in the class stream.

3. Click next to the name of the student whose grade you want to change.

4. Click the pencil icon next to the grade, and enter the new grade in the box.

5. Enter any additional feedback in the box and click *Update.*

6. After you click *Update,* the student receives an e-mail message letting him or her know that you've changed the grade.

To export grades to a csv file, click the *Download* button at the top of the assignment page.

USES OF GOOGLE APPS

BY ESTHER WOJCICKI

$$13$$

Here is the website for Google Apps for Education: www.google.com/a/edu. And this website—www.google.com/edu/training—will help you learn how to use these tools effectively.

1. Collaborate on lesson plans.
2. Keep a running record of meeting notes.
3. Create a shared lesson-plan repository. Create a folder for grade-level shared resources and store lesson plans in a folder shared by the school.
4. Improve the writing process.
- Have students work collaboratively from anywhere.
- Give students ongoing and simultaneous feedback.
- Use the revision history to hold students accountable for their work.
5. Set up a peer-review system. Give students the responsibility for providing feedback on other students' work. Students can easily tag one another's comments.

6. Publish students' work. Multiple sharing settings allow you to publish students' work by sharing it within your class, within the school, or within the district, or by making it public on the web.

7. Translate letters home. Use Google Translate to translate letters, permission slips, and newsletters for non-English-speaking parents and guardians.

8. Track student homework. Use Sheets to track student homework and share the results with parents. If you are using one spreadsheet, give each student a code name or number to protect his or her privacy.

9. Coordinate signups using spreadsheets. Have parents sign up for parent-teacher conferences or other meetings using a spreadsheet. Use revision history to ensure that everyone is using the sheet to schedule fairly.

10. Research while writing a document.

- Highlight the text you want to research.

- Navigate to Tools and click Research.

- Check out the bar at the right side for search results.

11. Create amazing presentations using Slides.

12. Use Google Forms to:

- Give your students a pre-assessment at the beginning of class. Modify your instruction based on the results. Then givestudents an "exit ticket" at the end of class to see what they learned.

- Survey your students at the beginning of the school year to find out their interests. Change the template to make it more exciting

- Have your students submit reading records online. Encourage them to read by having them complete their reading records electronically.

- Collect observational feedback from teachers and students using Forms on a tablet or smartphone. The data will automatically populate to a spreadsheet.

- Keep track of discipline referrals. Recognize discipline patterns and share with key stakeholders.

- Automatically grade forms with Flubaroo (www.flubaroo.com), an Apps Add-On that allows you to automatically grade assignments ((right?)) that have been submitted using a Google form.

13. Use Google Calendar to:

- Manage your schedule effectively. Look at your work schedule, personal calendar, and any other relevant calendars in one view. Easily change events listed.
- Share calendars with colleagues and students.
- Schedule the use of shared resources like rooms and equipment.
- Create a backwards map of the standards you need to teach by the end of the week/semester/year to ensure that you have covered them all.
- Use appointment slots to schedule parent-teacher conferences or guidance-counselor sessions.
- Teach your students time management by scheduling due dates and review dates.

14. Use Gmail to:

- Communicate in different language (using Translate).
- Give students access to pen pals in another state, province, or country. With Google Translate it doesn't matter if they don't speak the same language.

15. Use Google Groups to:

- Create groups for your classes or staff. Groups encourage discussion among peers and can be used to share resources and materials.
- Share docs and calendars with specific groups. Create classroom placement groups to better distribute differentiated materials and resources.
- Create parent support groups so that they can easily communicate with one another and share news and updates.

16. Use Google Talk to:

- Invite an expert into your class to do a guest lecture through Video Chat. Invite your students to ask a grandparent who lives in another state to read to the class during story time.

- Hold office hours to give help with homework. Let students know that you'll be available to help online at certain times. Video-conference with students who are absent.

17. Use Google Sites to:

- Create a site for your class. Embed a class calendar, videos, and presentations.

- Create and manage student e-portfolios. Showcase student work and pass it on from year to year.

- Submit student projects. Have students do projects or create reports using sites. You can also have them do their submissions for the Global Google Science Fair.

- Build a Curriculum Portal.

18. Use Google Blogger to:

- Run your classroom. Students can access their "Do Now" independent practice, and obtain exit slips through blog entry.

- Use Moderator to extend classroom discussions. Have students reflect on their daily learning through Google Moderator. Students can read one another's reflections and vote on the responses they like the best.

NETWORKS THAT SUPPORT TEACHERS

BY ESTHER WOJCICKI

14

Keeping Up with Edtech

Educational technology is changing on a daily basis, which is great for experimenting with your moonshots in the classroom. As we have been discussing throughout this book, there are many resources online to help you keep up with the latest and greatest innovations in education technology. In this chapter, we will review some of the ones we have found most helpful. Even more important, we will also discuss ways you can connect with like-minded individuals, both online and offline. We have found that the edtech community is supportive, collaborative, and creative. Growing your own Personal Learning Network, or PLN, can be a great way to help you reach your fullest potential as a teacher. Here are some ways you can build and grow your PLN:

EDSURGE

EdSurge[1] is the leading site for people interested in education technology. Its weekly e-mail newsletters are full of useful news and product recommendations for educators, entrepreneurs, and investors. Its signature *EdSurge Innovate* newsletter is published every Wednesday and reports on the latest product launches, investment news, and general happenings in the education world. *EdSurge Instruct* is a newsletter specifically aimed at K–12 teachers; it comes out every Thursday. On EdSurge.com, news is updated daily, and the site includes an extensive index of education-technology tools. Products are reviewed by educators and categorized by subject or skill area, whether they are used primarily by teachers or administrators, and various other criteria. The EdSurge news team is also active on social media; they share the latest headlines several times a day on Facebook and Twitter. Each post or article is also open to reader comments, which can lead to interesting discussions. EdSurge is open to reader contributions, and it often posts opinion pieces from educators and entrepreneurs.

Beyond its online community, EdSurge is also active offline. Events are listed on its site and in its newsletters, and the company hosts Tech for Schools Summits[2] around the country throughout the year. (See the Events and Conferences section below for more information.) These summits are a great way to network in person with people you might know through their Twitter handles or blogs, and each conference features product demos, student and teacher panels, and the opportunity to interact directly with people creating and using products for the classroom.

EDUDEMIC

If you are a fan of "listicles" like those on Buzzfeed, you might find Edudemic[3] interesting and fun to read. The site connects education and technology through articles like "The 15 Best iPad Apps for the

World Language Classroom[4]" and "30 Education Innovators Worth Following on Twitter."[5] You can also find teachers' guides on how to incorporate technology into the classroom, reviews of edtech products, opinion pieces, and resources for students and teachers. Edudemic's writers are also active on social media, and you can often find their articles tweeted and shared across networks of tech-savvy teachers.

GEORGE LUCAS EDUCATIONAL FOUNDATION

The George Lucas Educational Foundation[6], which runs the website Edutopia is dedicated to improving K–12 education through innovation and evidence-informed teaching strategies. Edutopia.org and its related social-media channels have as their mission inspiring, informing, and accelerating positive change in schools and districts. Edutopia.org provides a rich resource of articles, videos, and classroom guides to support the foundation's vision of a "new world of learning, a place where students and parents, teachers and administrators, policy makers and the people they serve are all empowered to change education for the better; a place where schools provide rigorous project-based learning, social-emotional learning, and access to new technology; a place where innovation is the rule, not the exception; a place where students become lifelong learners and develop 21st-century skills, especially three fundamental skills:

- how to find information;
- how to assess the quality of information;
- how to creatively and effectively use information to accomplish a goal."

GETTING SMART

Getting Smart[7] is a community focused on innovations in learning. Its website, GettingSmart.com, covers formal and informal topics in K–12, higher ed, and lifelong learning. These include developments in technology, entrepreneurship, research, and policy. Articles, videos, and infographics cover topics like the Common Core State Standards Initiative, gamification, and personalized learning, and how to choose digital tools for your classroom. The Getting Smart team is also active on social media.

MindShift[8] a blog launched by NPR and Northern California's KQED, explores innovations in education, with an eye on the future of learning. It covers trends in culture and technology, research, and policy. Some of its featured topics include games and leaning, children and media, and teaching strategies.

Many educators, entrepreneurs, and thought leaders also have their own personal blogs where they share anecdotes and their opinions on current issues in education. Chances are that these individuals are also active in networks on Facebook, Google+, and Twitter. Reading about others' experiences might spark some fresh ideas of your own to use in the classroom. Or perhaps you already have your own blog, or might become inspired to start one! Meanwhile, leaving comments on another teacher's blog or a site like EdSurge can be a great way to connect with others and get involved in the conversation. Don't be shy! Reaching out can also be a way to step outside your comfort zone and develop some great new ideas and personal connections as well.

Social Networks

TWITTER

As we've already mentioned, Twitter[9] can be a great place to keep up to date with the latest trends and innovations in education technology and teaching methods. If you're new to Twitter, you can start by following colleagues, friends, and thought leaders. But while becoming a consumer of information on Twitter is good, we have found that becoming an active participant in the conversation can be a true learning experience. So when you see something interesting—or, for that matter, something controversial—tweet your thoughts about it. Another way to get involved in education conversations on Twitter is to follow hashtags. There are many hashtags that are used across the network, and new ones pop up every day. The following are common and can be used in conjunction with others: #edchat, #edtechchat, #blendedlearning, #commoncore, #elemchat, #kinderchat, #k12. Explore your own interests and find what might be most useful to you. Also, keep an eye out for Twitter chats. Interesting conversations can happen in 140-character bytes! Some are regularly scheduled (e.g., weekly). You might even find yourself hosting a Twitter chat some day in the not-too-distant future!

GOOGLE+

If you are an active user of Google Apps or YouTube, Google+[10] might be a great social network for you. You can create circles for colleagues, students, and friends, and selectively share content with each of them, or share some content with all of them. Hangouts, Google+'s video-chat feature, can be used to collaborate when project teams cannot be in the same place. There are also many opportunities for you and your students to interact directly with interesting speakers featured on Hangouts on Air[11], a live streaming conversation. You can also broadcast your own Hangout on Air and take questions from around the world. Google+ is available on both mobile devices and desktop.

WIKISPACES

Wikispaces[12] Classroom is a free web-hosting space that boasts a user base of over 10 million teachers and students. It allows teachers to create a private social-classroom workspace where students can communicate and work on writing projects with other members of their team. In addition, the service has rich assessment tools to measure student contributions and engagement in real time. With familiar features like a social news feed, the service is easy to use and engage with. Wikispaces is commonly used for classroom management, project-based learning, safe social networking, professional and curriculum development, and online and remote learning. Wikispaces is accessible on any web-enabled device, and it has also developed its own iPad app.

BETTERLESSON

BetterLesson[13] is a network of Master Teachers that currently hosts over 1.3 million lesson plans, classroom materials, and other instructional resources, was founded by a group of teachers from Atlanta and Boston public schools to connect educators and help them create, organize, and share their curricula. The network focuses on aggregating and scaling innovative content and teaching practices from high-performing teachers across the country. BetterLesson operates on core principles that include universal access to high-quality instructional content, recognition for work, and collaboration. Its latest project, CC.BetterLesson, includes over three thousand Common Core–aligned lessons created by the 130 Master Teachers in the network. You can browse lesson plans by Common Core Standard, grade level, or subject.

Other Online and Offline Communities

GOOGLE TEACHER ACADEMY

Google Teacher Academy[14] (GTA) is a free professional-development program designed to help primary- and secondary-school educators from around the globe get the most from innovative technologies. It is designed to create a strong professional community of educators who support one another over the course of a year. Each GTA is an intensive, two-day event during which participants get hands-on experience with Google tools, learn about innovative instructional strategies, receive resources to share with colleagues, and immerse themselves in a supportive community of educators who are making an impact. GTAs are held around the world; those who would like to attend are invited to submit an online application. The application includes short-answer questions and a video, and participants—approximately fifty for each event—are selected on the basis of their professional experience, passion for teaching and learning, and successful implementation of technology in school settings. Educators who actively provide mentorship or training for other teachers are especially encouraged to apply. Interested in GTA? Consider becoming a Google Educator[15] before applying in order to better showcase your Google knowledge and experience. Educators who attend a GTA become Google Certified Teachers (GCTs). They model high expectations, lifelong learning, collaboration, equity, and innovation, and they act as ambassadors for change.

GRAPHITE

Graphite[16] is a free service from Common Sense Media[17], a non-profit organization whose mission is to improve the lives of kids and families by providing trustworthy information and education about media and technology. Graphite is a tool that allows educators to discover apps, games, and websites for the classroom. These are reviewed by experts and educators to determine criteria like Common Core State Standards alignment. Graphite's filters are easy to use in order to find products by standard and grade level. Reviews are also crowdsourced from the community in Graphite's Field Notes. Curious about how other teachers use a tool in their classroom? Check out the Field Notes. Once you are ready to join and participate, simply create a free profile and add Field Notes to help other teachers.

IMAGINE K12

Imagine K12[18] was founded by Silicon Valley entrepreneurs who believe that the future lies in preparing our children for twenty-first-century success. They believe that one way to make this happen is through the application of technology to K–12 education. Imagine K12 funds early-stage edtech startups and mentors their staff through an intensive three-month program. It also connects with passionate educators who provide feedback on early prototypes of products. The accelerator hosts a Teacher in Residence program, where experienced educators hold weekly office hours for people from startups and provide valuable insights on how products can be used in classroom settings.

If you are looking for continuing-education opportunities to supplement your own learning, there are many excellent Massive Open Online Courses (MOOCs) available for free to be completed on your own schedule. For example, "Blended Learning: Personalizing Education for Students"[19] was offered on Coursera in Fall 2013. And if you are inclined to create your own MOOC to inspire others, you can do so on Google Course Creator.[20]

Events and Conferences

In our experience, one of the best complements to integrating online learning into your classroom is going to an in-person event. There is nothing like interacting with people face to face, especially if you have been corresponding with them online for some time. Here are some great conferences and events that integrate the online and offline blended-learning experiences. To get an up-to-date list of online and offline education conferences go to edsurge.com/e.

DIGITAL MEDIA AND LEARNING RESEARCH HUB[21]

The Digital Media and Learning Research Hub[21] produces a collection of free and open resources on the emergence of digital technology and its effects on learning. Its annual conference in March aims to reach across boundaries between different disciplines in order to "reimagine the where, when, and how of educational practice."

EDMODOCON

Edmodo's online conference EdmodoCon[22] offers an international day of professional development. In 2012, EdmodoCon served 11,000 registrants from 117 countries. Sessions included talks on using iPads in the classroom, teaching digital citizenship, and using game-based learning. Videos from past conferences can be viewed on the EdmodoCon website.

EDUCATION INNOVATION SUMMIT

The Education Innovation Summit,[23] a collaboration between GSV Advisors and Arizona State University, is a yearly event that brings together entrepreneurs, investors, philanthropists, politicians, educators, and other advocates of education innovation. Michael Horn of the Clayton Christensen Institute has called this conference "the can't-miss education innovation event."

GOOGLE APPS FOR EDUCATION SUMMITS

EdTechTeam, a global network of educators, hosts Google Apps for Education Summits[24] all over the world. These events are intensive two-day conferences that focus on deploying, integrating, and using Google Apps for Education and other Google tools to promote learning for K–12 and higher-ed students. Each event features hands-on demos and dynamic keynote speakers. For resources from previous GAfE Summits, click on an event on the Summit homepage, and then click on Resources. There you will find an extensive list of links to tools and resources to integrate into your classroom.

IMAGINE K12 EDUCATOR DAY

Imagine K12 Educator Day[25] is an annual event for educators featuring new companies that are building innovative tools for K–12 education. With an audience of classroom teachers, administrators, and school-technology professionals, this demo day provides entrepreneurs with the rare opportunity to speak directly with the end users of their products. Interested? Sign up for an invitation by joining the Imagine K12 Educator Network[26].

ASCD ANNUAL CONFERENCE AND EXHIBIT SHOW

The Association for Supervision and Curriculum Development holds an annual conference and exhibit show that is considered one of education's premiere events. Its theme is "Challenging Convention: Leading Disruptive Innovations," and consists of over 350 sessions. Over 300 companies exhibit at ASCD, with displays of the latest education products and services for teachers, principals, superintendents, district and state administrators.

CUE

CUE (originally Computer User Educators) is a nonprofit organization that supports a community of educators and learners through meetings, grants, events, and mini-conferences. Its annual CUE conference is the largest and oldest technology conference in California, and among the largest in the United States. Educators, tech coordinators, and administrators attend to learn about the latest developments in student achievement supported by technology. In addition to their Annual and Fall conferences, CUE also partners with other organizations including Google Teacher Academy and CLRN (California Learning Resource Network) to produce professional development events for teachers throughout the year.

DIGITAL LEARNING DAY

The Alliance for Excellent Education holds an annual Digital Learning Day to actively spread innovative practices in K-12 educational technology. Started in 2012, Digital Learning Day encourages teachers to share lesson plans and effective digital tools online. Since its inception, over 30,000 educators have participated and learned about new classroom technologies each year. The fourth annual Digital Learning Day will take place on March 13, 2015.

ISTE

The International Society for Technology in Education (ISTE[27]) hosts a conference each summer to inspire new ideas and collaborations. The conference and expo bring together educators from all fields and grade levels to share discoveries and develop innovative classroom solutions. The four-day-long event[28] includes professional-learning and networking opportunities and demos of new edtech products and services from over five hundred companies.

NSVF SUMMIT

NewSchools Venture Fund[29], a philanthropic non-profit venture fund, aims to transform public education for low-income children through entrepreneurship. Its yearly NSVF Summit[30] is an invitation-only gathering of entrepreneurs, educators, and policymakers who are passionate about this mission. The Summit brings leaders together to share ideas, resources, and connections. Request an invitation on the Summit website.

SXSWEDU

SXSWedu[31] takes place annually, immediately prior to the popular SXSW Interactive[32] conference in Austin, Texas. Sessions and workshops focus on promising practices to improve teaching and learning. Participants include a diverse group of educators, entrepreneurs, administrators, policymakers, and investors. The LAUNCHedu competition features the debut of new products and services in edtech. Other highlights of the conference include an eduFILM festival; the SXSWedu Playground, which features innovative pursuits in the maker movement; STEM education, gaming, and arts; as well as a free Education Expo for students and families.

EDSURGE TECH IN SCHOOLS SUMMITS

EdSurge hosts Tech for Schools Summits across the United States to bridge the gap between educators and entrepreneurs. During these one-day events, educators and entrepreneurs have the opportunity to discuss the technologies and practices that will truly make a difference in learning. With the mission of bringing the community together with "no lectures" and "no spin," EdSurge Summits help support the genuine exchange of ideas and feedback that can lead to actionable insights in both product development and classroom teaching. EdSurge Tech for Schools Summit events are open and free for educators.

STARTUP WEEKEND EDUCATION (SWEDU)
[run by Education Entrepreneurs]

Startup Weekend Education[33] (SWEDU) was founded on the belief that entrepreneurship is the most powerful force for improving education outcomes. SWEDU brings people together during 54-hour events to pitch ideas and collaborate with one another with the goal of launching startups to solve important education problems. On Day 1, individuals can pitch ideas and form teams to begin fleshing out their ideas. Over the next two days, meaningful guidance and feedback is provided from experienced coaches and mentors. The event culminates in a launch event where teams pitch their ideas to esteemed judges. In just two years, SWEDU has expanded to every inhabited continent, and it is continuing to grow.

PART II

AN OVERVIEW OF DIGITAL EDUCATION IN AMERICA

BY LANCE IZUMI

⑮

More and more students across the country are obtaining their education using a new wave of technology tools. This changing reality can be termed the digital education revolution.

Digital learning can be defined in a number of ways. The Freedom Foundation's iLearn Project says: "Digital learning is either coursework or a comprehensive school program that takes place primarily online. Online learning is untethered, meaning students can participate from anywhere the Internet is available."[1]

The Georgia Governor's Office of Student Achievement (GOSA), using language from organizations such as Digital Learning Now and the Florida Virtual School, defines digital learning as "learning facilitated by technology that gives students some element of control over time, place, path and/or pace."[2] The GOSA then defines terms within the digital-learning definition:

> Time: Learning is no longer restricted to the school day or the school year. The Internet and a proliferation of Internet access devices have given students the ability to learn anytime.

> Place: Learning is no longer restricted within the walls of a classroom. The Internet and a proliferation of Internet access devices have given students the ability to learn anywhere and everywhere.

Path: Learning is no longer restricted to the pedagogy used by the teacher. Interactive and adaptive software allows students to learn in their own style, making learning personal and engaging. New learning technologies provide real-time data that gives teachers the information they need to adjust instruction to meet the unique needs of each student.

Pace: Learning is no longer restricted to the pace of an entire classroom of students. Interactive and adaptive software allows students to learn at their own pace, spending more or less time on lessons or subjects to achieve the same level of learning.[3]

The GOSA very accurately observes that digital learning "is more than providing students with a laptop." Rather, digital learning requires a combination of technology, digital content and instruction:

Technology: Technology is the mechanism that delivers content. It facilitates how students receive content. It includes Internet access and hardware, which can be any Internet access device—from a desktop to a laptop to an iPad to a smartphone. Technology is the tool, not the instruction.

Digital Content: Digital content is the high quality academic material which is delivered through technology. It is what students learn. It ranges from new engaging, interactive and adaptive software to classic literature to video lectures to games. It isn't simply a PDF of text or a PowerPoint presentation.

Instruction: Educators are essential to digital learning. Technology may change the role of the teacher but it will never eliminate the need for a teacher. With digital learning, teachers will be able to provide the personalized guidance and assistance to ensure students learn and stay on track—throughout the year and year after year—to graduate from high school. Teachers may be the guide on the side, not the sage on the stage.[4]

Given these definitions, how widespread is K-12 digital learning in America? The U.S. Department of Education's National Center for Education Statistics did a survey of school districts around the country and found that, in 2009-10 school year, 55 percent of the more than 2,000 districts surveyed reported having students enrolled in distance education courses. Distance education is usually defined as instruction and learning that occurs where the student and teacher are not located at the same site and at the same time.

Ninety percent of the districts with distance education enrollments reported having students enrolled in courses delivered over the Internet. Among these districts, 92 percent reported that students accessed Internet-delivered courses at school, 78 percent reported that students accessed these courses at home, and 15 percent reported that students accessed these courses at some other location such as public libraries or community centers.[5]

❝ An increasing number of states are requiring students to have digital-learning knowledge and skills. ❞

In terms of the number of students who are taking advantage of these distance education courses, it is estimated that there were more than 1.8 million enrollments in distance-education courses, most of which use digital learning. Nearly three-quarters of these enrollments were in high schools, 9 percent were in middle or junior high schools, and 4 percent were in elementary schools.[6]

The distance-education enrollment figure does not include students attending full-time online schools, such as state-sponsored virtual schools. In 2011-12, an estimated 275,000 students attended full-time online schools. [7]

An increasing number of states are requiring students to have digital-learning knowledge and skills. Michigan, Alabama, Florida, Idaho and Virginia have enacted digital-learning requirements for students to graduate from high school. Georgia, New Mexico and West Virginia recommend that students acquire digital-learning skills, but do not require it.

One of the goals of the U.S. Department of Education's 2010 National Technology Education Plan (NTEP) is that, "All students and educators will have access to a comprehensive infrastructure for learning when and where they need it."[8] NTEP says that this infrastructure "integrates computer hardware, data and networks, information resources, interoperable software, middleware services and tools, and devices, and it also connects and supports interdisciplinary teams of professionals responsible for its development, maintenance, and management, and its use in transformative approaches to teaching and learning."[9] Yet, much still needs to be done to meet that goal.

Indeed, one of the most highly publicized concerns regarding online learning is the so-called "digital divide," which centers on the ability of all students, regardless of their backgrounds, to access the Internet and online services. While this divide has shrunk in recent years, it still exists.

According to the NTEP, "A crucial element of an infrastructure for learning is a broadband network of adequate performance and reach, including abundant wireless coverage in and out of school buildings."[10] The U.S. Department of Commerce reported that an estimated 68 percent of American households had broadband Internet access in 2010, which was a 4 percent increase over 2009. Also, more than 77 percent of households reported having a computer. Income level, however, had a significant impact on digital connection.[11]

In households with an annual income under $30,000, only 45 percent reported having access to broadband Internet. For households with an annual income between $30,000 and $49,999, 67 percent reported having access. In households with income between $50,000 and $74,999, 79 percent had access. Finally in households with income over $75,000, 87 percent reported access to broadband Internet.[12] For households with young children, the statistics are similar. In households with children aged 0-8-years old, 72 percent have a computer at home. However, only 48 percent of these households with annual income of less than $30,000 had a home computer. In contrast, 91 percent of families with incomes over $75,000 had home computers.[13]

> " While the federal government has issued its periodic National Educational Technology Plans for the past decade and a half, California put out its policy blueprint for technology and education five years before the first Washington plan. "

In California, Internet usage and availability has grown significantly over just the past few years. According to a survey by the Public Policy Institute of California, in 2013, 86 percent of adult Californians reported using the Internet (nationwide, the percentage was a nearly identical 85 percent), up from 70 percent in 2008. Sixty-nine percent in 2013 said that they had broadband Internet access at their home, a considerable increase over the 55 percent in 2008. Despite these increases, the digital divide affects some groups and some areas more than others.[14]

While 81 percent of whites, 75 percent of Asians, and 71 percent of African Americans reported that they had broadband Internet access at home in 2013, just 52 percent of Hispanics said that they had such access. It should be noted, however, that even among Hispanics, the 2013 rate of Internet access was a 14 percent increase over the group's 2008 rate.

Like the rest of the country, income has a large impact on broadband access in Caliornia. Only 53 percent of adult Californians with incomes under $40,000 had broadband Internet access at home, versus 92 percent of those with incomes of $80,000 or more. In the San Francisco Bay Area, 80 percent had broadband Internet access at home, while just 60 percent in the Central Valley had such access.[15]

In 2013, among adult Californians with children under 18 years of age, 68 percent have broadband Internet access at home, a 14 percent increase over the 54 percent in 2008, but a 5 percent decrease since the 73 percent in 2012. Thus, while the large majority of children have access to broadband Internet at home, around three out of 10 do not.[16]

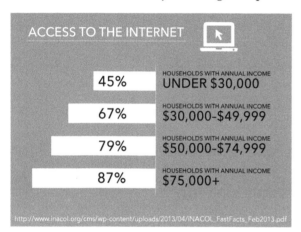

ACCESS TO THE INTERNET

45%	HOUSEHOLDS WITH ANNUAL INCOME UNDER $30,000
67%	HOUSEHOLDS WITH ANNUAL INCOME $30,000-$49,999
79%	HOUSEHOLDS WITH ANNUAL INCOME $50,000-$74,999
87%	HOUSEHOLDS WITH ANNUAL INCOME $75,000+

http://www.inacol.org/cms/wp-content/uploads/2013/04/iNACOL_FastFacts_Feb2013.pdf

While the federal government has issued its periodic National Educational Technology Plans for the past decade and a half, California put out its policy blueprint for technology and education five years before the first Washington plan. Enacted in 1991, the California Distance Learning Policy is now enshrined as California Education Code Section 51865.

According to one recent legal analysis, "California law does not draw formal distinctions among distance learning, online learning, and online instruction." The analysis continues, "Distance learning is a broadly defined term that means technology-enabled learning in which the instructor and student are not at the same location," while "online learning is learning from sources available on the Internet, including books, videos, lessons, and software." The analysis then says, "Online instruction is instruction between the instructor and the student via the Internet."

Thus, in California, distance learning could include options such as virtual charter schools, where much of the learning takes place using a computer and the student and teacher are miles away from each other, while online learning could include alternatives such as "hybrid" blended-learning charter schools, where a portion of the learning takes place in a traditional classroom and another portion takes place in a learning lab using the Internet and computer software programs.

For its part, California Education Code 51865, section (b), defines distance learning as instruction in which the student and the instructor are in different locations and interact through the use of computer and communications technology. Section (b) also addresses the digital divide by stating: "Equity in education, which requires that every pupil in California's public schools, and every adult in the state, have equal access to educational opportunities, regardless of where he or she lives or how small a school the pupil attends." Educational opportunities include digital learning, which have the potential to improve the achievement of students.

Section (f) of that same code further addresses the digital divide: ""In expanding the use of distance learning technology, the state should emphasize the delivery of education and training services to populations currently not receiving those services, the ease of access by educational institutions to the technology, and the lower cost over time of providing instruction through distance learning rather than on site."

Broadband Internet access and hardware such as laptop computers are part of the mix in closing the digital divide. However, California law also recognizes that high quality education for students requires high-quality teachers as well. California Education Code 51865, section (b)(2), says: "Quality in education, which would be enhanced through the creative application of telecommunications, as pupils are given the opportunity to interact with pupils from other cultures and geographical locations, and with outstanding educators from other institutions." The key question, however, is whether these "outstanding educators" are available to students or not.

Even if students have broadband access and adequate hardware, if they do not have teachers who have been educated in how to use and make the most out of digital-learning tools, then the full benefits to students will be unrealized. The NTEP says that optimally, "Educators and leaders at all levels of our education system also must be provided with support—tools and training—that can help them manage the assessment process, analyze relevant data, and take appropriate action." [17]

California Education Code 51865, section (d), emphasizes "providing educators with the opportunity to experiment with each alternative distance learning technology." Sadly, the current reality is that the vast majority of teachers in America and in states like California have never been trained in the use of digital-learning tools, whether in pre-service teacher credentialing programs or in-service professional development programs. They have never been given the opportunity "to experiment with each alternative distance learning technology" and, thus, cannot offer new learning opportunities to their students. The following chapter explores the dearth of digital-learning components in teacher preparation programs.

AN OVERVIEW OF TEACHER TRAINING IN DIGITAL EDUCATION IN THE U.S.

BY LANCE IZUMI

In the current National Education Technology Plan (NTEP), one of the key goals is to connect teachers "to the tools, resources, experts and peers they need to be highly effective and supported" when it comes to the digital education revolution."[1] "In a connected teaching model," says the NTEP, "classroom educators are fully connected to learning data and tools for using the data; to content, resources, and systems that empower them to create, manage, and assess engaging and relevant learning experiences; and directly to their students in support of learning both in and out of school."[2]

In addition, according to the NTEP, "Individual educators build online learning communities consisting of their students and their students' peers; fellow educators in their schools, libraries, and after-school programs; professional experts in various disciplines around the world; members of community organizations that serve students in the hours they are not in school; and parents who desire greater participation in their children's education."[3] The Plan says that support should be required for "a professional educator who can engage with educators on leveraging technology for improving their professional practice."[4]

In order to ensure that schools and teachers are ready to use this new connected teaching model, the NTEP calls for an overhaul of teacher-preparation programs:

> Episodic and ineffective professional development is replaced by professional learning that is collaborative, coherent, and continuous and that blends more effective in-person courses and workshops with the expanded opportunities, immediacy, and convenience enabled by online environments full of resources and opportunities for collaboration. For their part, the colleges of education and other institutions that prepare teachers play an ongoing role in the professional growth of their graduates throughout the entire course of their careers.[5]

While the NTEP states a very worthy goal for teacher education, the big question is whether teacher-preparation programs are meeting the challenge of providing pre-service and in-service teachers with the knowledge and skills to maximize the potential of that revolution and, in the process, raise the achievement of students.

In the coming years, more and more K-12 instruction and learning will use digital education tools. In their 2008 book , Clayton Christensen, Michael Horn and Curtis Johnson predict that a majority of high school courses will be delivered online by the year 2020. There are a variety of different delivery models that use online technology.

In their review of the academic literature, Wayne State University's Michael Barbour and his co-authors found that online instructors "needed advanced skills in the management of instructional activities and assessments, as well as stronger engagement skills."[6] In some ways, they say, "the online environment has its own issues—the teacher has to be both tech-savvy and be able to guide students."

Online teachers, according to Barbour, et al, "must be vigilant in keeping the student engaged," plus they need "advanced skills in the management of instructional activities and strong engagement skills."

Further, online teachers "need a genuine excitement for the course content and familiarity with the curriculum," and they will also need "to be able to select engaging content, rich multimedia for instruction, nontraditional content delivery methods, sound teaching philosophy, an understanding of the use of the Internet to teach and learn, and innovative teaching strategies."[7] These skills can then be applied in virtual, asynchronous and synchronous course models.

When students are in independent virtual course, where they do not attend a brick-and-mortar class but, rather, progress at their own pace using a structured program in which content and instruction are delivered over the Internet, Barbour and his colleagues observe that "the teacher needs to be skilled in the technical aspects of delivery and the organization of the course."

In an asynchronous course, there is little real-time interaction between the teacher and the student. The teacher provides lectures, assignments, assessments and other material to students who access them using the Internet. Barbour, et al point out that the lack of live interaction between students and teachers "does not mean that there is no communication between the teacher, student, and classmates." They point out:

> Teacher needs to provide feedback on assignments, and students must often interact with one another via discussion boards or group assignments. However, unless the student is taking an asynchronous course with classmates in a brick-and-mortar school, the potential for student isolation is still present. Therefore, online instructors in an asynchronous environment must be able to provide opportunities for interaction when convenient for the student, provide authentic feedback without ever coming in direct contact with the student, and be able to monitor students who are becoming isolated from the rest of the class.[8]

As opposed to the non-interaction between students and teachers in asynchronous courses, in synchronous courses students and teachers interact in real time using online tools. Although they are separated by distance, they come together during regularly scheduled periods. "Instructors," note Barbour, et al, "must have the capabilities to effortlessly work with the new communication technology and be able to integrate synchronous activities with any asynchronous events or discussions that occur when the class is working offline."[9]

The increasingly popular blended-learning model of instruction is a hybrid. According to the California-based Christensen Institute, formerly the Innosight Institute, "Blended learning is a formal education program in which a student learns at least in part through online delivery of content and instruction with some element of student control over time, place, path, and/or pace, and at least in part at a supervised brick-and-mortar location away from home." This first part of this definition is a simple explanation of online learning. It is the second part that is the crux of blended learning:

> The second component of the definition specifies that the learning must be "supervised" and take place "away from home." This is to distinguish it from students learning full-time online at a brick-and-mortar location such as a coffee shop, public library, or home. Someone associated with the brick-and-mortar setting provides the supervision, rather than parent or other adult who is associated primarily with the student.[10]

Within this definition of blended learning, the Christensen Institute cites four different models of blended-learning delivery: the rotation model, the flex model, the self-blend model, and the enriched-virtual model. In the rotation model, students rotate on a fixed schedule or at the teacher's discretion between learning modalities, "at least one of which is online learning," with other modalities potentially including "small-group or full-class instruction, group projects, individual tutoring, and pencil-and-paper assignments." This rotation may occur within a single classroom, between a classroom and an online learning lab on campus, between a classroom and a remote location such as the student's home (the so-called "flipped classroom"), or based on customized schedules for each individual student.[11]

In the flex model, "content and instruction are delivered primarily by the Internet," with students moving "on an individually customized, fluid schedule among learning modalities," and the teacher-of-record is on site and provides, along with other on-site adults, "face-to-face support on a flexible and adaptive as-needed basis through activities such as small-group instruction, group projects, and individual tutoring."[12]

> " These different blended-learning models need teachers who have different skills than teachers in exclusively brick-and-mortar classrooms. "

Under the self-blend model, individual students can "choose to take one or more courses entirely online to supplement their traditional courses and the teacher of record is the online teacher," which allows students to "self-blend some individual online course and take other courses at a brick-and-mortar campus with face-to-face teachers." The enriched-virtual model differs from the self-blend model in that students in an entire class/school may "divide their time between attending a brick-and-mortar campus and learning remotely using online delivery of content and instruction."[13]

These different blended-learning models need teachers who have different skills than teachers in exclusively brick-and-mortar classrooms. In a 2012 article for *The Journal*, Michael Horn and Heather Staker write: "Although it is hard to generalize across the landscape of blended learning because of the rapid pace of innovation in the models, the differences between the models, and the continued changes in technology, there are five common skills that teachers will likely need to be successful in a blended-learning environment." Those five skills include:

1. COMFORT WITH 'CHAOS'

One of the biggest shifts in a blended-learning environment is often that students will be engaged in different activities and working on different concepts and skills. Teachers must learn to be comfortable facilitating learning in this environment and creating a culture that sets high academic expectations and encourages students to own their learning.

2. STUDENT-LEARNING DATA ANALYSIS AND DECISION MAKING

Responding to individual student data in real time—or even on a daily basis, as happens in many blended-learning models today—is a significant and important shift for teachers to master. Not every teacher will become a data automaton of course, but what will help teachers is that increasingly they won't have to be the ones actively collecting every piece of data; instead they will be able to spend more time analyzing and figuring out what to do about it, coupled of course with their own "data" that they collect on students from their intuition and observations.

3. TARGETED LEARNING OPPORTUNITIES

Historically, teachers have been forced to deliver a relatively unified, monolithic educational experience. Teachers will now need new skills to learn how to support students who are learning different things, at different paces, through different approaches. They will need to be able to facilitate different learning opportunities for students—such as one-on-one tutoring, small-group instruction, project-based learning, and lectures. Given that leading small-group interventions will be a major part of this, becoming masterful at that skill rather than lesson planning for an entire class is a good starting point.

4. SPECIALIZATION

Teachers increasingly won't have to be all things to all people and will have opportunities to specialize. As blended-learning models mature, there will be opportunities for team teaching and differentiated roles for teachers. Some may be content experts, others learning coaches or facilitators, and still others might be non-academic teachers who look much more like caseworkers. Not every teacher may have to be a pro at data analysis, for example. As Public Impact has written, increasingly many elementary school teachers, for example, may need to learn to be specialists in particular subjects. For example, one teacher may be an expert in math and science, another in language arts and social studies, and paraprofessionals can support students with social and behavioral skills and watch students during lunch and recess.

5. TECHNOLOGICAL PROWESS

Because technology is becoming simpler to use and more ubiquitous in our daily lives, teachers won't actually need as much as people may think in the way of technology skills to teach in a blended-learning environment. Still, they will likely need a few basic skills. As the International Association for K-12 Online Learning's (iNACOL) National Standards for Quality Online Teaching documents, teachers will need to be able to communicate via a variety of mediums, explore, identify, and use a variety of online tools to meet student needs, and be able to do basic troubleshooting—such as helping students reset passwords, download plug-ins, and so forth. For many teachers, being able to teach effectively offline as well as online will be critical.[14]

Yet, despite the obvious and growing need for these specialized skills, teacher-training programs are not providing teachers with opportunities to acquire these skills.

Barbour, et al, found, "At present, there are very few examples of the preparation of teachers for the online environment."[15] Another study cited by Barbour, et al discovered that only a shockingly low one percent of K-12 teachers had been trained to teach online.[16]

Similarly, the NTEP observes, "Many of our existing educators do not have the same understanding of and ease with using technology that is part of the daily lives of professionals in other sectors."[17]

Frontline teachers testify that there is little training for the new digital-education age. Catlin Tucker is a young award-winning English teacher at Windsor High School in Northern California and is the author of the 2012 book *Blended Learning in Grades 4-12.* "When I first taught it was all pen and paper," she says. When she was getting her teacher education at the University of California at Santa Barbara, she recalls that she had one course that had to do with technology: "Yeah, and it was really just basic processing, Excel overview, maybe they taught us how to use Power Point." "I really retained nothing from that class because I wasn't asked to apply any of it when I was teaching," and, she laments, when she was student teaching "there was no technology; there was no way for me to even say, 'I might like to use a Word document.'"

And even though she has now jumped into the digital-education revolution, she says that most of her colleagues in the teaching profession are not weaving technology into their practice. "Not only are we teachers missing out on exciting opportunities," she explains, "but we are not really arming our kids with the tools set they're using or that they need to be successful."[18]

When asked about teachers' level of understanding of digital tools, Tucker estimates that about 10 percent of teachers have some general understanding, and "then you come into schools like mine and you are probably going to hit like 5 percent that have exposure to technology beyond like, 'Oh, I have a website.'" She laments, "I don't think there are a lot of teachers being armed coming into the profession with that knowledge."

Although she acknowledges, "I don't have a window into [teacher] credential school," she does see the lack of preparation of new teachers coming into the profession. She tells of a new teacher "and she was at credential school and all she had taken that was tech-focused at all was '100 Ways to Use Power Point.'" "So I don't know where some credential schools are, but I'm not seeing game-busters coming out of [credential] school armed with technology."

Asked for her view of the adequacy of digital-learning coursework at schools of education, Tucker is blunt:

> It's just not there. I just feel like we're behind the curve. Teachers, I don't think, should be leaving credential school without not only learning, but also having to engage with these tools as students. That necessitates the professors or whoever is teaching those courses to be quite fluent with the tools so they can engage their teacher-credential participants. Because when I do trainings, I want my teachers to be forced into the decision of a student. So you hit all the barriers a student hits, you have the same learning curve, you know what to expect when you're teaching it. That means all the way up the chain people have to be prepared to teach using these tools, and I don't see that happening right now. I think that a lot of changes need to happen in traditional school settings if we are going to even get close to preparing teachers to where they need to be.

Some teacher-credential programs have tried to address the technology revolution by tacking on a class here or there, or by trying to incorporate technology components in existing courses. Tucker says that such a strategy is wrongheaded and will not work. "The idea that you could elect to take a course," she warns, "or that it could be like, 'oh, your final project for this class is this piece of technology finished product,' is missing the whole point." "It has to be integrated from top to bottom," she urges, and, "It has to be the way that teachers and credential programs collaborate with one another and share ideas and have conversations and create products together that demonstrate learning." "And it needs to be throughout," she concludes, and "that's not happening."

In terms of the blended-learning model, Tucker says that teachers should be asking specific questions: "Shouldn't you figure out what pieces are going to happen in class? What pieces are happening online? What tools do I need? What makes the most sense?" Yet, "Most teachers don't think in that way."

> **" Only a handful of anomalous programs offer prospective teachers training in the biggest revolution in teaching and learning to ever hit the profession. "**

Despite authoring an excellent how-to book on blended learning, Tucker says that she is aware of only four university teacher-credentialing programs that are using her book, including Fresno State University and San Francisco State University. Otherwise, "There may just be copies of pages of my book going around, which is not that big of a deal." It is not surprising that Tucker has found few takers for her book among university credentialing programs. Around the country, only a handful of anomalous programs offer prospective teachers training in the biggest revolution in teaching and learning to ever hit the profession.

The reasons for the dearth of courses on digital learning in university credentialing programs are varied. According to Barbour, et al:

Existing pre-service teacher education initiatives for future teachers that attempt to support K-12 online learning are faced with a variety of challenges such as a lack of research and few models to guide their development. Other critical barriers to effective pre-service K-12 online learning teacher education arise from constrictive geographic regulations around the teacher certification process that vary from state to state. Such policies and procedures are more suited to traditional brick-and-mortar environments and complicate the reach of K-12 online learning's broad development.[19]

The bottom line, according to Barbour, et al, is that credential programs are failing to prepare incoming teachers for the digital-education revolution: "It is generally agreed that teacher education is currently unprepared for the burgeoning demand for K-12 online learning."[20]

It is indicative of the digital-learning void in university teacher credential programs that Barbour, et al only cite one example of a credential program focusing on digital learning. That program, a collaboration between Iowa State University, the University of Florida, the University of Virginia, Graceland University and Iowa Learning Online, created the Teacher Education Goes Into Virtual Schools (TE-GIVS) project that attempted to design "a national model for pre-service teacher education with an emphasis on K-12 online learning."

The TEGVIS project "sought to identify and develop online teaching competencies that would be valuable for all K-12 teachers to support K-12 online learning in the traditional setting, to develop tools that permitted engagement with K-12 online learning practices from multiple perspectives (e.g., the online student, the online teacher, the online course developer, and local school site facilitator), and, ultimately, to build a national community of K-12 peers who might constructively critique and challenge the model."[21] As promising as this description appears, Barbour, et al point out that funding for this project dried up in 2007 and the remnants of the program are only available in archives.

In California, there is a technology requirement for prospective teachers. That requirement can be satisfied, however, with taking just a single course, which many would say falls far short of the necessary instruction that new teachers should receive to be fully competent in digital-education delivery. The University of Southern California Rossier School of Education describes the technology requirement by recommending that prospective teachers "Take a Computer Class . . . or Two" and explains:

> All individuals who wish to obtain their California teacher credentials need to demonstrate fluency with computers and technology. According to the state's specific requirements, California teachers must "complete foundational computer technology coursework that includes general and specialized skills in the use of computers in educational settings." This can often be done while in college or enrolled at a Commission-approved teacher preparation program.[22]

A majority of California teachers receive their credentials through programs run by the California State University system. To meet the technology requirement for new teachers, some CSU campuses offer individual courses that focus on preparing would-be teachers for the world of digital education. At San Diego State University, the College of Education offers EDTEC 470, which is entitled "Technologies for Teaching." According to the school:

> This introductory course provides an exciting hands-on look at the possibilities and potentials of computer technology for education. The goal of this course is for pre-service teachers to begin to use a wide variety of computer-based technology for both professional and instructional use.

You will leave with both a sense of all that is possible using technology in teaching and concrete ideas about how to infuse technology into your teaching. The course meets the technology requirements for new California teachers.[23]

In addition, the school says that students in the "Technologies for Teaching" course will learn about a variety of technology-related issues:

- Developing a personal learning system
- Creative expression
- Today's ed tech context
- Assessing student learning
- Effective presentations
- Collecting and manipulating data
- Finding information
- Developing a complete Webquest
- Ethical, legal and social issues.[24]

Courses offered by the University of California system to satisfy the state's technology requirement are described similarly to those offered by the California State University.

The University of California at San Diego offers a course called "Integrating Technology in Education K-12, Level 1" that explores "the use of technology in education as a tool to enhance teaching & learning." Prospective teachers "will learn and demonstrate the effective use of computer hardware and software and fundamental hardware care operations to ensure safety." Topics in this course will include "legal aspects of technology in education, electronic communication tools, printed media, classroom and record management, introduction to technology uses across the curriculum & classroom, evaluation of electronic research tools and the maintenance of effective learning environments using technology in education."[25]

Interestingly, San Diego State University advises that its "Technologies for Teaching" course will not be offered after the spring 2013 semester. Also, and more important, while courses like "Technologies for Teaching" and "Integrating Technology in Education K-12, Level 1" are certainly better than no courses at all in credential programs, it should be remembered that experts and frontline teachers such as Catlin Tucker point out that the vast majority of new teachers coming into the profession seem to have virtually no exposure to the tools of the digital-education revolution or an understanding of how they may incorporate that revolution into their classrooms. Given that knowledge gap, one can ask just how effective the California technology requirement is in giving new teachers the knowledge and skills they will need to be effective users of technology to improve student learning and achievement.

While credential programs for incoming teachers have minimal educational technology requirements, states around the country are beginning to offer masters degrees, certificates and endorsements for digital education to teachers already in the profession.

For example, Dr. Dawn Poole, a professor of advanced studies in education at California State University Stanislaus describes how her campus addresses the rise of blended learning, including variants such as the flipped classroom (a model where students watch prerecorded videos at home or in some other non-classroom setting, which then allows class time in schools to be used for students working on problems, teachers working with students one-on-one or in small groups, and students working with each other on problems and projects):

> We address blended learning in our educational technology concentration within the MA in curriculum and instruction. There are five education technology courses in the concentration (plus other courses), with one of those courses offered per term. Three of the five courses are completely online, and the other two are blended. Students, therefore, learn about blended learning as the approach is modeled with the delivery of the concen-

tration courses. We more specifically address blended learning in several courses:

Technology in Society: Discuss online learning in general, flipped classrooms, evaluation of online courses and teachers, discussion of whether California should require completion of an online course as part of the high-school graduation requirements.

Advanced Integration Strategies: Students produce flipped lessons, focusing on the overall lesson.

Multimedia Development: Students produce a flipped lesson, focusing on the production element of the lesson.

The Technology Coordinator:
Discuss/Examine how a school's infrastructure can support technology-facilitated learning, which includes blended components.

Dr. Poole summarizes by stating, "We address innovative technologies in all of the courses in the education technology concentration, courses which are taken by students who have declared the concentration, as well as students in other concentrations who take one or two courses as electives."

San Francisco State University offers teaching professionals a masters of arts in education or a graduate certificate in training that "emphasizes the analysis, design, development and evaluation of instruction and materials utilizing multimedia, online, and emerging technologies." The program focuses on instructional design and development skills, such as, web design, graphics, animation, and video.[26]

The San Francisco State program offers a number of digital-education-focused courses, including ITEC 860, entitled "Distance Education." The course description states that students will explore "the field through demonstrations of telecommunications facilities, meeting of professional organizations, Internet capabilities, and teleconference classroom." "This course," says the school, "introduces the learner to the principles of learning at a distance, commonly called distance education, distance learning, distributed learning, e-learning, online learning, etc." One of the major elements of the course is the design of an actual instructional unit using distance education:

> Practice applying instructional design skills for distance learning by completing a comprehensive distance learning instructional unit design project. This project will be selected by you—working in conjunction with a small group of your peers. Your team will complete a formal design plan and produce a limited (short, but complete) instructional unit as the major assignment for the second half of the course.[27]

Outside of California, universities in other states are establishing masters and certificate programs in digital education. For instance, George Mason University (GMU) in Virginia has created a master of education (MEd) and graduate certificate concentrating in the Integration of Online Learning in Schools.

According to GMU, "The Learning Technologies in Schools (LTS) program provides the knowledge and skills needed to effectively integrate technology in the teaching/learning process whether in the face-to-face classroom, online, or a combination" and "prepares teachers to assume leadership roles in implementing, supervising, managing, and integrating technology resources in K-12 learning environments."[28]

In addition, the program provides an immersive and research-based understanding of how to teach K-12 students online. In every course, says the school, participants learn through a combination of research, exploration, reading, discussion, collaboration, practice, reflection, mentor-mentee dyad, and resources found on the course website. Required courses for both the certificate and masters degree include:

EDIT 760 - Online Teachers and Learners (1 credit hour):
Examines the attributes of teachers and K-12 learners with emphasis on attitudes, behaviors, and adaptations required by online teachers and learners.

EDIT 761 - Models for K-12 Online Learning (2 credit hours):
Identifies, explores, and evaluates a range of educational models for K-12 online learning.

EDIT 762 - Quality K-12 Online Learning (1 credit hour):
Examines and evaluates quality indicators for the design of online learning pointing to the six major areas for consideration: instructor-learner, learner-learner, learner-content, learner-interface, learner-instructional strategies, and social presence.

EDIT 763 - Tools for K-12 Online Learning (2 credit hours):
Examines tools that structure and support online learning with particular emphasis on the unique affordances of each tool including tools for producing, delivering, and supporting online learning.

EDIT 764 - The ART of Online Communication (3 credit hours):
Examines strategies to assess, respond to, and target online communication and develops expertise in questioning and listening, supporting self-regulation, and clarifying conceptual understanding using a series of case studies and role playing activities.

EDIT 765 - Facilitating K-12 Online Learning (2 credit hours):
Develops expertise in facilitating and moderating online learning to include synchronous and asynchronous environments, community building strategies, questioning strategies, prompting reflection, and facilitating conceptual understanding.

EDIT 766 - Understanding Online Presence (2 credit hours):
Examines impacts of distance on teachers and learners and develops strategies to establish teacher presence, to establish and express self, to promote learner-learner connections, and to compensate for the separation of teacher-learner and learner-learner.

EDIT 767 - Designing K-12 Online Learning (3 credit hours):
Develops frameworks for designing and structuring online learning opportunities and emphasizes course content and learning outcomes, selection of appropriate online models, and organization of online lessons and courses, online learning tools, and assessment and evaluation strategies.[29] For completion of the masters degree, the following courses are also required:

EDIT 768 - K-12 Online Design (1 credit hour):
Focuses on the creation of online learning activities, materials, and resources appropriate for K-12 learners and culminates in comprehensive design documents ready for the production phase.

EDIT 769 - K-12 Online Design II (1 credit hour):
Focuses on the creation of online courses appropriate for K-12 learners and culminates in comprehensive design documents that detail goals, assessments, learning tools, and detailed scripts or documents ready for the production phase.

EDIT 791 - Project Development Practicum I (6 credit hours):
Designed for students in the Division of Learning Technologies programs to facilitate the application of design and production processes to the solution of learning challenges with particular emphasis on the design and development phase of the design process.

EDIT 792 - Project Development Practicum II (6 credit hours):
Designed for students in the Division of Learning Technologies programs to facilitate the application of design and production processes to the solution of learning challenges with particular emphasis on the implementation and evaluation phase of the design process.[30]

While the GMU program is cutting edge compared to what is being offered (or not being offered) around the country, the program is relatively small, with a cohort of 24 students progressing through the coursework together a group. Also, the program requires that an MEd applicant have three years of teaching experience. Thus, while the university says that graduates of the program become local experts and change agents for technology in their schools, the reality is that most Virginia teachers will not receive anything approaching the training that the GMU teacher-students receive.

> **"This Checklist...includes 10 standards and accompanying performance indicators. "**

Boise State University in Idaho has a Department of Educational Technology that offers 21 courses in School Technology Coordination, Technology Integration, Emerging Technologies, Online Teaching, and E-Learning Design. In addition to their two Masters programs, the department also offers three graduate certificates (Technology Integration, Online Teaching, and School Technology Coordination), as well as a K-12 Online Teaching Endorsement Program.

The K-12 Online Teaching Endorsement Program, which requires students to have an existing Idaho teaching credential and at least one year of online teaching in the last three years, consists of six courses that aim to have teachers meet the K-12 Online Teaching Endorsement Competency Checklist. This Checklist, which was approved by the Idaho legislature, includes 10 standards and accompanying performance indicators:

Standard #1: Knowledge of Online Education–
The online teacher understands the central concepts, tools of inquiry, and structures in online instruction and creates learning experiences that take advantage of the transformative potential in online learning environments.

- The online teacher utilizes current standards for best practices in online teaching to identify appropriate instructional processes and strategies.
- The online teacher demonstrates application of communication technologies for teaching and learning.
- The online teacher demonstrates application of emerging technologies for teaching and learning.
- The online teacher demonstrates application of advanced troubleshooting skills.
- The online teacher demonstrates the use of design methods and standards in course/document creation and delivery.
- The online teacher demonstrates knowledge of access, equity (digital divide) and safety concerns in online environments.

Standard #2: Knowledge of Human Development and Learning–
The teacher understands how students learn, develop, and provides opportunities that support their intellectual, social, and personal development.

- The online teacher understands the continuum of fully online to blended learning environments and creates unique opportunities and challenges for the learner.
- The online teacher uses communication technologies to alter learning strategies and skills (e.g., Media Literacy, vicual literacy).
- The online teacher demonstrates knowledge of motivational theories and how they are applied to online learning environments.
- The online teacher constructs learning experiences that take into account students' physical, social, emotional, moral, and cognitive development to influence learning and instructional decisions.

Standard #3: Modifying Instruction for Individual Needs—
The teacher understands how students differ in their approaches to learning and creates instructional opportunities that are adapted to learners with diverse needs.

- The online teacher knows how adaptive/assistive technologies are used to help people who have disabilities gain access to information that might otherwise be inaccessible.

- The online teacher modifies, customizes and/or personalizes activities to address diverse learning styles, working strategies and abilities (e.g., provide multiple paths to learning objectives, differentiate instruction, strategies for non-native English speakers).

- The online teacher coordinates learning experiences with adult professionals (e.g., parents, local school contacts, mentors).

Standard #4: Multiple Instructional Strategies—
The online teacher understands and uses a variety of instructional strategies to develop students' critical thinking, problem solving, and performance skills.

- The online teacher evaluates methods for achieving learning goals and chooses various teaching strategies, materials, and technologies to meet instructional purposes and student needs (e.g., online teacher-gathered data and student offered feedback).

- The online teacher uses student-centered instructional strategies to engage in learning.

- The online teacher uses a variety of instructional tools and resources to enhance learning.

Standard #5: Classroom Motivation and Management Skills—
The teacher understands individual and group motivation and behavior and creates a learning environment that encourages positive social interaction, active engagement in learning, and self-motivation.

- The online teacher establishes a positive and safe climate in the classroom and participates in maintaining a healthy environment in the school or program as a whole.

- The online teacher performs management tasks.

- The online teacher uses effective time management strategies.

Standard #6: Communication Skills, Networking, and Community

Building—The online teacher uses a variety of communication techniques including verbal, nonverbal, and media to foster inquiry, collaboration, and support interaction in and beyond the classroom.

- The online teacher is a thoughtful and responsive communicator.
- The online teacher models effective communication strategies in conveying ideas and information and in asking questions to stimulate discussion and promote higher-order thinking.
- The online teacher demonstrates the ability to communicate effectively using a variety of mediums.
- The online teacher adjusts communication in response to cultural differences (e.g., wait time and authority).

Standard #7: Instructional Planning Skills—

The online teacher plans and prepares instruction based upon knowledge of subject matter, students, the community, and curriculum goals.

- The online teacher clearly communicates to students stated and measurable objectives, course goals, grading criteria, course organization and expectations.
- The online teacher maintains accuracy and currency of course content, incorporates Internet resources into course content, and extends lesson activities.
- The online teacher designs and develops subject-specific online content.
- The online teacher uses multiple forms of media to design course content.
- The online teacher designs course content to facilitate interaction and discussion.
- The online teacher designs course content that complies with intellectual property rights and fair use standards.

Standard #8: Assessment of Student Learning–
The online teacher understands, uses, and interprets formal and informal assessment strategies to evaluate and advance student performance and to determine program effectiveness.

- The online teacher selects, constructs, and uses a variety of formal and informal assessment techniques to enhance knowledge of individual students, evaluate student performance and progress, and modify teaching and learning strategies.
- The online teacher enlists multiple strategies for ensuring security of on-line student assessments and assessment data.

Standard #9: Professional Commitment and Responsibility–
The online teacher is a reflective practitioner who demonstrates a commitment to professional standards and is continuously engaged in purposeful mastery of the art and science of online teaching.

- The online teacher adheres to local, state, and federal laws and policies (e.g., FERPA, AUP's).
- The online teacher has participated in an online course and applies experiences as an online student to develop and implement successful strategies for online teaching environments.
- The online teacher demonstrates alignment of educational standards and curriculum with 21st century technology skills.

Standard #10: Partnerships–
The online teacher interacts in a professional, effective manner with colleagues, parents, and other members of the community to support students' learning and well-being.[31]

Each of the above bulleted performance indicators also comes with examples of ways to implement the indicator. Thus, the first bulleted performance indicator under Standard #2, which says, "The online teacher understands the continuum of fully online to blended learning environments and creates unique opportunities and challenges for the learner," includes a variety of implementation suggestions: multiple forms of delivery of the same content addressing multiple learning styles (text, audio, video, graphic); synchronous and asynchronous delivery of the content; individual and group learning; digital communities for extended learning activities; and application of learning theories and instructional principles to provide multiple learning opportunities.

> " While there is room for disagreement over specifics in the 10 standards, any teacher who met all the standards in the Checklist would certainly be ready to tackle a blended-learning classroom or other digital-education model. "

While there is room for disagreement over specifics in the 10 standards, any teacher who met all the standards in the Checklist would certainly be ready to tackle a blended-learning classroom or other digital-education model. Indeed, while Boise State's endorsement program is an excellent step forward in raising the digital competencies of teachers already in the profession, one must ask why prospective teachers who are getting their credentials are not required to meet all or some of these standards. With the prediction that large proportions of future students will be receiving all or part of the education through digital means, one wonders why incoming teachers across the country are not being asked to meet at least some or all of the Checklist's standards.

Wayne State University in Michigan offers a masters in education in K-12 technology integration. Since it requires an undergraduate degree and recommends teacher certification, it is primarily designed for in-service teachers. Following the completion of four information technology core courses, and before the required internship and practicum experience, students take eleven K-12 Integration core courses. Among the courses students take are Internet in the K-12 Classroom, Designing Web Tools for the Classroom, Facilitation of Online and Face-to-Face Learning, and Designing Interactive Courseware. Teachers can also take some of these courses and qualify for a certificate in online teaching.

A growing number of other states are starting to offer MEds, certificate and endorsement programs in online teaching for in-service teachers. In Arizona, Arizona State University offers a certificate in online teaching. In Colorado, the University of Colorado at Colorado Springs offers a certificate in online instructional technology that, among other things, teaches students how to incorporate the Internet into the K-12 curriculum and develop interactive multimedia lessons. In Florida, the University of Florida, the University of Central Florida, and the University of South Florida offer a variety of MEds, certificates and internships in online teaching.

In Georgia, Valdosta State University and Georgia Southern University offer endorsement programs in online teaching. In Massachusetts, Northeastern University offers a certificate in distance learning and Lesley University offers an MEd in educational technology. In Michigan, in addition to Wayne State University, Michigan State University offers a certificate in educational technology and a masters in educational technology, while Oakland University offers a certificate in digital literacies and learning. In Missouri, the University of Missouri offers an MEd and a certificate in online educator focus. In Ohio, Kent State University offers a certificate in online teaching and learning.

In Washington, Washington State University offers a certificate in teaching online. Finally, in Wisconsin, the state requires teachers to have 30 hours of professional development designed to prepare them for online learning. The University of Wisconsin at Stout offers a certificate in e-learning and online teaching, which includes five courses that allow teachers to meet the state requirement.

While these programs are a hopeful sign for the future preparation of teachers, much more needs to be done to ensure that all teachers, both prospective pre-service teachers and veteran in-service teachers, acquire the skills necessary to meet the challenges and ensure the benefits of the digital-education revolution. As Barbour, et al state:

> The [teaching] profession needs to have these aspects of what is now considered the domain of online instructional practice incorporated into the traditional teacher preparation curriculum of all teacher education programs. We are doing a disservice to all our students and teachers if we do not demand this. In much the same way that all teachers should be able to integrate technology into teaching (which means that endorsement to technology integration are redundant at best, demeaning to a professional at worst), all teachers should be able to design, deliver and support instruction in an online as well as a face-to-face environment.[32]

Yet, the gap between this ideal and the reality of little teacher preparation has reverberations throughout the education system. "The gap in technology understanding," says the National Technology Education Plan, "influences program and curriculum development, funding and purchasing decisions about educational and information technology in schools, and pre-service and in-service learning." Further, "This gap prevents technology from being used in ways that would improve instructional practices and learning outcomes."[33] Because the consequences of this gap are so devastating, the NTEP urges that "we need innovation in the organizations that support educators in their profession—schools and districts, colleges of education, professional learning providers, and professional organizations."[34]

Catlin Tucker and others on the teaching frontline would certainly agree with the NTEP's conclusion. It is time, therefore, for education leaders and policymakers to set a course that will make digital-education competency a must for all teachers in America.

HOW OTHER COUNTRIES ARE TRAINING TEACHERS IN DIGITAL EDUCATION

BY LANCE IZUMI

"I have noted that teacher education is a 'confused mess' in many parts of the world," writes Sir John Daniel, president and CEO of the Commonwealth of Learning, which is an intergovernmental organization created by the Commonwealth heads of government to encourage the development and sharing of open learning and distance education knowledge, resources and technologies. He warns of "the often incoherent goals of teacher education" and how "teacher education policy inherited from the 20th century has little relevance to the 21st century." A key part of the latter problem is that teacher-education policies "did not take into account the potential of open and distance learning and information and communication technology to do things differently."[1] International test results provide an interesting background to weigh Sir John Daniel's observations.

When the 2012 scores for the latest Programme for International Assessment (PISA) exams were released in late 2013, the results were not surprising. PISA exams, which are administered by the Organisation for Economic Co-operation and Development (OECD), are given in 65 countries. For the latest math, reading and science exams, the United States had a combined ranking of 36th.[2] Low student achievement in many countries has not been helped by the inadequate teacher training in the use of digital-learning tools for the classroom.

A report by Colin Latchem, president of the Open and Distance Learning Association of Australia and former head of the Teaching Learning Group at Curtin University in Western Australia, cites a study by the OECD and Sweden's Knowledge Foundation that found that while governments have invested heavily in information and communication technology (ICT) in schools, "so few teachers actually use it as intended." He writes:

> The interim findings are that ICT integration is not occurring regularly or systematically in the OECD countries reviewed because of the shortcomings in teacher training in ICT. It is recommended that teacher training institutions should: take far greater head of the technological world into which pupils need to be inducted; be much clearer on the role, aims and outcomes of the ICT in education theory and how to achieve these; and integrate ICT in all subject teaching training. The theory and practice of ICT integration must also be linked so that teacher trainers can make more and better use of ICT in their own teaching, and so that teacher trainers and classroom teachers can collaborate more closely during teaching practice.[3]

A Finnish study citing a review of the research literature found several paradoxes in the use of ICT at schools and in teacher education:

- National level ICT-strategies and national curriculum guidelines for ICT use have been prepared during the last two decades in several countries which had only minor influence on the visions and practice of the teachers on their use of ICT in education;

- There is research evidence about the influence of ICT to learning and students' motivation, but teachers do not rely much on research-based evidence to identify good practices;

- Students have rich experiences of the use of technology outside of school, but do not use technology for learning at school;

- Teachers are skilled technology users, but they are unable to take advantage of their competence and to apply it to the way they teach in school;

- ICT is available in schools, but teachers beliefs about teaching and learning (e.g., the belief about good practice in school) do not support the use of technology at school;

- A large amount of ICT material already exists, but teachers are not experienced in using these materials effectively within and outside regular classroom activities.[4]

As the Finnish report points out, governments in many countries recognize the importance of the digital-education revolution, but changing structures like teacher training programs to take advantage of this revolution has been difficult. Take New Zealand, for example. An official New Zealand government report on digital education recognized the advantages of this new mode of delivering education:

> The end point of e-learning is a reward well worth striving for. The potential is for New Zealand's primary and secondary schools to provide students with an education that is as good as, or better than in any other developed country. One where students are taught using the communication tools of their own generation rather than those of a past one. One where students can progress at their own pace regardless of the speed at which they learn, or whether their schools are low or high decile. The potential exists for schools to transform themselves so as to turn out the higher-educated students needed in the New Zealand we aspire to be in the 21st century.[5]

The report says that the digital-learning revolution could be a game-changer for students, since it "enables them to learn when they feel inclined to learn, in a style and at a pace that suits them" and they "can organise their lives accordingly." As a result, "Study, social and family time become far more flexible." In the new learning paradigm, "the term "homework" is now redundant—if the school network can be accessed then schoolwork of any kind can be done anywhere and anytime, inside or outside school hours."[6]

Yet, as in the United States, New Zealand's teacher training institutions have been too slow to recognize the advent of digital education and to respond to it. According to the government report, "One area that arose repeatedly as a serious concern in the interviews was the perception that our colleges of education are many years behind the times in teaching the teachers." One person interviewed by the author of the report said, "the way universities are teaching is essentially the same as 80 years ago, but the young people in front of the teacher are from a different paradigm." Further, "today's graduates know the pedagogy, but have little concept of modern e-learning practices" and there is "doubt whether the training institutions themselves are using the technology."[7] In sum, the report criticized teacher institutions "which are seen as behind the times and missing the opportunity to position themselves as thought leaders in the field."[8]

A blogger in New Zealand writes that the country's teacher-education programs "are mired in old school techniques" and "most of our learning was still firmly rooted around the old style of learning: lectures and textbooks." The blogger makes an important distinction between having teacher-training courses online and being able to use digital-learning tools in practice:

> For me the biggest take-away from experience as an online student is that using ICT, using ICT to learn and teaching with ICT are fundamentally different activities and I don't think Teacher Education providers have cottoned on to the latter two in particular. Having course content available online does

not mean students know how to implement e-learning pedagogy into their teaching practice.[9]

While teacher-training programs in places like the U.S. and New Zealand lag in arming teachers with knowledge about digital education, some Asian countries like South Korea, Hong Kong and Singapore, whose students do very well on international tests such as PISA, are in the forefront of educating their teachers in how to use digital-learning tools to improve the achievement of students.

In South Korea, according to a UNESCO report, pre-service teacher training in information communication technology (ICT) began in the mid-1990s at elementary and secondary teacher-training institutions.[10] In 2002, the South Korean government developed the ICT Skill Standards for Teachers that was then adopted for both pre-service and in-service training for teachers. Pre-service teachers are required to take from six to 20 credits of ICT courses. The government had both short-term and long-term goals when it pushed for digital-learning competency among its teachers.

In the short term, South Korea believed that effective adoption of ICT enhanced the quality of teaching, learning and pedagogy. Also, strengthening student teachers' competency in the use of ICT in education would better prepare them for rapid changes in the educational environment.[11] Long-term goals included strengthening international competitiveness of pre-service teacher institutions through state-of-the-art IT infrastructure, enhancing the quality of teaching and learning to reduce the information divide, and facilitating the introduction of pedagogy using ICT in pre-service training programs.[12]

In South Korea, there are 11 national universities that train elementary school teachers. All of these universities offer computer education courses either as major field or elective courses. There are also 40 colleges of education that train secondary school teachers. The UNESCO report found that in the pre-service teacher-training curriculum on ICT for elementary and secondary teachers, basic courses focused on how to apply ICT into teaching-and-learning methods in specific subjects. Advanced courses focused on advanced use of ICT to develop teaching-and-learning methods including knowledge of computers and networking. Both primary and secondary teachers are required to understand:

(1) PC and the peripherals, system software, application software,
(2) the concept of and the ability to develop course ware with multimedia authoring software, computer networks, and information ethics, and
(3) management and development of resources on the Internet and apply them to teaching.[13]

UNESCO says that for pre-service teachers in South Korea, "Teacher colleges and colleges of education are offering new courses on information and ICT use, updating teaching-learning methods, and integrating ICT use in all classes." Further, "A significant amount of funding has been allocated to teachers' colleges to install the necessary hardware and software and to provide a proper learning environment." Finally, for in-service teachers, "one-third of the teachers have received training every year since 2002."[14] All of these findings are in marked contrast to the U.S., where nothing approaching the Korean level of commitment to digital education exists in American teacher-training programs.

Hong Kong is also working to assure that its teachers are ready for the digital-education revolution. Its 1998-2003 plan entitled "Information Technology for Learning in a New Era Five-Year Strategy," states, "We will require all teacher training institutions to integrate in their pre-service programmes, IT competency such as producing courseware, applying the skills of computer-aided instruction, and using various electronic networks for peer support and collaborative learning."[15]

Thus, the Hong Kong Institute of Education offers a bachelor of education degree with a major in information and communication technology. According to the Institute:

This programme is aimed at providing students with a wide range of knowledge, concepts and applications of information and communication technology to develop problem-solving skills using Information and Communication Technology (ICT). It also provides students with opportunities to appreciate the impact of ICT on knowledge-based society, and equips students with pedagogical knowledge, subject knowledge, values, skills and practice essential to teach ICT.

On completion of the programme, students are expected to be able to:

- demonstrate understanding of basic concepts in major areas of ICT and use a range of applications software to support information processing and problem-solving;

- demonstrate an understanding of methods for analyzing problems, and planning and implementing solutions using ICT;

- realize the social, ethical and legal issues pertaining to the use of ICT and appreciate how information literacy and the sharing of knowledge using ICT to influence decision-making and shape our society; and

- learn to connect ICT knowledge to the teaching of ICT and develop approaches to help students learn ICT in exciting and effective ways.[16]

The Institute offers a similar bachelor of science education degree with a focus on science and web technology, which the Institute says should give students the ability to, among other things, "integrate knowledge and skills in Science Education and Web Technology and apply them creatively in the development of web-based applications, multimedia courseware for science learning, and computer systems and networks in educational and other related settings."[17]

For in-service teachers, the Hong Kong Education Bureau provides more than 100 professional development courses in ICT. According to one of the Bureau's goals, which was last revised in February 2012, "Teachers will be provided with professional development opportunities and support to undertake the challenge of using IT for curriculum and pedagogical innovations, and to facilitate, guide, administer and assess learning in ways that align with the goals of the Curriculum Reform."[18]

In the period from September 2013 to December 2013, the Bureau offered the following courses for K-12 teachers:

- IT in Education e-Leadership & Management Series: Microsoft "Partners in Learning" 2013-14 Programmes and Free Resources Briefing Session

- IT in Education Technological Series: Setup and Adopt Free Microsoft Cloud Service for Collaborative Learning and Teaching

- IT in Education Technological Series: Manage and Utilise Old PCs and Servers with Virtualisation Technologies and Management Tools

- IT in Education e-Learning Series: Dissemination of Selected School Projects under the Pilot Scheme on e-Learning in Schools—Practical Workshop on Collaborative Learning Platform for Liberal Studies

- IT in Education e-Leadership & Management Series: Leadership and Management for e-Learning—A Home-school Joint Venture

- IT in Education e-Leadership & Management Series: IT in Education Planning and Implementation in Schools with Illustrative Examples—Some Proposals for Open Source Learning Management System Management and Configuration

- IT in Education e-Learning Series: Foundation Course for Effective Use of Tablet PC (Android) in Learning and Teaching

- IT in Education e-Learning Series: Drama in Education

- IT in Education e-Learning Series: Learning and Teaching with Motion Sensing Technology

- IT in Education e-Learning Series: Using Cloud System for Interactive Learning and Teaching in General Studies

- IT in Education e-Learning Series: The Development of Mobile Learning and e-Learning in Hong Kong Primary School

- IT in Education e-Learning Series: Briefing on Internet Learning Support Programme (ILSP)—i Learn at Home [19]

The Hong Kong Education Bureau acknowledges that teacher training courses provided under the 1998/99-2002/03 Five-Year Strategy plan "were mostly skewed towards the training of generic IT skills." "Teachers," noted the Bureau, "wish to know more about how to apply IT in the learning and teaching of different key learning areas (KLAs), or even subjects." In addition, "after receiving training, teachers still need to overcome further hurdles in implementing new teaching approaches using IT in the classroom." Thus, "New models of professional development should be developed to build in mechanisms that will encourage and support the new teaching approaches."[20]

To further its stated goal of empowering teachers with information technology, the Bureau in 2012 proposed the following reforms and initiatives:

- *Revamping the existing training framework on the use of IT in education*—the existing training framework was drawn up in 1999, a time when Hong Kong was starting to use IT in education on a large-scale. The framework will need to be revamped and updated having regard to the experiences gathered and studies conducted. The focus of training will be on ways to facilitate exploratory learning, guide collaborative enquiries, provide learning resources, administer learning tasks, tailor teaching to students' varied abilities and conduct assessment. The revamped framework should seek integration into the Continuing Professional Development Framework for teachers developed by the Advisory Committee on Teacher Education and Qualifications.

- *Supporting KLA or subject-based training and professional development courses*—tertiary institutions, qualified private firms, professional bodies and experienced teachers will be brought together to develop quality KLA [key learning areas] or subject-based training in the context of continuing professional development for teachers. A course evaluation mechanism will be put in place. Teachers' feedback on the usefulness of the courses, quality of the training materials, pedagogies of the trainers will be collated and evaluation results will be used to improve future courses to be provided.

- *Continuing and enhancing the "train the trainers" scheme*— this will bring the state of the art technology to teachers, riding on the innovation and strengths of the private sector.

- *Introducing a voluntary certification system by IT organizations and subject associations*—A voluntary certification system will be set up to recognize competencies and commitment of teachers who have received training. The system should provide extra, and higher, recognition for the provision of evidence and examples of how the training has led to pedagogical changes in the classroom. A "certification ladder" may be established with the assistance of IT organizations as well as subject associations to encourage continuing professional development of teachers.

- *Developing more online training for teachers*—we will develop, through HKEdCity [Hong Kong Education City], an online training platform and more instructional software for teachers. This will offer greater flexibility in training scheduling and cater for individual learning differences. The HKEdCity will also set up mutually supportive teacher communities to undertake and share pedagogical innovations, through online and face-to-face contacts.

- *Continuing the sharing and collaboration among teachers*—exemplars emerged and software that are proven to be effective in enhancing learning and teaching will be recognized and disseminated. Sharing will be enhanced in terms of scale, frequency and depth. We will jointly organize with tertiary educators, the private sector and the school sector, flagship conferences on IT in education to enhance sharing of information and dissemination of good practices. Incentive schemes will also be conceived to encourage collaboration amongst schools and relevant organizations in harnessing IT in learning and teaching. [21]

The Bureau says it "will no longer organize training on generic IT skills, as virtually all teachers have acquired the basic skills and such courses are abundant in the market." Instead, the Bureau will transform two of its existing "Centres of Excellence" to become "Learning Centres" that aim "to facilitate teachers to develop, share and disseminate innovative learning and teaching methods using the latest information technologies."[22]

Finally, the Hong Kong Institute of Education offers a post-graduate diploma in primary education that integrates ICT across the curriculum; delivers an IT course; helps develop student teachers' confidence, creativity, and capacity to explore educational ICT applications; and requires participants to pass the Information Technology Competence Test before graduation. Specifically, the ICT component of the diploma "empowers participants with the pedagogical knowledge and skills and the necessary attitude in implementing the IT curriculum for primary school children in line with the strategic documents published by the Education Bureau." The Institute says, "On completion of the courses of this subject study, participants will be competent and confident in helping the primary school students to attain the different levels of the IT learning targets, developing innovative IT learning environments and activities to facilitate children's learning and personal development as well as managing the resources and on-going development of IT in a primary school."[23]

Singapore, which usually scores at the top of international math tests, is also known for the widespread use of ICT in the classroom. Discussing a survey of countries done by her organization, Susan Patrick, president and CEO of the International Association for K-12 Online Learning (iNACOL), says that 100 percent of secondary schools in Singapore use online learning. Specifically, there is blended/hybrid learning going on in every classroom. All Singaporean teachers know how to teach online.[24]

A report by Singapore's National Institute of Education (NIE), which is the country's official teacher education entity for all teachers across subject disciplines and from primary to junior college, says that data shows "a progressive increase in the use of technology for e-learning." "Campus-wide e-learning weeks," notes the report, "have been conducted since 2007 and this initiative has helped build faculty's confidence in using e-platforms for teaching."[25] A key pedagogical goal of the NIE is to integrate technology in the learning process by working "with the [Ministry of Education] to integrate technology in the learning process in our ITP and professional development programmes."[26]

The philosophy and focus of teacher training in ICT in Singapore has evolved over the years. According to Shanti Divaharan, Wei-Ying Lim and Seng-Chee Tan of Nanyang Technological University in Singapore, from 2000 to 2003 the focus was technology skills. This focus was apparent in the NIE's mandatory course in ICT use, which is required for all pre-service teachers. According to the Nanyang researchers:

> NIE's ICT course in the early 200s focused on the development of ICT skills of student teachers. The underlying assumption was that student teachers, when equipped with relevant ICT skills, coupled with an awareness of the various instructional strategies, will be competent designers of ICT integrated lessons. The course was entitled *Introduction to Instructional Technology*. A learning management system (LMS) was used as a medium to deliver the course materials and to communicate with student teachers. [27]

Student teachers had to design a computer-based lesson and had to incorporate various computer features such as animation, graphics, sound and interactivity to enhance teaching and learning. "A range of instructional activities such as simulations, games and problem-solving activities were incorporated," note the Nanyang researchers.[28]

From 2004 to 2009, the focus of the mandatory ICT course shifted to "putting the learner at the center of all activities that were designed." Singapore's 2003-08 Master Plan for ICT emphasized "(i) learners use ICT effectively for active learning; (ii) connections between curriculum, instruction and assessment are enhanced using ICT' and (iii) teachers use ICT effectively for professional and personal growth." The name of the course was changed to "ICT for Meaningful Learning." Student teachers were exposed to various pedagogical approaches which could be used to support ICT integration such as case-based learning, inquiry-based learning, project-based learning, resource-based learning, and game-based learning. [29]

Finally, the current focus of the mandatory course is on knowledge creation with Web 2.0. The goal of the course is now "to nurture our student teachers to become 21st century teachers skilled at using technology for facilitating school learners' knowledge creation":

> The third *Master Plan* (mp3) for ICT in education was instituted in 2009 and will end in 2014. The main goal of mp3 is to foster in learners the competencies of self-directed learning (Tan, Divaharan, Tan and Cheah, 2011) and collaborative learning (Chai, Lim, So and Cheah, 2011) through effective use of ICT. Concurrently, the plan aims to develop learners to be discerning and responsible ICT users. Among the enablers is the capacity for the teachers to plan and deliver ICT-enriched learning experiences for students to become self-directed and collaborative learners, as well as to become discerning and responsible users of ICT (MOE, 2011).[30]

The Nanyang researchers observe that the current design framework of mandatory ICT course is underpinned by "the five *Dimensions of Meaningful Learning*, which include (i) Engaging prior knowledge; (ii) Learn by doing; (iii) Real world knowledge; (iv) Collaborative learning; and (v) Self-directed learning." Singapore's goal, according to the researchers:

> These dimensions were introduced as considerations for student teachers when designing technology integrated lessons. In order to truly comprehend these aspects of learning, and to be able apply them effectively, the student teachers were taken on a learning journey of a repertoire of technology tools enabling them to apply the knowledge acquired to design technology integrated lessons to replicate similar experiences for their learners. In sum, the use of ICT tools shifted from a content delivery tool (*Power Point*), to

learning management and collaborative tool (LMS and discussion forum), and finally to the current form of integrated suite of technologies, including Web 2.0 technologies. [31]

Besides Asian countries such as South Korea, Hong Kong and Singapore, there are some noteworthy efforts going on in other parts of the world.

In Finland, which scores well on PISA and other international exams, eight universities train pre-service teachers for primary and secondary schools. According to a Finnish government report, Finland has a national goal "that more than half of teachers should have a good competence in the educational use of ICT or that they can use a text processor, e-mail and an Internet browser well, make web-pages, use distance learning tools and that they also know the pedagogical principles for using ICT."[32] Although universities in the country are autonomous, their policies are guided by the national strategies and goals.

Finnish teacher education is operating under the national strategy entitled "Information Society Programme 2007-2015." Under this strategy, "Teachers should have outstanding information society skills, and ICT should be a part of multiform teaching at all levels of education." In order to implement this strategy, Finnish policymakers envision, "Close integration of the use of ICT in teaching with basic and further education of teachers," and, further, encouraging "institutions to implement new, innovative learning styles and methods."[33] The Finnish government report notes that each university is supposed to formulate strategies of their own that are in harmony with the national strategies. These university strategies "do have continuous obvious effects on the planning of curricula as well as [teacher education] programmes."[34]

At the University of Helsinki's Department of Teacher Education, goals have been set for educating pre-service teachers in ICT use in schools. For instance, in the primary school teacher-education program:

Student teachers in the subject teacher learn to use basic ICT tools at their home departments. The goals for learning pedagogical use of ICT are described among the aims for specific pedagogical courses. For example, in the course *"Theoretical, psychological, and didactical basis related to teaching and learning particular subject"* these student teachers should learn to use versatile teaching methods and ICT in the teaching of their subject.[35]

Thus, as opposed to many teacher education courses in the U.S. where there is often little, if any, mention of ICT and digital learning, in Finland many of the courses incorporate ways teachers can use ICT to better teach subject matter.

A survey of Finnish pre-service teachers found that the majority had a positive attitude towards ICT and were satisfied with their acquisition of ICT skills. Students noted, however, that courses for attaining basic ICT skills were recommended, but were not always compulsory. The equipment they used was new, which "allowed them to use new and interesting technologies in their teaching practice" and there was "a general positive opinion of the possibilities to use modern technologies when in teacher education." For their part, faculty members teaching pre-service teachers were highly motivated "to use ICT in their teaching and showing student teachers how to use modern technologies." Interviews with faculty members "indicated a most serious effort to promote ICT use in [teacher education]."[36]

Although Finland is ahead of many countries in emphasizing ICT competency in its teacher training programs, the country still must ensure that its strategies and goals translate to practical changes in the classroom. As a Finnish government report concludes, "it is apparently not enough that the strategies have been implemented in writing the curricula and formulating the goals of different courses and teaching practice but it has to be ascertained that their influence is brought down to the level of the teaching-learning processes."[37] As a consequence, the report recommends that "ICT should be integrated to all courses and teaching practices in teacher education programmes and, moreover, well planned courses or activities supporting the use of ICT in teaching and learning at school should be offered."[38]

In the United Kingdom, unlike many OECD countries, basic ICT training is compulsory and is delivered primarily in higher education institutions for pre-service teachers or during employment for in-service teachers.

Open University in the U.K. offers a postgraduate certificate, postgraduate diploma and master-level programs in online and distance education. The university says it offers students "the unique opportunity to study the theory and practice of online and distance education through modules designed by experts from the Institute who are now using information technology to reinvent open distance learning."

THESE MODULES INCLUDE:

Accessible online learning: supporting disabled students
Examine the learning experiences of disabled students, the technical aspects of accessibility, and the current debates and discussions about disability and accessibility in educational contexts.

Openness and innovation in elearning
With an emphasis on exploring innovation, you will look at both the latest developments in educational tools and current debates around the concept of openness.

Practice-based research in educational technology
Develop research and evaluation skills in technology-rich environments by learning about new methods of data collection and analysis, and the philosophical assumptions underlying educational enquiry.

Technology-enhanced learning: practices and debates
Engage with elearning or 'technology-enhanced' learning by exploring the processes of designing, implementing and evaluating, and become a creative and effective elearning professional.

The networked practitioner
This course enables you to experience producing resources related to online and distance education and then improving them through engagement with others in peer reflection. [39]

Perhaps the best summary and recommendation for the future comes from the report on ICT and teacher education by the Finnish Ministry of Education and Culture, which stated: "We may sum up that there is a need for university departments of education to design the ICT-related goals of the programmes of teacher education and related courses on a more concrete level and to create a systematic way for systematic follow-up for reaching these goals." That recommendation should apply not just to Finland, but to teacher education institutions in the U.S. as well. [40]

CONCLUSION

We are deeply humbled and grateful that you have read this far. More importantly, we are also *excited* about the possibilities that lie ahead in education. As the original moonshot took audacious thinking and a great deal of preparation before the ultimate goal was reached, we believe that small changes today can lead to major systemic change in the future and better learning for students. What this means is that each and every one of us—teachers, administrators, and parents—can play an important role in preparing today's students to be productive members of the twenty-first-century workforce. The status quo was developed for another culture, another world, starting at the beginning of the twentieth century. It was preparing kids for the factory model; today we are preparing kids for a world we cannot even conceptualize. They need to think, not follow directions. We need to move forward, take a risk; we have the tools and the skills to change the classroom and make learning exciting and relevant for all students.

We invite you to share your moonshots with us at moonshotsineducation.com.

ENDNOTES

Moonshots in Education

Chapter 1 Notes

1. http://articles.latimes.com/2013/sep/30/local/la-me-1001-lausd-ipads-20131001

Chapter 1 Sources

http://www.edutopia.org/blog/evaluating-quality-of-online-info-julie-coiro

Fletcher, A. *Meaningful Student Involvement: Guide to Students as Partners in School Change.* Olympia, WA: CommonAction, 2005; p. 4.

http://www.innosightinstitute.org/innosight/wp-content/uploads/2012/05/Classifying-K-12-blended-learning2.pdf

http://blogs.kqed.org/mindshift/2014/04/teachers-most-powerful-role-adding-context/

McCombs, B. L., and J. E. Pope. *Motivating Hard to Reach Students.* Washington, DC: American Psychological Association, 1994. https://www.edsurge.com/n/2014-04-02-no-silver-bullets-hybrid-high-learns-a-tough-edtech-lesson

Newmann, F., et al. *Student Engagement and Achievement in American Secondary Schools.* New York: Teachers College Press, 1992.

Reeve, J., H. Jang, D. Carrell, S. Jeon, and J. Barch. "Enhancing Students' Engagement by Increasing Teachers' Autonomy Support."*Motivation and Emotion*, 28, 2004, pp. 147–169.

Skinner, E. A., and M. J. Belmont. "Motivation in the Classroom: Reciprocal Effects of Teacher Behavior and Student Engagement across the School Year." *Journal of Educational Psychology*, 85(4), 1993; p. 572

Chapter 4

1   Staker, Heather and Michael B. Horn, "Classifying K-12 Blended Learning", Innosight Institute, May 2012. See http://www.innosightinstitute.org/innosight/wp-content/uploads/2012/05/Classifying-K-12-blended-learning2.pdf.

2   See http://www.christenseninstitute.org/wp-content/uploads/2013/04/Classifying-K-12-blended-learning.pdf. Partnership for 21st Century Skills, see www.p21.org.

3   Duckworth Lab, see https://sites.sas.upenn.edu/duckworth/pages/research-statement.

4   Common Core State Standards Initiative, see http://www.corestandards.org/Math/Practice/MP1.

5   Illinois State Board of Education, see http://www.isbe.net/ils/social_emotional/standards.htm.

6   APA PsycNET, see http://psycnet.apa.org/journals/psp/21/2/204/.

7   Roediger, Henry L. and Jeffrey D. Karpicke, "Test-Enhanced Learning: Taking Memory Tests Improves Long-Term Retention, *Psychological Science*, 2006.

8   McDaniel, Mark A., Paula J. Waddill, and Giles O. Einstein, "A Contextual Account of the Generation Effect: A Three Factor Theory." *Journal of Memory and Language*, v. 27, Issue 5, October 1988, p. 521-536, see http://www.sciencedirect.com/science/article/pii/0749596X8890023X.

9   Smith, Steven M., Arthur Glenberg, and Robert Bjork, "Environmental Context and Human Memory," *Memory & Cognition*, v.6, 1978, see http://bjorklab.psych.ucla.edu/pubs/Smith_Glenberg_Bjork_1978.pdf.

10 Spiegel, Alex, "Struggle For Smarts? How Eastern and Western Cultures Tackle Learning." National Public Radio, November 12, 2012, see http://www.npr.org/blogs/health/2012/11/12/164793058/struggle-for-smarts-how-eastern-and-western-cultures-tackle-learning.

11 Kahn, Jennifer, "Can Emotional Intelligence be Taught, *New York Times*, Sept. 11, 2013, see: http://www.nytimes.com/2013/09/15/magazine/can-emotional-intelligence-be-taught.html?pagewanted=all&_r=1&.

12 See http://edutopia.org.

13 Society for Research in Child Development, "Social Policy Report Brief: New Approaches to Social and Emotional Learning in Schools", v. 26, Issue 4, 2012 see: http://www.srcd.org/sites/default/files/documents/washington/sel_2013_2.pdf.

14 Graziano, Paulo A., Rachael D. Reavis, Susan P. Keane, and Susan D. Calkins, "The Role of Emotion Regulation and Children", National Center for Biotechnology Information, Feb., 1, 2007, see http://www.ncbi.nlm.nih.gov/pmc/articles/PMC3004175/.

15 Schwartz, Barry, "Attention Must Be Paid!" *Slate*, see http://www.slate.com/articles/life/education/2013/09/paying_attention_is_a_skill_schools_need_to_teach_it.html.

16 Best, J.R., P.H. Miller, and J.A. Naglieri, "Relations between Executive Function and Academic Achievement from Ages 5 and 17 in a Large, Representative, National Sample", PubMed.gov, 2011, see http://www.ncbi.nlm.nih.gov/pubmed/21845021.

17 The Woodcock-Johnson Revised, see http://en.wikipedia.org/wiki/Woodcock%E2%80%93Johnson_Tests_of_Cognitive_Abilities.

18 Hart, Betty and Todd R. Risley, "The Early Catastrophe: The 30 Million Word Gap by Age 3", see https://www.aft.org/pdfs/americaneducator/spring2003/TheEarlyCatastrophe.pdf.

19 Fernald, Anne, and Virginia A. Marchman, and Adriana Weisleder, "SES differences in language processing skill and vocabulary are evident in 18 months, *Development Science*, 8 December 2012, see http://onlinelibrary.wiley.com/doi/10.1111/desc.12019/abstract.

20 Gilliam, Walter and Golan Shahar, "Preschool and Child Care Expulsion and Suspension: Rates and Predictors in One State, 2006; *Infants and Young Children*, v. 19 no. 3, 2006, see http://www.researchgate.net/publication/232198215_Preschool_and_Child_Care_Expulsion_and_Suspension_Rates_and_Predictors_in_One_State; Raver, C. Cybele, Jane Knitzer, "Read to Enter: What Research Tells Policymakers About Strategies to Promote Social and Emotional School Readiness Among Three- and Four-Year-Old Children", National Center for Children in Poverty. 2002; see http://www.son.washington.edu/centers/parenting-clinic/opendocs/ProEmoPP3.pdf; Rimm-Kaufman, Sara, Robert Pianta, and Martha Cox. "Teachers' Judgements of Problems in the Transition to Kindergarden, *Early Childhood Research Quarterly*, v. 15 no. 2, 2000.

21 Hart, Betty and Todd R. Risley, "Meaningful Differences in the Everyday Experience of Young Children," *Early Education for All, 1995*, see http://www.strategiesforchildren.org/eea/6research_summaries/05_MeaningfulDifferences.pdf.

22 The Thirty Million Words Project, see http://tmw.org.

Chapter 8

1   See: http://www.slate.com/articles/newsand_politics/hey_wait_a_minute/2012/09/
harvard_cheating_scandal_everyone_has_it_wrong_the_students_should_be_cele-
brated_for_collaborating_on_an_unfair_test_.html

Chapter 11

1   http://www.chromebook.com/
2   http://www.siliconschools.com/
3   http://www.christenseninstitute.org/
4   https://www.khanacademy.org/
5   https://www.khanacademy.org/partner-content/ssf-cci
6   https://www.edsurge.com/
7   https://www.edsurge.com/guide/how-teachers-are-learning-professional-de
velopment-remix
8   https://www.google.com/enterprise/apps/education/
9   http://www.freetech4teachers.com/2013/04/how-to-add-voice-comments-to-
google.html
10 http://www.google.com/edu/classroom/
11 http://hapara.com/
12 http://theanswerpad.com/index.php/go-interactive/
13 http://exitticket.org/
14 https://www.masteryconnect.com/
15 http://all4ed.org/issues/project-24/
16 http://all4ed.org/
17 http://ed.ted.com/
18 http://www.techsmith.com/camtasia.html
19 https://www.coursera.org/
20 https://www.edx.org/
21 https://www.udacity.com/
22 https://www.edmodo.com/
23 http://www.classdojo.com/
24 http://classbadges.com/
25 https://www.google.com/edu/tablets/
26 https://www.apple.com/education/it/
27 http://www.nearpod.com/

28 http://www.averusa.com/education/tablet-solutions/tabcam.asp?ref=gateway

29 https://www.zaption.com/

30 http://educade.org/

31 http://www.pinterest.com/teachers/

32 http://www.teacherspayteachers.com/

33 https://www.blendspace.com/

34 http://www.achieve3000.com/

35 http://www.headsprout.com/

36 http://www.mindsnacks.com/

37 http://elevateapp.com/

38 https://www.newsela.com/

39 https://www.noredink.com/

40 http://www.shmoop.com/

41 http://www.launchpadtoys.com/toontastic/

42 http://www.aleks.com/

43 http://www.dragonboxapp.com/

44 http://www.dreambox.com/

45 https://www.luckybirdgames.com/

46 http://www.mangahigh.com/en-us/

47 https://www.sokikom.com/

48 https://www.khanacademy.org/

49 http://www.mathalicious.com/

50 http://motionmathgames.com/

51 http://web.stmath.com/

52 http://www.tenmarks.com/

53 http://www.ck12.org/

54 https://itunes.apple.com/us/app/monster-physics/id505046678?mt=8

55 http://science360.gov/

56 http://www.hmhco.com/shop/education-curriculum/science/elementary-science/sciencefusion

57 https://itunes.apple.com/us/app/videoscience/id333284085?mt=8

58 http://www.nationalgeographic.com/

59 http://www.studentcpr.com/en/

60 http://www.usfirst.org/roboticsprograms/frc

61 http://mindstorms.lego.com/

62 http://makewonder.com

63 https://code.google.com/p/blockly/

64   http://scratch.mit.edu/

65   http://appinventor.mit.edu/

66   http://appinventor.mit.edu/explore/resource-type/curriculum.html

67   http://www.virtualnerd.com/

68   https://www.duolingo.com/

69   http://www.mindsnacks.com/

70   http://www.rosettastone.com/

71   http://www.mindsnacks.com/subjects/us-geography

72   https://itunes.apple.com/us/app/stack-the-states/id381342267?mt=8

73   https://itunes.apple.com/us/app/stack-the-countries/id407838198?mt=8

74   https://itunes.apple.com/us/app/u.s.-geography-by-discover/
      id374922243?mt=8

75   https://www.khanacademy.org/better-money-habits

76   https://creative.adobe.com/

77   https://www.google.com/culturalinstitute/project/art-project

78   http://www.apple.com/creativity-apps/mac/

79   http://www.moma.org/learn/kids_families/labs

80   https://www.fiftythree.com/paper

81   http://www.apexlearning.com/courses

82   http://www.getfueled.com/

83   http://www.brainpop.com/

84   https://www.thelearningodyssey.com/

85   http://www.k12.com/

86   http://www.shmoop.com/

87   http://www.oercommons.org/

88   http://oeru.org/

89   https://phet.colorado.edu/

90   http://globallives.org/

Chapter 12

1   http://googleforwork.blogspot.com/2014/02/littleton-public-schools-uses-goo-
     glehtml.

2   https://docs.google.com/file/d/0B__OTXR_u3RbclVVcUE2R0tjbUk/
     edit?pli=1

3   https://docs.google.com/file/d/0B__OTXR_u3RbclVVcUE2R0tjbUk/edit?pli=1

4   https://www.youtube.com/watch?v=2Y0Gm02XGis

5   https://docs.google.com/file/d/0B5AOHQcS-cAeOTA3YjExYTEtZjg5NS-00M2RiLWE3NWMtZmVkMjRiOTJkOTdk/edit?pli=1

6   https://docs.google.com/file/d/0B5AOHQcS-cAeOTA3YjExYTEtZjg5NS-00M2RiLWE3NWMtZmVkMjRiOTJkOTdk/edit?pli=1

7   https://docs.google.com/file/d/0B__OTXR_u3RbclVVcUE2R0tjbUk/edit?pli=1

8   https://www.youtube.com/watch?v=sHMCyg-zKjY

9   https://sites.google.com/site/techsherpas/[9]

Chapter 14

1   Visit EdSurge at http://www.edsurge.com.

2   http://www.edsurge.com/summits

3   http://www.edudemic.com/

4   http://www.edudemic.com/12-best-ipad-apps-world-language-classroom/

5   http://www.edudemic.com/education-innovators-twitter/

6   http://www.edutopia.org/

7   http://gettingsmart.com/

8   http://blogs.kqed.org/mindshift/

9   https://twitter.com/

10   https://plus.google.com/

11   https://www.google.com/+/learnmore/hangouts/onair.html

12   https://www.wikispaces.com/

13   http://betterlesson.com/

14   http://www.google.com/edu/programs/google-teacher-academy/

15   https://www.google.com/edu/training/certifications/

16   http://www.graphite.org/

17   http://www.commonsensemedia.org/

18   http://www.imaginek12.com/

19   https://www.coursera.org/course/blendedlearning

20   http://code.google.com/p/course-builder/

21   http://dmlhub.net/

22   http://www.edmodocon.com/

23   http://edinnovation.asu.edu/

24   http://www.gafesummit.com/

25   http://www.imaginek12.com/educator-day.html

26   http://www.imaginek12.com/teachers.html
27   http://www.isteconference.org/
28   http://events.launch.co/festival/
29   http://edu.launch.co/
30   http://www.newschools.org/summit
31   http://sxswedu.com/
32   http://sxsw.com/interactive
33   http://www.swedu.co/

Chapter 15

1   See http://ilearnproject.com/digital-learning/
2   See http://gosa.georgia.gov/defining-digital-learning#_ftn1
3   See http://gosa.georgia.gov/defining-digital-learning#_ftn1
4   See http://gosa.georgia.gov/defining-digital-learning#_ftn1
5   See http://nces.ed.gov/pubs2012/2012008.pdf
6   See http://nces.ed.gov/pubs2012/2012008.pdf
7   See http://www.inacol.org/cms/wp-content/uploads/2013/04/iNACOL_Fast-Facts_Feb2013.pdf
8   U.S. Department of Education, "Transforming American Education: Learning Powered by Technology," 2010, p. 51, available at http://www.ed.gov/sites/default/files/netp2010.pdf
9   U.S. Department of Education, "Transforming American Education: Learning Powered by Technology," 2010, p. 52, available at http://www.ed.gov/sites/default/files/netp2010.pdf
10   U.S. Department of Education, "Transforming American Education: Learning Powered by Technology," 2010, p. 52, available at http://www.ed.gov/sites/default/files/netp2010.pdf
11   See http://www.inacol.org/cms/wp-content/uploads/2013/04/iNACOL_Fast-Facts_Feb2013.pdf
12   See http://www.inacol.org/cms/wp-content/uploads/2013/04/iNACOL_Fast-Facts_Feb2013.pdf
13   See http://www.inacol.org/cms/wp-content/uploads/2013/04/iNACOL_Fast-Facts_Feb2013.pdf

14 Mark Baldassare, Dean Bonner, Sonja Petek, and Jui Shrestha, "California's Digital Divide," Public Policy Institute of California, June 2013, available at http://www.ppic.org/main/publication_show.asp?i=263

15 Mark Baldassare, Dean Bonner, Sonja Petek, and Jui Shrestha, "California's Digital Divide."

16 Mark Baldassare, Dean Bonner, Sonja Petek, and Jui Shrestha, "California's Digital Divide."

17 U.S. Department of Education, "Transforming American Education: Learning Powered by Technology," 2010, p. xi, available at http://www.ed.gov/sites/default/files/netp2010.pdf]

Chapter 16

1   See   http://www.ed.gov/news/press-releases/us-department-education-releases-finalized-national-education-technology-plan

2   U.S. Department of Education, "Transforming American Education: Learning Powered by Technology," 2010, p. xii, available at http://www.ed.gov/sites/default/files/netp2010.pdf

3   See http://www.ed.gov/sites/default/files/netp2010-execsumm.pdf

4   U.S. Department of Education, "Transforming American Education: Learning Powered by Technology," 2010, p. 60, available at http://www.ed.gov/sites/default/files/netp2010.pdf

5   See http://www.ed.gov/sites/default/files/netp2010-execsumm.pdf

6   Michael Barbour, Jason Siko, Elizabeth Gross and Kecia Waddell, "Virtually Unprepared: Examining the Preparation of K-12 Online Teachers" in Richard Hartshorne, Tina Heafner and Teresa Petty, *Teacher Education Programs and Online Learning Tools: Innovations in Teacher Preparation* (Hershey, PA: Information Science Reference, 2013), p. 62.

7   Michael Barbour, Jason Siko, Elizabeth Gross and Kecia Waddell, "Virtually Unprepared: Examining the Preparation of K-12 Online Teachers" in Richard Hartshorne, Tina Heafner and Teresa Petty, (Hershey, PA: Information Science Reference, 2013), p. 78.

8   Michael Barbour, Jason Siko, Elizabeth Gross and Kecia Waddell, "Virtually Un-prepared: Examining the Preparation of K-12 Online Teachers" in Richard Harts-horne, Tina Heafner and Teresa Petty, (Hershey, PA: Information Science Refer-ence, 2013), p. 62.

9   Michael Barbour, Jason Siko, Elizabeth Gross and Kecia Waddell, "Virtually Un-prepared: Examining the Preparation of K-12 Online Teachers" in Richard Harts-horne, Tina Heafner and Teresa Petty, (Hershey, PA: Information Science Refer-ence, 2013), p. 62.

10   Heather Staker and Michael Horn, "Classifying K-12 Blended Learning," Chris-tensen Institute, May 2012, p. 3, available at http://www.christenseninstitute.org/wp-content/uploads/2013/04/Classifying-K-12-blended-learning.pdf

11   Heather Staker and Michael Horn, "Classifying K-12 Blended Learning," p. 8-12.

12   Heather Staker and Michael Horn, "Classifying K-12 Blended Learning," p. 12.

13   Heather Staker and Michael Horn, "Classifying K-12 Blended Learning," p. 14.

14   Michael Horn and Heather Staker, "5 Skills for Blended-Learning Teachers," Oc-tober 4, 2012, available at http://thejournal.com/articles/2012/10/04/5-skills-for-blended-learning-eachers.aspx

15   Michael Barbour, Jason Siko, Elizabeth Gross and Kecia Waddell, "Virtually Unprepared: Examining the Preparation of K-12 Online Teachers" in Richard Hartshorne, Tina Heafner and Teresa Petty, *Teacher Education Programs and On-line Learning Tools: Innovations in Teacher Preparation* (Hershey, PA: Information Science Reference, 2013), p. 61.

16   Michael Barbour, Jason Siko, Elizabeth Gross and Kecia Waddell, "Virtually Unprepared: Examining the Preparation of K-12 Online Teachers" in Richard Hartshorne, Tina Heafner and Teresa Petty, *Teacher Education Programs and On-line Learning Tools: Innovations in Teacher Preparation* (Hershey, PA: Information Science Reference, 2013), p. 63.

17   U.S. Department of Education, "Transforming American Education: Learning Powered by Technology," 2010, p. xii, available at http://www.ed.gov/sites/default/files/netp2010.pdf

18   Interview with Catlin Tucker on August 6, 2013.

19   Michael Barbour, Jason Siko, Elizabeth Gross and Kecia Waddell, "Virtually Un-prepared: Examining the Preparation of K-12 Online Teachers" in Richard Harts-horne, Tina Heafner and Teresa Petty, (Hershey, PA: Information Science Refer-ence, 2013), p. 63

20 Michael Barbour, Jason Siko, Elizabeth Gross and Kecia Waddell, "Virtually Unprepared: Examining the Preparation of K-12 Online Teachers" in Richard Hartshorne, Tina Heafner and Teresa Petty, (Hershey, PA: Information Science Reference, 2013), p. 63.

21 Michael Barbour, Jason Siko, Elizabeth Gross and Kecia Waddell, "Virtually Unprepared: Examining the Preparation of K-12 Online Teachers" in Richard Hartshorne, Tina Heafner and Teresa Petty, *Teacher Education Programs and Online Learning Tools: Innovations in Teacher Preparation* (Hershey, PA: Information Science Reference, 2013), p. 64.

22 See http://rossieronline.usc.edu/7-steps-to-become-a-teacher-in-california/

23 See http://edweb.sdsu.edu/Courses/EDTEC470/

24 See http://edweb.sdsu.edu/Courses/EDTEC470/

25 See http://extension.ucsd.edu/studyarea/index.cfm?vAction=singleCourse&vCourse=EDUC-30150

26 See http://www.sfsu.edu/~itec/

27 See http://www.sfsu.edu/~itec/program/courses/860.html

28 See http://learntech.gmu.edu/learning-technologies-schools/

29 See http://iols.gmu.edu/proginfo/descriptions/

30 See http://iols.gmu.edu/proginfo/descriptions/

31 See http://edtech.boisestate.edu

32 Michael Barbour, Jason Siko, Elizabeth Gross and Kecia Waddell, "Vitually Unprepared: Examining the Preparation of K-12 Online Teachers" in Richard Hartshorne, Tina Heafner and Teresa Petty, (Hershey, PA: Information Science Reference, 2013), p. 78.

33 U.S. Department of Education, "Transforming American Education: Learning Powered by Technology," 2010, p. xii, available at http://www.ed.gov/sites/default/files/netp2010.pdf

34 U.S. Department of Education, "Transforming American Education: Learning Powered by Technology," 2010, p. xiii, available at http://www.ed.gov/sites/default/files/netp2010.pdf

1   John Daniel, "Preface," in Patrick Alan Danaher and Abdurrahman, *Teacher Education through Open and Distance Learning* (Vancouver, BC: Commonwealth of Learning, 2010), p. vi, available at http://www.icde.org/filestore/Resources/Reports/PERSPECTIVESONDISTANCEEDUCATION-TeacherEducationthrough.pdf?page=75

2   "Pisa 2012 Results: which country does best at reading, math and science?", *The Guardian*, December 3, 2013, available at http://www.theguardian.com/news/datablog/2013/dec/03/pisa-results-country-best-reading-maths-science

3   Colin Latchem, "Using ICT to Train Teachers in ICT" in Patrick Alan Danaher and Abdurrahman, *Teacher Education through Open and Distance Learning* (Vancouver, BC: Commonwealth of Learning, 2010), p. vi, available at http://www.icde.org/filestore/Resources/Reports/PERSPECTIVESONDISTANCEEDUCATION-TeacherEducationthrough.pdf?page=75

4   Veijo Meisalo, Jari Lavonen, Kari Sormunen, Mikko Vesisenaho, "ICT in Finnish Initial Teacher Education," Finnish Ministry of Education and Culture, 2010, p. 10, available at http://www.minedu.fi/export/sites/default/OPM/Julkaisut/2010/liitteet/okm25.pdf?lang=en

5   Ernie Newman, "Demand from Primary and Secondary Schools," New Zealand Commerce Commission, December 2011, pp. 4-5.

6   Ernie Newman, "Demand from Primary and Secondary Schools," New Zealand Commerce Commission, December 2011, p. 6.

7   Ernie Newman, "Demand from Primary and Secondary Schools," New Zealand Commerce Commission, December 2011, p. 19.

8   Ernie Newman, "Demand from Primary and Secondary Schools," New Zealand Commerce Commission, December 2011, p. 3.

9   See http://traintheteacher.wordpress.com/category/education-2-0/

10 "Pre-service Teacher Training on ICT use in Education: Republic of Korea," UNESCO, 2005, p. 1, available at http://www.unescobkk.org/fileadmin/user_upload/ict/Misc/TT_Korea.pdf

11   "Pre-service Teacher Training on ICT use in Education: Republic of Korea," UNESCO, 2005, p. 1, available at http://www.unescobkk.org/fileadmin/user_upload/ict/Misc/TT_Korea.pdf

12 "Pre-service Teacher Training on ICT use in Education: Republic of Korea," UNESCO, 2005, p. 1, available at http://www.unescobkk.org/fileadmin/user_upload/ict/Misc/TT_Korea.pdf

13 "Pre-service Teacher Training on ICT use in Education: Republic of Korea," UNESCO, 2005, p. 2, available at http://www.unescobkk.org/fileadmin/user_upload/ict/Misc/TT_Korea.pdf

14 See http://www.unescobkk.org/education/ict/themes/training-of-teachers/overview/south-korea/

15 "Information Technology for Learning in a New Era Five-Year Strategy 1998/99-2002/03," Hong Kong Education Bureau, available at http://www.edb.gov.hk/en/about-edb/publications-stat/major-reports/consultancy-reports/it-learning-1998-2003/ch4.html

16 See http://www.ied.edu.hk/degree/bed_s_dse.htm

17 See http://www.ied.edu.hk/degree/bsed_wt_dse.htm

18 See http://www.edb.gov.hk/en/edu-system/primary-secondary/applicable-to-primary-secondary/it-in-edu/the-second-it-in-edu-strategy-goal2.html

19 See http://www.edb.gov.hk/en/edu-system/primary-secondary/applicable-to-primary-secondary/it-in-edu/pdp-ited.html

20 See http://www.edb.gov.hk/en/edu-system/primary-secondary/applicable-to-primary-secondary/it-in-edu/the-second-it-in-edu-strategy-goal2.html

21 See http://www.edb.gov.hk/en/edu-system/primary-secondary/applicable-to-primary-secondary/it-in-edu/the-second-it-in-edu-strategy-goal2.html

22 See http://www.edb.gov.hk/en/edu-system/primary-secondary/applicable-to-primary-secondary/it-in-edu/the-second-it-in-edu-strategy-goal2.html

23 See http://www.ied.edu.hk/acadprog/pgde/PGDE_Pri.htm#p11

24 Susan Patrick, "The Future of Education: A Global View," iNACOL, p. 5, available at http://www.legis.nd.gov/files/committees/61st%20NMA/appendices/he033110appendixe.pdf?20130930081952

25 Singapore National Institute of Education, p. 82, available at http://www.nie.edu.sg/files/TE21%20online%20version%20-%20updated.pdf

26 Singapore National Institute of Education, p. 85, available at http://www.nie.edu.sg/files/TE21%20online%20version%20-%20updated.pdf

27 Shanti Divaharan, Wei-Ying Lim and Seng-Chee Tan, "Walk the Talk: Immersing pre-service teachers in the learning of ICT tools for knowledge creation," *Australasian Journal of Educational Technology*, 2011, 27 (Special issue, 8), p. 1306, available at http://www.ascilite.org.au/ajet/ajet27/divaharan.pdf

28   Shanti Divaharan, Wei-Ying Lim and Seng-Chee Tan, "Walk the Talk: Immersing pre-service teachers in the learning of ICT tools for knowledge creation," *Australasian Journal of Educational Technology*, 2011, 27 (Special issue, 8), p. 1306, available at http://www.ascilite.org.au/ajet/ajet27/divaharan.pdf

29   Shanti Divaharan, Wei-Ying Lim and Seng-Chee Tan, "Walk the Talk: Immersing pre-service teachers in the learning of ICT tools for knowledge creation," *Australian Journal of Educational Technology,* 2011, 27 (Special issue, 8), p. 1307, available at http://www.ascilite.org.au/ajet/ajet27/divaharan.pdf

30   Shanti Divaharan, Wei-Ying Lim and Seng-Chee Tan, "Walk the Talk: Immersing pre-service teachers in the learning of ICT tools for knowledge creation," *Australasian Journal of Educational Technology*, 2011, 27 (Special issue, 8), p. 1308, available at http://www.ascilite.org.au/ajet/ajet27/divaharan.pdf

31   Shanti Divaharan, Wei-Ying Lim and Seng-Chee Tan, "Walk the Talk: Immersing pre-service teachers in the learning of ICT tools for knowledge creation," *Australasian Journal of Educational Technology* 2011, 27 (Special issue, 8), pp. 1315-1316, available at http://www.ascilite.org.au/ajet/ajet27/divaharan.pdf

32   Veijo Meisalo, Jari Lavonen, Kari Sormunen, Mikko Vesisenaho, "ICT in Finnish Initial Teacher Education," Finnish Ministry of Education and Culture, 2010, p. 20, available at http://www.minedu.fi/export/sites/default/OPM/Julkaisut/2010/liitteet/okm25.pdf?lang=en

33   Veijo Meisalo, Jari Lavonen, Kari Sormunen, Mikko Vesisenaho, "ICT in Finnish Initial Teacher Education," Finnish Ministry of Education and Culture, 2010, p. 22, available at http://www.minedu.fi/export/sites/default/OPM/Julkaisut/2010/liitteet/okm25.pdf?lang=en

34   Veijo Meisalo, Jari Lavonen, Kari Sormunen, Mikko Vesisenaho, "ICT in Finnish Initial Teacher Education," Finnish Ministry of Education and Culture, 2010, p. 23, available at http://www.minedu.fi/export/sites/default/OPM/Julkaisut/2010/liitteet/okm25.pdf?lang=en

35   Veijo Meisalo, Jari Lavonen, Kari Sormunen, Mikko Vesisenaho, "ICT in Finnish Initial Teacher Education," Finnish Ministry of Education and Culture, 2010, p. 24, available at http://www.minedu.fi/export/sites/default/OPM/Julkaisut/2010/liitteet/okm25.pdf?lang=en

36   Veijo Meisalo, Jari Lavonen, Kari Sormunen, Mikko Vesisenaho, "ICT in Finnish Initial Teacher Education," Finnish Ministry of Education and Culture, 2010, p. 43, available at http://www.minedu.fi/export/sites/default/OPM/Julkaisut/2010/liitteet/okm25.pdf?lang=en

37   Veijo Meisalo, Jari Lavonen, Kari Sormunen, Mikko Vesisenaho, "ICT in Finnish Initial Teacher Education," Finnish Ministry of Education and Culture, 2010, p. 53, available at http://www.minedu.fi/export/sites/default/OPM/Julkaisut/2010/liitteet/okm25.pdf?lang=en

38   Veijo Meisalo, Jari Lavonen, Kari Sormunen, Mikko Vesisenaho, "ICT in Finnish Initial Teacher Education," Finnish Ministry of Education and Culture, 2010, p. 58, available at http://www.minedu.fi/export/sites/default/OPM/Julkaisut/2010/liitteet/okm25.pdf?lang=en

39   See http://www3.open.ac.uk/study/postgraduate/qualification/c23.htm]

40   Veijo Meisalo, Jari Lavonen, Kari Sormunen, Mikko Vesisenaho, "ICT in Finnish Initial Teacher Education," Finnish Ministry of Education and Culture, 2010, p. 59, available at http://www.minedu.fi/export/sites/default/OPM/Julkaisut/2010/liitteet/okm25.pdf?lang=en

Acknowledgements

The authors would like to thank the Koret Foundation for its support of this project. We would like to thank Pacific Research Institute (PRI) summer research intern Alex Silverman for his invaluable research-gathering efforts. In addition, the authors would like to thank creative director Dana Beigel for her excellent layout of this book and Linda Bridges for her copyediting of the book manuscript. Finally, the authors would like to acknowledge the contributions of the dedicated staff of PRI, including Rowena Itchon, senior vice president and Sally Pipes, president and CEO. In addition, the authors would like to acknowledge the efforts of Christine Hughes and Chrissie Dong, formerly members of PRI's development department, and Laura Dannerbeck, director of events and marketing for PRI. The authors of this study have worked independently and their views and conclusions do not necessarily represent those of the board, supporters, or staff of PRI.

We would also like to thank the following people for their feedback, conversations, and support of the book: John Merrow, Education Correspondent for PBS News-Hour and President of Learning Matters, David Kelley, professor at Stanford University and founder of IDEO and the d school at Stanford; Michael Horn, Co-Founder of the Christensen Institute; Maggie Johnson, Director of Education and University Relations at Google for her continued support throughout the years. We would like to thank Dan Russell, Google Research Scientist, for his excellent chapter on Search and my colleague at Palo Alto High School Paul Kandell for his insightful chapter on motivation.

We would like to thank Tad Taube, President Emeritus of the Taube-Koret Foundation for being such an amazing supporter of our work and our program; Tina Frank, Vice President and COO of the Koret Foundation for her support through the years; Palo Alto High School Principal Kim Diorio for her support and vision to help make schools better for all students. Esther Wojcicki would also like to thank the following teachers for their being such great teachers and allowing us to include them and their work in our book: Suney Park, Eastside College Prep; Cynthia Ambrose and Jennifer Janes, Horry County Schools (Whittemore Park Middle School);

Joyce Tang, Milpitas USD (Thomas Russell Middle School); Josh Paley, Gunn High School teacher; Dan Maas, CIO for Littleton Public Schools, Colorado; Mike Hathorn, teacher Hartford High School, Vermont; Wendy Gorton, educator, Portland, Oregon; Andi Kornowkski, teacher at Kettle Moraine High School, Wisconsin; Lucie deLaBruere, teacher at St. Albans, Vermont; Kevin Brookhauser, teacher of Humanities and Digital Citizenship, California.

Esther Wojcicki would also like to thank her former student Maya Kitayama, co-editor in chief of the *The Campanile* 2013-14, for her chapter on AP Music teacher Michael Najar. She would like to thank the Google education team for their continued support: Jonathan Rochelle, Google Docs/Drive Co-Founder & Tech Optimist; Zach Yeskel, Google Classroom Product Manager: Jennifer Holland, Google Apps for Education Product Manager. She would like to thank Betsy Corcoran, founder and CEO of EdSurge, for her help in finding her editorial assistant Alicia Chang who did an amazing job. She would also like to acknowledge the Knight Foundation for its support of her work through the years. So many people supported her including all her students who help her understand the needs of teenagers everyday. Thank you to all of you.

About the Authors

Esther Wojcicki

Esther Wojcicki, known as "Woj" to her students, has never been interested in convention. So, when she left a career in newspapers to teach journalism at California's Palo Alto High School in 1984, one of the first things she did was to discard all of the traditional textbooks in her classroom. Since then her thought leadership on education as well as its intersection with technology has not only transformed the school where she still teaches, it has succeeded in grabbing global attention.

Wojcicki, a scheduled speaker at DLDwomen, is credited with building Palo Alto High's journalism program from a small group of 20 students in 1985 to one of the largest in the nation with 600 students and six electives including three magazines, two television shows, one website and one video production class. Over the past 20 years, the publications have won Gold and Silver Crowns from Columbia Scholastic Press Association, the PaceMaker Award and Hall of Fame Award from National Scholastic Press, and best in nation from *Time* Magazine in 2003. That's not all: the school's online magazine was honored with two Webby Awards in 2005. All of this has earned Wojcicki a number of teaching awards. Most recently she was honored nationally on the U.S.'s Digital Learning Day, as one of a small group of "great teachers" who use technology effectively in the classroom.

Says Gady Epstein, a China correspondent for the *Economist*, who was first exposed to journalism in Wojcicki's class while still in high school: "She was very popular with students, the coolest teacher on campus. Once you entered her gravitational pull you didn't want to leave it."

Epstein said Wojcicki treated students like adults. "She would talk to us as equals. Although people looked up at her she did not talk down to them. She expected students to make decisions and be responsible for them and granted a lot of freedom."

Wojcicki may have inspired students like Epstein but she is not content with training the next generation of journalists. Her aim is to create better students. Her thesis—one she shared with an international audience at a June education conference at the Paris-based Organization for Economic Cooperation and Development—is that journalism skills can be used to teach students to think more clearly and do better in a variety of subjects. "Journalism can be an umbrella for learning everything including spelling, grammar, concise writing, interviewing, statistics, ethics and civic engagement," Wojcicki said in an interview with Informilo.

Interest in her approach to education led to an invitation by the Academy of Singapore Teachers to be part of the Outstanding Educator in Residence program. Under the program renowned educators from around the world are invited to spend several weeks in Singapore lecturing to Singapore educators.

Invites to Paris and Singapore are not the norm for most U.S. high school teachers, but then again Wojcicki is anything but ordinary. The daughter of Russian immigrants, Wojcicki, whose maiden name is Hochman, was valedictorian of her high school class and went on to become the first person in her family to earn a college degree. She graduated from UC Berkeley with a B.A. in English and Political Science; received a secondary teaching credential from UC Berkeley, as well as a graduate degree from the Graduate School of Journalism at Berkeley. She also has an advanced degree in French and French History from the Sorbonne, and both a Secondary School Administrative Credential and a M.A. in Educational Technology from San Jose State University.

She married Stanley Wojcicki, a well-known physicist and former Stanford University professor, worked for a number of newspapers, including the *Los Angeles Times*, bore three daughters (she is now grandmother to nine), started teaching high school and served as a consultant to Google, helping to do outreach to schools with a variety of the search engine giant's products, including spreadsheets, gmail and groups. She served as Chair of Creative Commons and is currently a vice-chair of Creative Commons and an advisor to The University of the People, a global online non-profit free university.

Wojcicki's ties to Google run deep. Her daughter Susan bought a house nearby in Menlo Park soon after she was married. Susan and her husband needed to sublet rooms in the house to make the mortgage. The tenants were Sergey Brin and Larry Page and they famously ended up starting Google in Susan's house. Susan, who was working at Intel, joined Google in 1999 as the company's first marketing manager. Today Susan is senior vice president of advertising at Google, where she is responsible for the design and innovation of all of Google's advertising and measurement platform products, including AdWords, AdSense, DoubleClick, and Google Analytics.

The close proximity to Google's founders had other consequences: daughter Anne, an investment banker-turned-entrepreneur focused on health, ended up marrying Brin. Today she is CEO of 23andMe, a genetics testing company.

Wojcicki no longer formally advises Google on the application of technology to the classroom. But her early thought leadership in education and tech caught the attention of the board of Creative Commons, a group devoted to allowing people to share their creativity and knowledge. Creative Commons offers a range of Open Content licenses, which makes sharing content legally on the Internet easier. As education moves on-line, a legal framework needs to be put in place so that course materials can be shared, explains Joi Ito, Chairman of Creative Commons and Director of the MIT Media Lab. "Ito doesn't hesitate to sing Wojcicki's praises. "She is full of ideas, is always going a mile a minute and is connected to everyone," he says, describing her as "hyper-connected, hyperactive and hyper-practical."

These qualities and her expertise led to her involvement with University of the People. "I asked Esther to be a member of the advisory board because she has vast experience in the intersection of technology and education and openness—she is one of the leaders of the open educational resources movement," says Shai Reshef, UoPeople's founder.

There is a shift in thinking that needs to take place to change classrooms both on-line and offline, says Wojcicki. Teaching journalism can play a role in making learning more interactive and effective. But teachers also have to continuously embrace and evaluate new technologies and adapt their classrooms accordingly, instead of relying on outdated skill sets. And if they don't want to become invisible and irrelevant they will be open to sharing their course materials online, helping to democratize education. Thanks in part to Wojcicki, the message is now being heard far beyond the corridors of Palo Alto High.

– *Written by Jennifer L. Schenker*

LANCE T. IZUMI, J.D.

Lance Izumi is Koret Senior Fellow and Senior Director of Education Studies at the Pacific Research Institute. He is the author of the highly praised 2012 book *Obama's Education Takeover* (Encounter Books), which details the centralization of education policymaking in Washington under President Obama. His most recent work is the 2013 PRI report, "One World School House vs. Old World Statehouse: The Khan Academy and California Red Tape."

He is the co-author of the 2011 PRI book *Short-Circuited: The Challenges Facing the Online Learning Revolution in California* and is the executive producer and narrator of a *National Review Online*-posted short film based on the book.

Lance is also the co-author of the groundbreaking book *Not as Good as You Think: Why the Middle Class Needs School Choice* and co-executive producer of the award-winning 2009 PBS-broadcast film documentary *Not as Good As You Think: The Myth of the Middle Class School*. He also appears in Academy Award-winning director Davis Guggenheim's 2010 education film documentary *Waiting for Superman*, which was voted best U.S. documentary at the prestigious Sundance Film Festival.

In 2008, *The New York Times* selected Lance Izumi to be one of its online contributors on the presidential race and education issues. In 2009, *The New York Times* posted *Sweden's Choice*, a short film on Sweden's universal school-choice voucher system, which he wrote and narrated. Mr. Izumi continues to contribute to *The New York Times*' "Room for Debate" opinion series.

He is also the co-author of the 2005 PRI book *Free to Learn: Lessons from Model Charter Schools*, which was used as a guidebook for creating high-performing charter schools in New Orleans after Hurricane Katrina. He has also authored numerous PRI studies and reports, plus innumerable op-ed pieces in top U.S. and international publications.

Mr. Izumi is a member of the Board of Governors of the California Community Colleges, the largest system of higher education in the nation. First appointed to the Board in 2004, he is now the Board's longest serving member. He served two terms as president of the Board of Governors from 2008 through 2009.

Mr. Izumi served as chief speechwriter and director of writing and research for California Governor George Deukmejian. He also served in the administration of President Ronald Reagan as speechwriter to United States Attorney General Edwin Meese III.

Mr. Izumi received his juris doctorate from the University of Southern California School of Law. He received his master of arts in political science from the University of California at Davis and his bachelor of arts in economics and history from the University of California at Los Angeles.

ALICIA CHANG, Ph.D.

Alicia Chang is a cognitive and developmental psychologist (Ph.D., UCLA), specializing in cognitive and language development and applications of cognitive science to STEM education. Since completing her doctorate and postdoctoral research fellowships at the University of Pittsburgh and the University of Delaware, Alicia has been working in the field of education technology. She lives and works in the San Francisco Bay Area, and serves as a researcher at the Pacific Research Institute.

ALEX SILVERMAN

Alex Silverman served as a research intern for the Pacific Research Institute in 2013. He received his bachelor of arts in economics from the University of Rochester, where he received various honors and awards.

ELLIOTT PARISI

Elliott Parisi served as a research fellow for the Pacific Research Institute. He is a graduate of George Fox University in Oregon and will be receiving his master in public policy from the Pepperdine University School of Public Policy in spring 2015.

About Pacific Research Institute

The Pacific Research Institute (PRI) champions freedom, opportunity, and personal responsibility by advancing free-market policy solutions. It provides practical solutions for the policy issues that impact the daily lives of all Americans, and demonstrates why the free market is more effective than the government at providing the important results we all seek: good schools, quality health care, a clean environment, and a robust economy.

Founded in 1979 and based in San Francisco, PRI is a non-profit, non-partisan organization supported by private contributions. Its activities include publications, public events, media commentary, community leadership, legislative testimony, and academic outreach.

Education Studies

PRI works to restore to all parents the basic right to choose the best educational opportunities for their children. Through research and grassroots outreach, PRI promotes parental choice in education, high academic standards, teacher quality, charter schools, and school-finance reform.

Business and Economic Studies

PRI shows how the entrepreneurial spirit—the engine of economic growth and opportunity—is stifled by onerous taxes, regulations, and lawsuits. It advances policy reforms that promote a robust economy, consumer choice, and innovation.

Health Care Studies

PRI demonstrates why a single-payer Canadian model would be detrimental to the health care of all Americans. It proposes market-based reforms that would improve affordability, access, quality, and consumer choice.

Environmental Studies

PRI reveals the dramatic and long-term trend toward a cleaner, healthier environment. It also examines and promotes the essential ingredients for abundant resources and environmental quality: property rights, markets, local action, and private initiative.

Moonshots in Education

Moonshots in Education

CPSIA information can be obtained
at www.ICGtesting.com
Printed in the USA
LVHW071620020419
612699LV00021B/872/P